Joseph Wood Krutch

A WRITER'S LIFE

Joseph Wood Krutch,

A WRITER'S LIFE.

by John D. Margolis

THE UNIVERSITY OF TENNESSEE PRESS
KNOXVILLE

Copyright © 1980 by The University of Tennessee Press / Knoxville.
All rights reserved.
Manufactured in the United States of America.
First edition.

Clothbound editions of University of Tennessee Press books are printed on
paper designed for an effective life of at least 300 years, and binding materials
are chosen for strength and durability.

Library of Congress Cataloging in Publication Data

Margolis, John D
   Joseph Wood Krutch, a writer's life.

   Bibliography: p.
   Includes index.
   1. Krutch, Joseph Wood, 1893–1970. 2. Critics—
United States—Biography. 3. Naturalists—United
States—Biography. I. Title.
PS29.K7M3   809 [B]   80-182
ISBN 0-87049-292-6

To my mother and father

CONTENTS

ILLUSTRATIONS

 ACKNOWLEDGMENTS

In the course of preparing a biographical study of a contemporary figure, an author inevitably incurs many debts. My greatest is to Mrs. Joseph Wood Krutch, who has not only generously shared with me memories of her late husband, but has also on several occasions extended to me her exceptionally gracious hospitality. Mrs. Krutch also gave me access to numerous family papers and photographs. All but one of the photographs included in this book were made available to me by her. I am likewise grateful to Gerald Green, who has provided constant encouragement and various other kinds of assistance during my preparation of this book.

Much of my research was conducted at the Library of Congress, where many of Krutch's papers are deposited. I am grateful to the staff of the Manuscript Division for its tolerance of my many impositions, and to the staffs of the following libraries, where other portions of the research for this book were carried out: the Columbia University Library, the Houghton Library at Harvard University, the University of Iowa Library, the New York Public Library, the Northwestern University Library, and the University of Tennessee Library.

The *Atlantic Monthly* and the *Nation* kindly granted me access to their files. Other of Krutch's publishers have also generously responded to my queries, and I should record my special appreciation for the information provided by two of Krutch's editors, the late Hiram Haydn and the late William Sloane.

I also thank Mrs. Mark Van Doren and Charles and John Van

Doren for having shared with me their recollections of Krutch; the latter also kindly provided a photograph of his late father and Krutch. Mrs. Robert Ogg and her late husband, Kenneth Bechtel, were also extraordinarily generous to me in many ways. The hours they spent with me in conversation about Krutch and their other kinds of assistance leave me greatly in their debt.

My account of Krutch's professorial years at Columbia is based on materials in the Columbiana Collection of the Columbia University Library, made available to me by the curator, Alice H. Bonnell; and upon the recollections graciously shared with me by Krutch's former colleagues and students: Quentin Anderson, Jack N. Arbolino, Melvin Hershkowitz, Carl Hovde, Marjorie Nicolson, Richard Rowland, Edna L. Steeves, H.R. Steeves, Richard C. Sterne, as well as the late James Clifford, F.W. Dupee, Alfred Harbage, and Lionel Trilling. I am grateful to all of them.

At various stages in its preparation my manuscript was read by Wallace Douglas, Gerald Graff, and Samuel Hynes. Thanks to their helpful suggestions, the book is better than it might otherwise have been. I am also greatly indebted to Lee Edelman. As an undergraduate at Northwestern, he assisted me in my preliminary research; some years later he provided a painstaking and thoughtful critique of a late draft of the manuscript. It is a pleasure to record my appreciation for his many kinds of help.

I am also grateful to Mary Wardle, who typed the manuscript with such skill and good cheer, and to Judith Leon and Jeannette Weimer.

Finally, I want to record my appreciation to the Belvedere Scientific Fund and the Research Committee of Northwestern University for grants which made it possible for me to pursue my research and then to take leave of my university responsibilities in order to write this book.

John D. Margolis
Evanston, Illinois
16 September 1979

 PREFACE

When, in 1928, Joseph Wood Krutch wrote his publisher about *The Modern Temper,* the book he was then completing, he pointedly remarked that it was "distinctly high-brow." For the young Krutch, the term lacked the opprobrium Van Wyck Brooks had attached to it in his famous 1915 discussion of "lowbrow" and "highbrow." Indeed, it was with pride that Krutch thus described his essays — and, implicitly, himself. For some years he had been laboring to fashion himself into a literary highbrow; the publication of his brilliant study of post-War despair seemed clearly to have marked the success of his endeavor.

That famous book had been preceded by other, similar efforts. In 1920 he had begun his literary career with a display of his free-thinking cleverness in a witty *Smart Set* essay on suicide. As the *Nation*'s correspondent at the Scopes trial, he had proudly rejected the narrow-minded illiberalism of his native Tennessee. As the author of a pioneering psychoanalytic biography of Poe, he had shown his understanding of the latest literary and intellectual fashions of the day. And as a reviewer for the *Nation* and other leading periodicals, he had established himself as one of the foremost interpreters of modern fiction and drama.

With *The Modern Temper* he sought to consolidate his already considerable reputation as a literary highbrow. Describing himself as a man of "robust but serious mind," Krutch was writing to other such people who shared his fastidious intellectual refinement; who, like him, were aloof from the workaday realities of the common life;

and whose exceptional sensibilities seemed to afford them insights unavailable to the ordinary man. Luxuriating in his despair, Krutch portrayed himself as a tortured spirit unlike any who had lived before. Refusing to accept what he viewed as the comfortable platitudes of the middle class and dissenting from philistine notions of progress, he insisted that the apparently meaningless world revealed by science was the real world; that the traditional values of western civilization were empty ones; and that man must adjust to the necessity of living maturely, without illusions, in a hostile, spiritually incommodious universe. As Granville Hicks predicted when Krutch's book appeared in 1929, *The Modern Temper* was to become "one of the crucial documents of his generation."

In the eight chapters of his book, Krutch had not of course presented a comprehensive analysis of *the* modern temper. Modernism is a complex, many-sided affair—one of the most elusive and protean movements in intellectual history. Encompassing many different sensibilities and styles, modernism includes various tempers, from among which Krutch chose to concentrate on one which best served his literary ends: the apocalyptic, nihilistic strain. He wrote less as a scholar than as an artist. The book then was partly a literary performance, of a piece with Krutch's earlier efforts to display his highbrow iconoclasm; and its literary effect was stunning. But at the same time it was a poignant expression of that radical skepticism—and consequent despair—which, in his effort to become "distinctly high-brow," Krutch had made his own. However useful they were artistically, the thoroughgoing doubt, moral nihilism, and self-contented pessimism of *The Modern Temper* hardly offered any satisfactory philosophy of life. The books and essays which followed reflect Krutch's journey beyond the despair he had so eloquently described there.

In fact, the reputation Krutch had sought to achieve in the twenties was inconsistent with the man himself—a studied attempt to make himself into something other than he truly was. That he felt it necessary in 1928 to insist that he was "distinctly high-brow" suggests his uncertainty as to his achievement. Having spent his first twenty-two years in Knoxville, he had arrived in New York City only a decade before writing the first of his famous "Modern Temper" essays; and the intellectual sophistication that he so proudly displayed there was in fact a recent acquisition. Even while laboring to affect the fashionable attitudes of the advanced thinkers of the day, he could not wholly shake off the legacy of his turn-of-the-century East Tennessee youth: bourgeois, conservative, and fundamentally middlebrow.

As was everywhere implicit in the book, the modern temper was not something Krutch could happily accept as his own. What he later said of Dr. Johnson could equally be said of Krutch himself: he "clung to old-fashioned ways of feeling even more than he did to old-fashioned ways of thinking." Indeed, his sense of alienation from the social and intellectual currents of his day became ever greater during the following decades. Having begun by trying to encompass fashionable attitudes and thus to become a herald of the new, he presently assumed a different role, as a critic of many aspects of a society which he felt was dangerously awry in its denial of human dignity, its willingness to minimize the importance of human liberty, its lack of respect for the value of individualism, its obsession with what can be scientifically quantified and verified, and its lack of appreciation of the natural world. Krutch was in the end a man of his century less in his enthusiastic proclamation of those new values gladly embraced by many of his contemporaries than in his courageous affirmation of older, more fundamental values he discovered as he resisted the hurly-burly of his day. As a man and as a thinker he found ways of coping with a world in many ways uncongenial; and in his works he outlined a path which others of like mind might follow.

During the forty years following the publication of *The Modern Temper*, Krutch would enjoy many other reputations—far different from, but hardly less great than, that which he had earned at the beginning of his career. As a biographer, nature writer, and social critic, to name only a few of his later achievements, he found an audience far larger and no less admiring than that which so enthusiastically greeted his early work as an interpreter of modern thought. His career as a whole offers a moving account of a man's quest for values and for a style of life which would be more temperamentally congenial, more authentically his own, than those which brought him his earliest literary fame. This study seeks to describe the distinctive shape of that career, and the place of Krutch's various literary activities in the larger pattern of that quest.

After his meteoric rise to fame in the twenties, Krutch's reputation as a literary highbrow waned during the 1930s. As one of the earliest American interpreters of Proust, he continued briefly to associate himself with the latest intellectual fashions in the years immediately following the publication of *The Modern Temper*; but at the same time he found himself increasingly alienated from those whose admiration he had once sought, and whose enthusiasm for radical art and politics was far greater than his own. If he was unsatisfied by the apparently purposeless universe he had described in the 1920s, he was equally unable to embrace the single-minded purposefulness of those young modernists who had now turned Marxists. As the widely respected drama critic of the *Nation*, he expressed his distaste for the new political stage. As that journal's literary editor, he incurred the wrath of the Left for his insufficient respect for communism. In a series of eloquent essays on contemporary politics, he registered his dissent from what passed for advanced thought. And, as an unreformed liberal in a radical decade, he argued a cautiously affirmative answer to the question: *Was Europe a Success?*

That many of those who had so bitterly attacked Krutch in the 1930s came eventually to share his own misgivings over communism was perhaps a belated vindication of the quiet wisdom and massive common sense that characterized all of his later writing. But for Krutch the thirties marked a turning point in both his thought and his career. Disillusioned with the intellectual arrogance and intolerance of those highbrows with whom he had once sought to associate himself, as a writer he ceased straining to win their esteem; and as a man he began to seek something beyond the mere literary prestige which, for the moment, seemed to have eluded him.

From the Greenwich Village apartment where he had done much of his early writing, he moved to rural Connecticut—to find, as a student of nature, satisfaction far greater than any he had enjoyed as a student of contemporary art or thought. From his editorship on the politically charged *Nation* he moved to a professorship at Columbia. And from the skeptical modernism he had embraced in the 1920s he turned as a humanist to rediscover the significance of the traditional values that he had thought in *The Modern Temper* to be unavailable to a man of "robust but serious mind."

While seeking mentors in that rediscovery, he looked to writers from that past whose relevance he had earlier doubted. In the life and works of Samuel Johnson he found not only confirmation of his own growing conviction that "the cure for the greatest part of human miseries is not radical, but palliative," but also a model of the bracing common sense that he had come to recognize was absent from both modernist doubt and Marxist conviction. And through Henry David Thoreau he came further to recognize that the natural universe could be rich in a human significance which modernism denied it, and that a humanely scientific perspective like Thoreau's could richly illuminate that meaning.

The admiring—and widely admired—biographies of Johnson and Thoreau which Krutch published in 1944 and 1948 were not only his tributes to those men's literary and personal achievements, but also implicitly Krutch's efforts at self-definition. Celebrating an English Augustan and an American Romantic, he was celebrating as well something beyond the modernism with which he was still popularly associated. Wholly lacking the highbrow pretension of much of his earlier writing, these books were addressed to "the general reader" who would presently become Krutch's largest audience. The great popular success of the works marked a new beginning in his literary career. As he turned to write essays on nature and contemporary society, the influence of Thoreau and Johnson continued to be apparent.

As one of the most widely read nature writers of his day, Krutch brought his Thoreauvian inspiration first to an account of the life he had, over many years, come to enjoy among the plants and animals of New England, and then, after his retirement to Tucson, to an account of the beauty and reassurance he found in the flora and fauna of the southwest. As a modernist, he had seen nature as cold and humanly meaningless; now he saw it as "the great reservoir of energy, of confidence, of endless hope, and of that joy not wholly subdued by the pale cast of thought." Through his many books and essays, others came to see it thus as well; and Krutch's nature writing anticipated (in some measure, doubtless encouraged) that renewed interest in the environment which has swept America since the 1960s.

As a social critic, Krutch became a writer and thinker of consequence for hundreds of thousands of general readers in the 1950s and

60s—just as he had been for the highbrows of the 1920s. Drawing upon the insights gained from his deeply felt experience of nature and respecting anew the evidences of Johnsonian common sense, he argued in two books and numerous essays that man was a more estimable creature than either modernism or various determinist philosophies suggested. His moralistic observations on a society obsessed with technological progress and the accumulation of material goods echoed—though far more gracefully and thoughtfully—the social critiques of the hippies and other spokesmen of the then-blossoming counterculture. As at the beginning of his career, so too at the end he found that man was, "for all his wealth and power, poor in spirit." But Krutch was no longer willing to acquiesce in modernism's passive resignation to the inevitability of man's spiritual poverty. As a humanist who had once again come to believe in "old-fashioned human nature," he tried to lead others beyond the doubt and despair he had so eloquently expressed in *The Modern Temper*. After the Depression and World War II, many Americans thirsted for the reassurance and quiet wisdom he offered.

By the time of his death in 1970, Krutch's standing was higher than ever. Most of his two dozen books were in print, many of them in paperback; and in conferring upon him numerous honors, the literary establishment had confirmed the great popular reputation he enjoyed. In fact, by then he had achieved not one, but many distinguished reputations: as drama critic, book reviewer, literary scholar, modernist, biographer, naturalist, and social critic. During his fifty years of writing he had addressed himself boldly to a variety of subjects each of which, in an age of increasing specialization, seemed destined to become the exclusive province of the expert. His was a protean mind, and with his extensive and often miscellaneous learning and wide-ranging curiosity he had become a complete citizen of the world of ideas. The achievement of his various individual works was often great, and scholars and general readers alike will doubtless continue to turn to many of his books and essays for instruction, inspiration, and the delight of his exceptionally fine prose. But the achievement of Krutch's career as a whole is greater even than the sum of his various reputations. He was and will continue to be recognized as one of America's leading men of letters.

Joseph Wood Krutch
A WRITER'S LIFE

I.

A KNOXVILLE YOUTH

Nestled picturesquely in the foothills of the Appalachians, turn-of-the century Knoxville was a peaceful—by some standards, even languid—East Tennessee town. Manufacturing and wholesaling provided a comfortable economy; a generous supply of churches ministered to the social and spiritual life; the state university constituted a modest center of learning; and a few theaters and a subscription library afforded the cultural resources for the 25,000 people who called Knoxville home. Its quiet streets were lined with poplars, cottonwoods, and other stately shade trees, while white frame houses sat unpretentiously on well-tended lawns.

The texture of life there was memorably portrayed by James Agee in his prose-poem, "Knoxville: Summer of 1915." Young Agee was only six then, and his family, living in the western part of town, barely knew the Krutches, who lived near the center. But Agee's evocation of a summer evening captures well the untroubled domesticity of Knoxville life as felt by a young person at the time: "There were few good friends among the grown people . . . , but everyone nodded and spoke, and even might talk short times, trivially, and at the two extremes of the general and the particular, and ordinarily next-door neighbors talked quite a bit when they happened to run into each other, and never paid calls." After the family dinner, rarely more than half an hour, "People sit on their porches, rocking gently and talking gently and watching the street. . . . People go by; things go by. A horse, drawing a buggy, breaking his hollow music on the as-

3

phalt: a loud auto: a quiet auto: people in pairs, not in a hurry, scuf-
fling, switching their weight of aestival body, talking casually. . . .
A street car raising its iron moan; stopping, belling and starting."[1]

It was a routine which, that summer of 1915, the young Joseph
Wood Krutch was happily preparing to exchange for what promised
to be a richer, more ample life in the metropolis. Having just graduated from the University of Tennessee, he was about to depart for
New York, where he would begin graduate work at Columbia and
then embark on a literary career. During the ensuing fifty-five years
he was rarely nostalgic about his Knoxville childhood. But however
vigorously he soon sought to distance himself from the kind of world
he had known as a youth, and however earnestly the Tennessee provincial endeavored to become a fashionable Eastern intellectual, those
first twenty-two years had unmistakably shaped his mind and character. The Knoxville child was in many ways the father of the celebrated New York and Tucson man of letters.

Arrested in a civic adolescence between its village origins and
the urban maturity to which it aspired, the Knoxville of Krutch's
youth was like hundreds of other small towns in America at the time.
Even the southernness which it enjoyed as an accident of geography
had made little impression. During the Civil War, Unionist sympathies had prevailed there, and as an adult Krutch could at best remark
that he was "a critic who sometimes remembers that he himself is a
Southerner."[2] On Krutch's birthday, November 25, 1893, the local
newspaper mirrored the typical interests of the town's citizens: an al-
dermanic election, the opening of a new shop downtown, the activities of church and fraternal groups, and the news—high on page one
—that "The University footballists are working hard preparatory to
their great Thanksgiving game." A week later the *Evening Sentinel* rejoiced with other Knoxvillians that "The University team has at last
punctuated its history with a victory. Coaching and training will
tell," the lead editorial went on. "May victory ever hereafter perch
upon her banner."[3]

The footballists that fall provided some excitement in the generally uneventful life of the town, but during Krutch's youth most
citizens were quite content with the conventional amenities of Knoxville life and thought; they neither expected nor desired a different

sort of existence. Conformity, Krutch recalled, was "taken for granted as the almost inevitable effect of a slow-moving community where no one thought of radical change, desirable or undesirable, because it was assumed that things would go on much as they always had. Members of the new generation would grow up to marry neighbors, follow in their father's footsteps, and quite probably go on living in the houses where they had been born."[4]

Krutch's parents gladly shared the assumptions of others in the community. Their home was a model of Knoxville respectability and reflected their deep, if unreflective, commitment to the small-town values that tacitly informed life there. The horizons of their world barely extended beyond the Knox County faithfully chronicled by the *Evening Sentinel.* Joe's father, Edward Krutch, had been born there in 1854 and died sixty-nine years later, in an elevator accident in a downtown building. His wife, born Adelaine Wood, had moved to Knoxville in 1860 at the age of six; she died in the family home at ninety-three. Apart from an occasional summer holiday in North Carolina or Maine, the two rarely ventured either intellectually or physically beyond East Tennessee. Their pretensions were few. They were both solid citizens of a community which, as Krutch recalled, "was not . . . much given to questioning things as they are."[5]

Like many of his fellow townsmen who had made Knoxville the commercial capital of the region, Krutch's father worked in merchandising as a trusted functionary in a large wholesale drug firm. He was — in the original, neutral French sense of the word — thoroughly bourgeois. His mode of life was stable, his income sufficient, and his attitudes conventional. His interests, Krutch recalled, "hardly extended beyond his business (at which he was only moderately successful), his home, and his children. . . . His position was in the very middle of the middle class." Like his wife, whose father had run a tannery, he was "intelligent but neither especially intellectual or artistic." "They were," Krutch later explained, "well enough educated by the modest standards of the community but 'intellectual ferment' was hardly a part of its prevailing atmosphere. . . . Awareness of such preliminary stirrings of doubt, dissatisfaction, and anxieties as affected intellectual centers had hardly reached Knoxville."[6] Mr. Krutch devoted his leisure to bridge and occasionally to Dickens, while Mrs.

Krutch looked after the house, doted on her sons, and participated in the church and other civic activities that characterize small-town life.

For young Joe, the bourgeois conventionality of his parents contrasted sharply with the artistic interests and disregard for convention of his paternal grandmother and her three other children. Uncle Oskar, a piano teacher in Washington, was famous in Knoxville for having once performed at the White House. Aunt Lou was also a piano teacher, and her recitals were among the highlights of Knoxville's cultural calendar. She was celebrated as well for occasionally going (unlike most other Knoxville ladies, unaccompanied) on ambitious camping trips in the mountains. Uncle Charlie was a portrait photographer by profession and a painter by avocation; each summer he too went into the Smokies, where he stayed with a mountain family, partaking generously of their corn liquor and fellowship, and making sketches for landscapes which were highly esteemed in East Tennessee.

Joe's grandmother was an even greater presence in his early life than the aunt and uncles with whom his parents were on cordial but hardly intimate terms. "Grossmother," he recalled, was "an intelligent, strong-minded woman of independent convictions who had brought into the provincial atmosphere of Knoxville and had managed to maintain . . . something of the sophisticated and aristocratic disregard of convention acquired from the world into which she had been born."[7] From that world of minor German nobility she had, at sixteen, run away with her music teacher to America, where they settled in a small German community near Knoxville. After she had borne him four children, Herr Krutzsch deserted her, and she supported the family by singing and teaching music.

A Sunday afternoon visit to Grossmother was a great treat for the young Krutch. He delighted in exploring her small backyard greenhouse and in observing her parrot and canaries; "I suspect it was her example," he later wrote, "which taught me the interest in animals and plants which was later to become a major concern." Moreover, his visits seemed "an excursion into an atmosphere quite different from that of my own more conventional home."[8] Grossmother was carefree and witty, while his parents were preoccupied with their domestic responsibilities and were essentially humorless. She was in-

6

terested in art and ideas, while they were not much concerned with either. Indeed, she rejected the bourgeois values of Knoxville as fully as they accepted them. In Grossmother, Aunt Lou, and Uncle Charlie, young Joe caught a glimpse of a kind of sophistication absent in his parents. When he left home for New York, Krutch would try to achieve something of the sort himself.

But these other Knoxville Krutches existed largely on the periphery of Joe's life. Edward Krutch had imbibed neither the artistic interests nor the venturesome nonconformity of his mother and older siblings. Indeed, he had been recognized early on as the one wholly dependable member of his fatherless family, and even as an adolescent he had served as effective head of the household. When Edward married at twenty-eight and set up his own home, he fashioned for himself a life as conventional as his family's seemed to him strangely eccentric; he honored the small-town values in the same measure that they scorned them. And it was of course his influence, along with that of his like-minded wife, which molded Joe most profoundly.

Joe was the youngest of three boys. The eldest, Alfred, shared some of the eccentricity but none of the artistic interests of his uncles and aunt. Partial to drink, cheap women, and the passing of bad checks, he parted ways with his family before Joe, ten years younger, came to know him well. As an impressionable youngster, however, Krutch doubtless saw in his family's rejection of Fred an admonitory example of the tolerable limits of nonconformity.

The Krutches' second son, Charles, six years Joe's senior, was, on the other hand, all one could hope for in an older brother. Unlike Fred, he was content with the pleasures of his middle-class Knoxville childhood, and he served as a model of quiet conformity which Joe would for many years follow. Dogged as a youngster by chronic ill health, he lacked the formal education which might have rendered him an intellectual mentor as well. But in many ways he helped Joe take advantage of what life in Knoxville offered. "During my youth," Krutch recalled, "he hovered over me to protect, comfort, and encourage, sharing or promoting my hobbies, praising me when I needed praise, and helping whenever he could."[9]

The Krutch family circle was hardly a close one; children and parents were no more given to quarrels than to lively displays of affec-

7

tion, living together in respectful but never intimate harmony. Joe and Charles rendered the filial tributes expected of them, and they received in turn the gifts of a secure, if uninspiring, middle-class boyhood. His parents bestowed upon Joe no rich cultural endowment — no love of literature or appreciation of music or sense of history. But they did inculcate in him, more deeply than he recognized, an appreciation of those ordinary bourgeois values and of those conventional, essentially middlebrow tastes according to which they had comfortably lived and made their unexceptional life a modest but unmistakable success. Many of their assumptions about life and conduct inevitably became his. Even as an adolescent, Krutch aspired to a different sort of life; and when he went up from the provinces to live and make his career as a writer in New York, he strained to adopt a perspective different from theirs. But he eventually discovered that his values and tastes were more nearly those of his parents and his Knoxville neighbors than of the advanced thinkers in the city with whom he was eager to associate himself, and who accorded him his initial fame as a spokesman of modernism. The commonsense conservatism and stability of his hometown would, in time, come to seem far preferable to what passed for intellectual and social progress elsewhere.

His debt to his own bourgeois childhood was one Krutch himself never fully acknowledged. He was curiously ungenerous when in 1962 he wrote in his autobiography: "I have no nostalgia for my childhood and I do not idealize the kind of lives Knoxvillians lived in my day. Adults and children alike were unadventurous both physically and intellectually. Their world was thoroughly provincial and lacked stimulation as well as excitement." But he added, "I cannot help remembering at the same time how relatively free it was from both the public and the private pressures, tensions, and anxieties of today."[10] As he wrote those lines in Tucson, nearly fifty years after leaving Knoxville, Krutch was seeking just such freedom himself. And he achieved it by embracing again many of the attitudes and something of the way of life of which he wrote so harshly.

❧ If life in Knoxville was not challenging, it was also not traumatic, and the young Krutch grew up uneventfully, hardly exceptional among other youngsters whose subsequent achievements would be far fewer than his. He was perhaps more given to the solitary pursuit of hobbies than to participating in games with playmates. By the generous standards of the Knoxville schools, he was a successful pupil; but he was, by his own admission, "no prodigy,"[11] and one would have been hard pressed to see in the boy the makings of a leading man of letters.

Lacking the encouragement of literary parents or access to an inviting library in his home, Krutch's childhood reading was desultory and self-directed. Some years later he wrote, "Many a time have we listened with shame to the stories told by our contemporaries and regretted that we could not boast like them of precocious taste, that we could not add our own story of how we devoured Pope's 'Homer' at the age of eight or like Max Beerbohm preferred 'Marius the Epicurean' to 'Two Years Before the Mast' because the former, containing no nautical terms, was easier to understand."[12] Such literature as he stumbled upon was more likely to have been the *Youth's Companion* or the Horatio Alger books, "probably the thinnest fare ever fed to children."[13]

In fact, his earliest interests were scientific rather than literary. In the back room of the town's small library he pored over bound volumes of the *Scientific American*, and at home he pursued such experiments as his modest knowledge and equipment allowed. He gathered together electric batteries, doorbells, and induction coils to form an imaginary Swastika Electric Company; he examined pond water under a microscope lent him by a local physician; he sprouted a bean in sawdust between two pieces of glass. Marvelling at the protrusion of the root and the unfolding of the embryo leaflets, young Joe discovered "a miracle more impressive than any I had heard of involving water and wine."[14]

The palpable evidences of science were more compelling to Krutch than were the abstractions of religion. Hearing in Sunday school of the great day when the lion and the lamb would lie down together, he observed silently, "If the lion ever tries it he will starve to death." "This was not," he acknowledged years later, "a very polished epigram, but I have never forgotten the moment when it seemed as significant as any remark that could possibly be made and it fur-

9

nished the starting point for an essential part of all the thoughts about the universe I have ever had since."[15] Even as a youngster Krutch was skeptical of utopianism, sensing the inevitability of predation in nature's scheme.

Such youthful skepticism was reinforced when he was packed off to hear the bishop during his annual visitation to the family's Episcopal church. Intrigued by a disapproving reference to Herbert Spencer, he found in the local library a volume by this godless author. For the twelve-year-old Krutch, a single chapter was sufficient to make him, for several years at least, "a devout Spencerian." Realizing, as he suddenly did, that he "no longer believed what [he] had been told in Sunday School and church," he was confirmed in an "assured, rather narrow rationalism" which required the better part of several decades' thinking to undo.[16] His skepticism, however, was for the moment his secret; to all appearances, he remained an ordinary Knoxville child.

The Knoxville schools, Krutch recalled, "were so traditional that they had all but forgotten what the tradition was supposed to be about," and few children were ever "overstimulated" there.[17] In history classes Joe "memorized a textbook, paragraph by paragraph, each of which I promptly forgot when, for the next day, I memorized the succeeding paragraphs."[18] In science and mathematics classes he occasionally came to the aid of his teacher, who understood a difficult problem less well than he. And for English he wrote uninspired "themes" on uninspiring topics, while reading bits of the literary staples: Shakespeare, Milton, *Silas Marner*, and the *Spectator* papers. It was, in fact, more a training than an education. Characteristically, the part of Joe's performance which most concerned his teachers and parents was his egregious penmanship and spelling. In these literary mechanics he seemed hopelessly ineducable. He protested reassuringly that, as an adult, he would not require these skills, since he would have a secretary. To the dismay of editors years later, he never did.

Even at school, as indirectly at church, Krutch found occasional inspiration. Reading the *Spectator* papers on Sir Roger de Coverley, he was attracted to "the character of the Spectator, who had embraced observation and reporting as his role in life. . . . The first impulse I ever had to write anything was in imitation of the Sir Roger de Coverley papers."[19] He doubtless wrote all the more enthusiastically knowing that those words, at least, would escape the schoolmarm's censorious eye.

Despite the educational and cultural deficiencies of Knoxville, Krutch's childhood there was not wholly impoverished. Only a few blocks from his home were three theaters to which many national touring companies paid regular visits. When Charles took his five-year-old brother to his first show, a matinee of "a rural melodrama" called *Si Plunket*, he opened up for Joe a world far more spacious than any other that small town could offer. The nourishment for the imagination which he failed to receive from his family or in books or at school he found in the halls of the Grand, the Bijou, and Staub's. There was art to be entertained by, not to be parsed and memorized; and there began that love of the theater which only a quarter-century of professional play-going could wholly dispel.

Most of Knoxville's theatrical life at the turn of the century was vaudeville, and young Joe found ample delight in "Bailey's Pantomime Dogs," "Powder and Chapmann: Songs, Sayings, and Sprightly Steppers," "Rozell's Minstrels," "McNamee: Comedy Clay Modeler," "Laypo and Benjamin: Hebrew Comedy Acrobats," and "Pat Hanrahan's Trained Goats." Compared with the "Ten-Twent'-Thirt'" vaudeville at the Bijou and the Grand, the offerings at Staub's were high art. To that elegant theater, which seated 1,800 patrons, people came from throughout the region to see some of the most famous actors and actresses of the day. Most of the fare was romantic drama, melodrama, farce, or musicals—the latter with choruses of as many as eighty. But serious drama also reached Staub's, and during Krutch's youth Ibsen could be seen, as well as Shakespeare, Shaw, or Restoration comedy. Going to the theater, and especially to Staub's, was for Krutch "a grand luxury, almost a debauch."[20] In the midst of a virtual Sahara of the Bozart, he had access to a world of art which satisfied needs he might not otherwise have known he had.

Attending the theater became a regular habit for Krutch, but supporting that habit on his modest allowance posed a problem. Charles helpfully provided the solution: as Knoxville correspondent for the *Dramatic Mirror*, a national theatrical weekly, he had been reporting on the box office receipts of the shows appearing in town; a perquisite of the job was a pass entitling him to free admission. Joe followed his brother's helpful example and became correspondent for a similar publication, *The Footlight*. Although his weekly dispatches to Atlanta were as ephemeral as the box office receipts they recorded, they earned him the desired pass and mark not only the beginning of Krutch's long association with the theater but also, in a way, the start of his career as a professional writer.

For young Krutch, the touring companies that visited Knoxville and the films shown in its nickelodeons became an umbilical to a great world beyond East Tennessee. The metropolis whence such marvels came must, he thought, be all that Knoxville was not—lively, creative, and cosmopolitan. He became impatient to see for himself New York, which seemed as exotic as some foreign land. Had he been given to mischievousness, he might have run away to the big city; but such was not in his character. Instead, at the dinner table he and Charles began persuading their parents to underwrite an excursion. Some months later their persuasive skills bore fruit. Barely in his teens, Joe set off, accompanied only by Charles, for the first of what would be a number of summertime trips to New York.

Though now paying for admission, the two brothers feasted on a theatrical diet far richer than that of Knoxville, occasionally attending as many as three films and plays per day. Restaurants offered culinary pleasures they had never imagined. As the two youths on their "Krutch tours" sought to exhaust the delights of Manhattan, they discovered that those delights were inexhaustible. Marveling at the skyscrapers, thrilled to be part of the bustling crowds, and excited by a vision of an existence far more ample than that of Knoxville, Joe at once became a confirmed lover of the city. Knoxville seemed suffocatingly provincial by comparison, and as he returned during successive summers he resolved that New York must someday become his home. That day, he realized, would not come until he had completed his undergraduate study at the University of Tennessee, several blocks from his home. But by the time he began his studies there he at least enjoyed (thanks to his summer trips) a conviction shared by few of his classmates: that there was world beyond East Tennessee. He knew, moreover, that his college study must prepare him somehow to enter that greater universe.

⁂ The University's role in the Knoxville of 1911 was suggested by the 1893 *Sentinel* item extolling the achievements of the footballists. The town was proud of the prominence it enjoyed as the seat of the state university; but for most citizens the University was noted more for its social and athletic activity than for academic distinction. It was, in short, like the town itself, an unlikely place for the development of a young man who was to become a distinguished scholar and a celebrated man of letters.

Most of the school's six hundred students were enrolled in such programs as agriculture and engineering. As the 1920 student magazine suggests, the ideal of liberal education was not widely accepted: "A person should positively decide just what he intends to make his life's work before entering college," prospective freshmen were advised, "because in all probability his four years will be wasted if he has studied one course and decides to follow a different profession."[21] Fewer than 5 percent of the students came from out of state; most were from East Tennessee, and the majority of those from Knoxville.

Sports (in which Krutch was never interested) and Greek societies (which were never interested in him) dominated student life. Again the student magazine is revealing: "The social life of the University . . . has always been one of the most attractive features of the institution. Young people love their good times, and have lots of them."[22] During his years there, Krutch recalled, the University was "for the most part sleepily conventional. Students — pupils would be a more accurate word — seldom read anything not required. The bookstore stocked absolutely nothing except textbooks and I can remember only one of my fellows who ever bought a book of any other kind."[23]

At the University, however, Krutch did find some activities which proved more rewarding than any he had been offered at school, and as a freshman he joined the Chi Delta Literary Society — in fact, a debating group. Required to "work up" a variety of topics and argue persuasively whatever position he took, he developed the intellectual and verbal agility which would stand him in good stead some years later as a literary journalist. From the beginning he showed obvious talent; in his first year he won the Society's medal for an oration on "International Peace," having defeated contestants expounding on "Napoleon" and "Life." But after two years arguing such issues as the establishment of a single six-year presidential term, immigration policy, currency reform, and President Wilson's policies in the Philippines, Krutch wearied of the niceties of politics, finding it (as he would throughout his life) an uninteresting topic.

He hoped that writing might prove more congenial, and as a junior he became associate editor of the student paper, *Orange and White*. Doubtless he was the author of the plaintive one-sentence editorial which asked, "How about a Dramatic Club?"[24] But he wrote more frequently of campus events that actually did (rather than ideally might) take place, and in a survey of various student clubs he reported that "The student activities . . . are many and varied. There are twelve organizations of students devoted to all manner of purposes, so that almost any one finds something to his taste. . . . There is no reason why any student should pine for employment even though his studies are too light to occupy his time."[25] The modest academic demands of the University left Krutch ample free time.

Eager for still further extracurricular employment, at the end of his junior year Krutch applied for the editorship of the *University of Tennessee Magazine*, the monthly publication of student writing. Facing what could hardly have been severe competition, he was appointed. As editor he enjoyed recognition of the sort that he had missed in the fraternities and on the playing fields, and he set about his new job with obvious relish. Before the end of his term he would leave his mark.

Shortly after his appointment, Krutch issued a call for contributions in the student newspaper. Even in this first official pronouncement he spoke like a man of long literary experience:

> A foolish horror of rejections seems to be the greatest obstacle which the editor has to overcome in securing contributions. Nothing could be more foolish. The number of rejections which successful magazine writers receive would no doubt surprise many students. After a story goes begging for several months it is finally accepted with high praise

by one editor after being refused by several others. Rejections are considered simply as a matter of course and have absolutely no discredit connected with them.

(That "foolish horror" was one from which Krutch was rarely to suffer.) He concluded his call for contributions saying, "As Thackeray has somewhere remarked, one never knows how many thoughts he has until he starts to write them down. Try it."[26]

In the literary career on which he was to embark several years later, Krutch followed that advice. From the beginning, writing was for him less an art than a craft; less a sacrament to be undertaken only upon the arrival of some elusive inspiration than an act of skillfully gathering together paragraphs on whatever topic was at hand. He was for most of his career less a creative artist than an enormously gifted literary journalist, and it is appropriate that his earliest undergraduate writing should be not a poem, story, or other more typical adolescent work, but a topical essay.

His very first editorial essay contains many of the elements which would characterize his work a half-century later. "We feel about editorials somewhat as Mr. Dickens did about prefaces," he began, recalling the preface to *Pickwick Papers*. "We are inclined to wonder just how widely and eagerly they are read and to suspect that they are usually regarded more as a conventional and ornamental appendage than as something to be actually read." Where one might most expect it—in an inaugural editorial—there was no sense of stuffy self-importance or literary pretension. Krutch was writing candidly, cordially and in his own voice to the people among whom he had grown up. From the beginning he also manifested the conservatism which was by then a fundamental part of his character. Despite his doubts about the importance of editorials, he had "no intention of being 'the first by whom the new is tried,'" and he added "the sanction of our acceptance to the general custom."

For all that, he was not so cowed by his background that he was incapable of asking original questions. Confident that "the field has been pretty well covered," he set aside such conventional topics as "college spirit" to take up "subjects that have been less thoroughly discussed."[27] In his next editorial he addressed himself to the value of a liberal arts education. After three years at the University he felt that the topic was important: " 'If an education cannot be put into use of what good is it?' " he had recently heard a local high school principal demand. A fair enough question, Krutch allowed, "if we could only agree as to what 'use' includes." To him it was clear that "use" must include the achievement of happiness. By that criterion he proposed — what must have seemed a novel, if not subversive, idea to many of his fellow students — that "The cultivation of the appreciation of beauty is distinctly utilitarian because it produces happiness, the only ultimate end of any useful thing."

Along with the tendency at universities like Tennessee "to push the ideal element, the element of art and literature, into the background," Krutch objected to the lowering of standards which had followed from recent educational "reform" and had "reacted unfavorably upon the best students, and inclined them to be satisfied to stand only a little above the general low standard. . . . It is in the college," he concluded, "that the counter revolution should be started."[28] Even in his earliest writing he showed his concern for values, his impatience with a narrow and shallow utilitarianism, his skepticism of change in the guise of "progress," and his readiness to challenge the received truths of the day in order to suggest other, more fundamental truths. Already, as a college essayist, he spoke with the assured voice of the moralist.

In another editorial he objected to the lowering of standards in the theater as well. If the theater was threatened by films, he said, it was because of the unprincipled willingness of producers to "give the public just what they want. . . . The people have wanted or seemed to want such frivolous stuff that they have not only ruined their taste for more substantial things but, as the managers might have foreseen, they have become completely cloyed upon what they thought they wanted and now they do not want anything."[29] The sentiments in this early writing anticipate remarkably similar statements in the social commentary with which, many years later, he ended his career.

Writing as editor of the college magazine, Krutch was not only finding out how many thoughts he had, but also testing his literary talents. The publication of *Androcles and the Lion* provided an occasion for him to try his hand at literary criticism. Some weeks earlier he had read his first Shaw play, when "some unfavorable references to his absurd impudence" in the *Literary Digest* prompted him to seek out Shaw's works in the library. At random he pulled from the shelf *Man and Superman*; by the end of the first act he was a Shavian. Krutch recalled that he "closed the book to sit for a while reveling in the discovery of what literature could be." He was thrilled not so much by Shaw's ideas themselves as by the discovery "that any one allowed to get into print could say such mischievously pertinent things."[30] Literature, he found, could be contemporary in a way that the standard classroom authors had never been. "It was only from that day forward," he said, "that I could take literature seriously or believe that an author was being candid with his readers."[31] As a young essayist, candor was a quality for which Krutch himself was striving. Years later he referred to that experience with *Man and Superman* as "the light which broke upon me on my way to Damascus."[32] Notwithstanding the hyperbole, the event was momentous. Krutch's biography is less the record of dramatic actions than of such intellectual experiences as his discovery during his senior year of Shaw—and, through Shaw, of literature.

Shortly after his illumination, the text of *Androcles and the Lion* appeared in *Everybody's Magazine*, and Krutch was eager to share his new enthusiasm with his readers. Though his acquaintance with Shaw's work was but recent and slight, he began with a sweeping generalization worthy of the seasoned critic: "George Bernard Shaw again bursts before his admirers with brilliance undimmed and with fresh proof of a solidity which many persist in denying him." His essay was partly summary, partly advertisement, and partly an effort to rescue Shaw from the fate of "all preachers of new doctrines [who] have to bear the effects of the distortion of their views by the ignorant and the malicious." In the relation between the early Christians and the conventional, pagan elements of their society, Krutch saw a parallel between Shaw and his contemporaries: "All that it is necessary for the Christians in his play to do in order to secure their release is to simply drop a pinch of incense on the altar and the patricians cannot understand the idealism that prevents them from performing this simple ceremony. Today, thinks Mr. Shaw, many people are dropping their incense upon the altar of conventionality and it is just this that he is unwilling to do."³³ In this respect as well, Krutch was becoming a Shavian.

The intention, stated in his first editorial, to treat "subjects that have been less thoroughly discussed" reflected Krutch's precocious understanding of at least one path to literary recognition. His essays on liberal education, the theater, and Shaw were innocuous when compared with two on Prohibition, both written shortly before his graduation. Part of his motivation was doubtless a principled objection to the hypocrisy of the movement. Furthermore, he was registering, as he prepared to leave for New York, a youthful protest against a symptom of the provinciality he hoped to escape. But above all one imagines he was eager—as he would be when beginning his career as a writer—to gain the attention which comes from saying the wrong thing at the right time. He succeeded, and in an essay and an accompanying editorial he created a minor scandal in the otherwise placid life of the University of Tennessee.

"Many good people," Krutch wrote, "appear to believe that when anybody pursues a line of conduct which does not command their approval, it is their duty to use even violent means to make that person comport himself according to their own ideas of right." Against the prevailing moral absolutism, the free-thinking young essayist proposed a contrary relativism: "In so abstract a matter as ethics, one person's opinion is about as good as another's." University authorities could perhaps tolerate this error of a misguided youth, but they were less tolerant of his imputation of hypocrisy to the right-thinking members of the community. "Most people," Krutch continued, do not

> feel so anxious about their own moral condition anyhow. It is the ways of other people that gives them the most concern. . . . Many strong prohibitionists do not hesitate to have a bottle of their own in the house because, after all, it is only their neighbor who is in danger. . . . It is not our duty to run about passing laws against everything that we do not do ourselves and founding societies for the suppression of things-in-general. We ought to be our brother's keeper with love and not with a club. We are not animal trainers.

"The ideas presented in this essay," he added with no slight satisfaction, "do not fall in with the spirit of the times."[34]

In the accompanying editorial, Krutch considered the Prohibition movement among his fellow students. "We hope that it will not be successful but we are inclined to believe that it will. There is a narrowness about it all that is not surprising in the ordinary man, but which is painful to see in those supposed to have a 'liberal' education." Citing authors from Shakespeare to Keats, he added playfully: "One can hardly read the literature of the world without seeing that the juice of the grape has played an important role and that great men have used it and done it honor."[35]

In Tennessee, however, and especially at the University, Prohibition was not taken lightly. Though enforcement generally lagged somewhat behind, Prohibition legislation had recently made significant headway in the state. While the Prohibition lobby was successfully wooing legislators' votes, the energetic president of the University, Brown Ayres, was no less eagerly seeking appropriations. Since the *Magazine*, modest though it was, was one of the University's proudest non-athletic achievements — distributed as an advertisement of sorts to more than 250 colleges and universities throughout the nation, and to nearly as many high schools around the state — it was embarrassing for Ayres to find there sentiments so alien to "the spirit of the times."

Krutch was summoned by the dean and warned that, though he was only a few months from graduation, he would be summarily expelled if he published any further offensive articles. If he was still unwilling to contribute his pinch of incense to the altar, Krutch at least recognized the practical limits of dissent. In the April editorial he took "'Spring' as the subject of [his] cogitations because the evidence of the almanac removes the subject from the list of those labeled 'controversial' and because it is the thing (aside from something that is nameless here for evermore) about which the poets love most to sing."[36]

In his undergraduate writing about Prohibition, Krutch was doubtless himself enjoying what he had found so attractive in Shaw: "that any one allowed to get into print could say such mischievously pertinent things." Recalling the affair, he said, "I had established myself as what my literary hero called a Devil's Disciple."[37] Behind those essays lay a young writer's eagerness to shock, and the knowledge that his impious reflections would command greater attention than more sober writing on some locally acceptable theme.

But one can also see in his remarks on Prohibition the earnestly moralistic and conscientiously libertarian Krutch of much of his subsequent writing. Whether discussing theatrical censorship in the twenties, Marxism in the thirties, or behaviorist theories of psychological determinism in the fifties and sixties, Krutch believed deeply in the reality, and necessity, of individual liberty. Shortly after his indiscretions on Prohibition, he wrote editorially of his uneasiness over the "odium" that "has come to be attached to the epithet 'individualist'": "We have indeed fallen into the pernicious habit of minimizing personal achievement and talking only of lumps; of forgetting that there is such a thing as 'a simple, separate person' and talking loosely of that indefinite modern catch word 'society' . . . . Real success or failure comes only from within and society cannot impress it from without. Only the individualist succeeds for only self-realization is success."[38] Even as an undergraduate Krutch had come to value that individualism. Some years later—after he felt he had failed to win stunning literary success—he turned within, to achieve the self-realization through which he made his life a "real success."

Though by his senior year Krutch had earned a certain recognition as editor of the *Magazine*—and notoriety for his writing on Prohibition—his undergraduate career was generally unexceptional. He enjoyed few of the "good times" the University promised its students; by his own reckoning, he "had only two even moderately intimate friends." Among his classmates, he recalled, he "enjoyed no reputation except as a rather tiresomely assiduous student."[39] At graduation his industry was recognized by his election to Phi Kappa Phi, the academic honorary.

Like his childhood interests, the academic direction which Krutch had been taking before his Shavian illumination was largely scientific. While also studying physics, botany, and chemistry, he concentrated on mathematics and hoped someday to teach it. "I did not know how else one with my lack of interest in the practical application of anything could make a living," he recalled.[40] Years later, when his interests turned from literature to nature, he would be grateful for such scientific literacy as he acquired when an undergraduate.

To prepare himself for teaching, Krutch took a number of required courses in history, education, and psychology. For two years he also participated in the obligatory military science program. In order to achieve the liberal education that he had championed as an editorialist, he also took each year at least two arts courses: in German language and literature, and in English. In the required freshman course he worked his way laboriously through Genung's *Working Principles of Rhetoric,* studied the application of Genung's principles in essays in the *Atlantic Monthly*, and memorized a meager ration of poetry. Freshman English at Tennessee was designed to nurture discipline rather than imagination; but the mastery of Genung's rhetorical principles and the imitation of them in weekly themes was perhaps not the worst possible preparation for a young man who would make his career as a writer of nonfiction.

As a sophomore he took the first of what would be three year-long courses with James D. Bruce, the chairman of the five-member English department. The initial course was a historical survey of English literature. As a junior Krutch studied romantic and Victorian poetry, and in his final year, Shakespeare and Chaucer. While the would-be mathematics teacher's nose was being "rubbed into a small but respectable portion of the best of English literature,"[41] his feelings were generally less of enthusiasm than of "bored resentment. The pearls which were cast lavishly before me, I trampled under foot," he recalled a decade later. "The glittering gems in 'Ward's English Poets' were no more than so many acorns."[42]

During his final year of college, however, Krutch took a new delight in works he had previously endured, at best. As a sophomore he had read *Hamlet* and "decided that it was 'pretty good' but that it certainly did not deserve all the fuss that had been made over it." Two years later he reread the play, and found it a new thing. "I could hardly believe that I had once dismissed with tolerant contempt the same phrases which now thrilled me. There was a magic in the words and a spell was woven about me."[43] His rediscovery of *Hamlet* coincided with his discovery of Shaw—and also, during that senior year, with his decision to go on for graduate work, not in mathematics, but in English, at Columbia University in New York.

The decision was made less because of his newfound love of literature than because he recognized he had modest prospects in mathematics. As he later recalled, he reasoned with himself at the time: "'If out of a class of three in a small college I am not outstandingly the best . . . it is not likely that I will ever distinguish myself in the field. I had better go in for something else.'"⁴⁴ As editor of the *University of Tennessee Magazine*, he had discovered that he could manipulate words more skillfully than numbers. But ultimately perhaps another consideration, characteristically practical, was decisive in his sudden change of plans: "One of the attractions of Literature as opposed to Mathematics was simply that the best place to study the latter was said to be Chicago and Chicago, to the imagination of most provincials —especially Southern provincials—was not to be compared with New York as an embodiment of everything the home town was not." Literature, then, was less a calling than an excuse to fulfill his long-standing ambition to live in New York City.

By the time he graduated from college, he had "never met a man or a woman who had written a book addressed to other than an academic audience, and never, with the exception of one touring pianist, anyone of more than local reputation in any of the arts and sciences. Those who did write books, paint pictures, or perform in public seemed to me members of a species different from that to which I, my family, and my acquaintances belonged." In choosing English, Columbia, and New York, Krutch was hardly presuming to join that species. "The most I hoped for myself was that I too might become a minor college professor," he recalled. "But at least I could also hope for a closer view of what writers and artists were like."⁴⁵ If he had no expectations of making sweets himself, he nonetheless looked forward in New York to pressing his nose against the sweet-shop window.

As he boarded the train in September 1915, Krutch was exhilarated by the prospects of his new life in New York. His memories of Knoxville were not unpleasant, however. As a graduate student and later as a young writer, proud of the sophistication he had suddenly acquired in the metropolis, he would look back on his provincial childhood and youth with different and less generous feelings, although even then the legacy of Knoxville would remain with him. He had been stamped, more deeply than he himself recognized, with the fundamentally conservative, middle-class, middlebrow mentality of his family and his community. After his early meteoric success as one of the fashionably sophisticated young writers of the 1920s, Krutch would come to find that the sweet-shop of the New York literary world was cloying, and that the attitudes of those who lived there were none he could honestly share. In the end he would recognize that he was more a middlebrow Knoxvillian than a highbrow New Yorker, and as a writer he would eventually find his greatest and most appreciative audience among those ordinary, commonsensical, intelligent but not strenuously intellectual people among whom he had grown up and toward whom he was shortly to condescend.

2.

⚘ SOME APPRENTICESHIPS

Returning to Knoxville for the summer after his first year at Columbia, Krutch felt "proudly, if not a bit unjustifiably, that [he] now inhabited a different world."[1] Residence in New York and graduate study at a major university were even more thrilling than he had imagined. His apprehension the previous fall had proven unfounded, and he was flourishing personally and academically as he never had in Knoxville.

Ambitious to succeed, he applied himself diligently to his courses. His own undergraduate preparation in literature was meager at best, and the challenges he faced at Columbia were far greater than any he had met at Tennessee. He was reassured to find himself apparently equal to the task. Even in the first year he mined a publishable article from his master's thesis on the nineteenth-century Philadelphia playwright George Henry Boker, which appeared in the *Sewanee Review* the following year. "When the history of the American drama comes to be written," he began solemnly, "there will emerge from obscurity no man of more interest to the general reader than . . . Boker. . . . A biographical and critical treatment of Boker is still a desideratum."[2] If his judgment of Boker's importance was mistaken, he nonetheless showed in his first appearance in a journal of national circulation that, for the moment at least, he took scholarship very seriously indeed, as he strained to affect what he imagined to be a proper academic voice.

During a seminar on Restoration drama in his second year,

24

Krutch resolved to concentrate his further studies there. The decision was partly, of course, a function of his continued delight in plays, a feeling he had first experienced years earlier at Staub's in Knoxville. Moreover, it was a sign of his effort, increasingly deliberate during the next decade, to transform himself from a Tennessee provincial into a New York sophisticate. The same "adolescent desire to shock" which had partly prompted his undergraduate essays on Prohibition led him "to pretend to like even more than I actually did both the raffish and also the 'decadent' . . . . The comic drama of the Restoration was notoriously the naughtiest section of English literature. Who could treat it with profounder understanding than I?"[3] In its hard, cynical disillusionment, Restoration comedy resembled the spirit even then defining itself as "modern". Krutch labored to make this spirit his own.

Among his fellow graduate students he was also laboring to fashion for himself a distinct and vivid personality such as life in Knoxville had never encouraged. The summer before he arrived at Columbia, he grew a little mustache — not only to disguise his boyish looks, but also to give him at least the appearance of the sophistication he hardly felt as he came up from the provinces to the metropolis. His new companions — many of them more adrift in the city than he — admired his familiarity with New York, and he was pleased to point them to some of the local spots with which he was already acquainted from his summer excursions. "I was astonished as well as delighted," he recalled, "to discover that I was considered 'sophisticated,' an amusing if somewhat reckless talker, and even a bit of a wit. I promptly adopted the new role which I found very congenial and played it in a fashion which must have been extremely callow but seemed to be effective among those who were, no doubt, almost equally so, each in his own way."[4]

Surrounded by an appreciative audience, Krutch excelled as a talker; in discussions among the graduate students at Columbia, he was invariably at the center. Though his nervous pacing of the floor belied his apparent self-confidence, he held forth with wit and at least the pretense of authority on a broad range of topics, literary and otherwise. Years later, writing of Dr. Johnson and his Club, he must have recalled his own formative experiences as an earnest conversationalist at Columbia. "Every member of the group tried to do well, tried within the limits of his capacity to shine. Good things were applauded, the abilities of the players were estimated, and certain sessions were remembered as particularly brilliant."[5] Krutch was eager to shine, and he savored the applause he received.

However, beneath the artfully self-created image of the witty sophisticate lay a deeply shy young man who, notwithstanding the admiration of teachers and colleagues, remained uncertain of his academic talents. In his third year at Columbia his uncertainty was compounded when he was appointed as a part-time instructor in the College, only to discover how ill suited he was for the teaching which he still imagined would be his career. The verbal prowess he displayed in conversation with his fellow students disappeared when he stood before a class of freshmen. Always ill at ease among strangers, he now found himself paralyzed with nervous anxiety and unable to relate to the students—who were doubtless, in their way, as nervous as their teacher. His efforts to draw them into discussion were met with stony silence, and each new meeting of his class built upon the failures of the last. Visibly upset by his students' innocent undergraduate pranks, he unwittingly encouraged more of the same. None of the devices he desperately seized upon worked; in his first effort at teaching he was as unhappy as he was ineffective.

Compared with the ordeal of teaching, even the army seemed attractive, and in the spring of 1918 he enlisted, resigning his instructorship and taking leave of his graduate study. For Krutch, the War had been a distant reality at best; excited by his new life in New York and willing to have others win the lasting peace which he was confident would follow victory, he had been content to continue writing his seminar papers in Morningside Heights. But his disastrous performance in front of the classroom and the increasing likelihood of his being drafted like so many of his colleagues led him to accept a friendly congressman's offer to secure him a stateside assignment.

Characteristically, Krutch sought to avoid, rather than to embrace, the strenuous self-testing of combat which attracted so many others of his generation. That he was a somewhat frail young man was doubtless significant. Moreover, he shared a quality which he later attributed to the Knoxvillians of his youth: a spirit which resisted physical adventure. Even in intellectual matters, as during the political debates of the 1930s, Krutch remained a reluctant combatant. He was relieved, then, to be able to perform his service in the Psychological Corps at Ft. Travis, Texas, testing and classifying new recruits. Seven months after his enlistment the Armistice was declared, and he was mustered out of the army as little affected by the war as a soldier could possibly be.

In January 1919, Krutch returned to Columbia. After passing his doctoral examination that spring, he returned to Knoxville, to begin such research as was possible there toward the dissertation which remained the final hurdle of his program. He also anxiously awaited word on his application for the English department's Cutting Traveling Fellowship which, if awarded, would allow him to spend the following year working on the dissertation in Europe—and, not incidentally, exploring cities even more romantic than New York. When a telegram announced his success, he was, of course, delighted. But his pleasure was tinged with misgiving: Mark Van Doren, his closest Columbia friend, had also applied for the fellowship, and the success of one seemed obviously to imply the failure of the other. While Krutch fretted in Knoxville about breaking the news to his friend, Van Doren in Urbana was similarly uneasy; he too had received the grant. Since none had been awarded during the War, two fellowships had been granted for 1919-20. Krutch's and Van Doren's apologetic letters to each other—written in ignorance that the other shared his own good fortune—crossed in the mail. The two young men promptly booked passage together on a ship to England that August.

Of all the gifts of his Columbia years, none was more precious to Krutch than his friendship with Van Doren. Having had only a handful of "even moderately intimate friends" in all his years in Knoxville, during the first weeks of his new life as a graduate student he discovered the joy of deeply intimate friendship founded upon great mutual respect. Although he was renowned as a talker among colleagues to whom he callowly displayed his sophistication, Krutch enjoyed with Van Doren the richer pleasure of true conversation.

Though his brother, Carl, was on the Columbia faculty, Mark Van Doren shared something of his friend's apprehension when he arrived in the fall of 1915 from his home in Urbana and his previous study at the University of Illinois. One Saturday the two provincials set off downtown on the Broadway subway, intending to explore the city. Over the noise of the train they talked with (and, as necessary, shouted at) each other. As Van Doren later wrote, they delighted to find "that we had a good deal to say to each other, and that each was really interested in what the other said; also that each was eager to speak when it came his turn, and was confident that what he said would be worth hearing . . . . Joe Krutch from this moment was famous company for me."[6]

For Krutch, Van Doren was not only the appreciative listener craved by the talker, but also the intellectual helpmate required by the conversationalist. His friend, Krutch recalled, could be counted upon to respond to his statements "with something which [was] not merely sympathetic and understanding but [was] also a new insight from some different point of view or perspective."[7] For more than fifty years their conversation "ranged without apology from the grandest to the meanest subjects."[8]

In some respects the two were quite similar. Long before arriving in New York, both had been imbued with the middle-class values, the middlebrow attitudes, and the belief in commonsense reason that characterized life in the small towns where they had been born and reared. But the friendship of Van Doren and Krutch was not founded merely on the self-congratulatory communion of like minds and personalities. They were, in important ways, different — and thus richly complementary.

Van Doren was a poet throughout, even in his almost classical physical features. Gifted with great sensitivity to the nuances of verse, he was more interested, as a critic, in the dynamics of art and the nature of the poetic sensibility than in the philosophical aspects of literature. Early on he abjured the use of the word *values*, which figured so centrally in Krutch's own writing.[9] Van Doren's greatest discoveries were intuitive, and he presented them in his volumes of verse. By contrast, Krutch's medium was invariably prose, and his approach was largely analytical and philosophical. Ideas, rather than the texture of experience, concerned him in most of his writing.

Temperamental as well as intellectual differences distinguished these two best of friends. Acting out the part in which he delightedly found himself cast at Columbia, Krutch was an entertaining wit and an aspiring sophisticate; Van Doren, in comparison, seemed earnest and vaguely humorless. Lacking the capacity to relate easily and intimately to other people, Krutch was reserved and appeared self-centered. Van Doren, on the other hand, became legendary for his extraordinary sweetness and generosity, and for many years he—and his brother Carl, who had supervised Krutch's master's thesis, and Carl's wife Irita—assisted Krutch materially at various stages in his literary career.

As he set off with Van Doren for England in August 1919, Krutch's ambitions were still scholarly rather than literary. The ostensible purpose of the traveling fellowship was, after all, to allow him to research and write his dissertation on Restoration and early eighteenth century drama. He spent a respectable number of hours quarrying through documents in the Public Record Office, examining materials in the Archbishop of Canterbury's library at Lambeth Palace, and exploiting the resources of the British Museum. But Van Doren had nearly completed his dissertation on Dryden even before their departure for England, and Krutch was not unwilling to be distracted from his scholarship. Together they visited the Lake District and saw the sights of London; unabashed tourists, with guidebooks in hand, they were delighted at last to see places whose associations with English literature they were proud to know. In the *Times* they placed an advertisement: "Two young Americans, literary, but interested in everything, desire London friends."[10] They were happily and unpretentiously small-town American innocents abroad.

In February they set off for Paris, and from their rooms on the Left Bank across from the Odéon they visited the cafes, museums, theaters, and bookstores which made Paris, to their minds, even more thrilling than London. But theirs was not the bohemian Paris of Tristan Tzara's Dada manifestations which, even by 1920, had lured many young Americans there. The young men from Knoxville and Urbana were more impressed by monuments of the past than by harbingers of the future. The antiquities of Paris seemed to them "more graceful and . . . also somehow more assured" than those of London —"less like preserved relics than a still integral part of the city." Krutch delighted in "the sense of stability which . . . is something that no one brought up in an American community can have experienced at home. It is," he recalled some years later, "the antithesis of Progress but, when met for the first time, it may strike those of a certain temperament as something reassuringly better."[11] A child of Knoxville, Krutch instinctively preferred stability to Progress, even as he was self-consciously trying to shake off the legacy of his provincial past.

Temperamentally conservative, neither Krutch nor Van Doren thought of joining the hundreds of their countrymen who had come to Paris during the War and stayed on, rejecting America. Both had teaching positions awaiting them that fall—Van Doren at Columbia, and Krutch at Brooklyn Polytechnic Institute. Krutch, moreover, had a dissertation to complete. Their funds nearly exhausted by April, they departed for America, traveling back to a world of responsibility at the very time when many of their contemporaries were flocking to Europe to escape it. In Knoxville that summer—where he neither suffered nor enjoyed the distractions of London and Paris—Krutch completed his thesis.

The controversy following the publication of Jeremy Collier's *Short View of the Immorality and Profaneness of the English Stage* (1698) is one of the livelier episodes in the literary history of the period, and on that topic Krutch was writing his dissertation. With all his nonjuring furor, Collier had denounced most leading comic playwrights of the Restoration. While he was hardly the first to have objected to the immorality of stage dialogue, the unflattering portrayal of clergymen like himself, or the apparent tendency of the theater to promote rather than correct folly and vice, his vigorous rhetoric won for his tract unprecedented attention, and it soon became the focus for a spirited battle of the books. Such controversies are inherently interesting, and the rehearsal of the charges, countercharges, and rejoinders offers the dissertation writer the opportunity to display his scholarly talents in coping with a mass of source material and fashioning it into a coherent narrative. Krutch's study ranged widely over various literary and social influences which he showed to converge upon both the publication of the *Short View* and the new sentimental comedy which presently arose. Adorned with all the obligatory trappings, his dissertation provides what remains the most comprehensive study of the

Collier controversy itself, as well as a rich quarry of material about English theater and society between 1660 and 1725.

Like his essay on Boker, Krutch's dissertation was largely a scholarly performance. But even through the forest of his doctoral scholarship shone the light of the new sophistication that Krutch had studiously acquired, and his appreciation for the hard, intellectual, often cynical way in which the Restoration playwrights, like the moderns of his own day, contemplated their world. Rather than corrupting morals, Krutch insisted, the comedy of the period merely reflected them: "The Restoration stage was a fashionable entertainment where the most reckless of the upper class saw their follies and vices wittily and realistically presented."[12] His lively description of the attitude of the Restoration wits glowed with admiration: "They wished to make the time to come in every way the reverse of the time that was past . . . ; to pull down all that had been set up, and set up all that had been pulled down; to hate all that had been loved and love all that had been hated. The Puritans had tended to regard all pleasure as sinful, and they determined to regard no pleasure as such." It was an attitude Krutch was trying to make his own.

Considering the vigorous hedonism of many of his contemporaries, Collier seemed to Krutch a grotesque Malvolio unnerved by the festivity of his times and all but blind to the charms of art. "He was a narrow-minded fanatic apparently as much shocked by wit as he was by blasphemy," he wrote. "No conceivable stage could have pleased him, since he was fundamentally an enemy to imaginative literature." The sentimental comedy favored by Collier was "not a spontaneous expression but a machine-made product . . . stereotyped and artificial," and the rise of that dramatic style demonstrated "the triumph of morality and criticism over wit." Krutch was firmly on the side of wit. For him, Collier's name "is the one most closely associated with the literary triumph of morality and dullness."[13]

Although it was readily accepted by his dissertation committee, Krutch's display of both his scholarship and his modern sophistication languished at the Columbia University Press for three years before the editors finally decided to require a publication subsidy from the author. Since such publication was prerequisite to his receiving the Ph.D., Krutch could only consent. Ironically, a man who would later support himself largely by his literary earnings underwrote the publication of his first book. *Comedy and Conscience After the Restoration* appeared in 1924 to mixed reviews, but the reviews and the Ph.D. itself were, for Krutch, by then anticlimactic. His ambitions had become literary, rather than academic.

When he returned to America in late spring 1920, Krutch brought with him a small bronze bust of Voltaire which for many years sat on his desk and presided over his writing. Although his acquaintance with Voltaire's works was slight, in Voltaire he saw a model of the iconoclasm, rationalism, liberalism, and even epicureanism to which he himself aspired. Moreover, mindful of his pedagogic failures at Columbia and fearful of similar failures in his new position at Brooklyn Polytechnic, Krutch had lately begun to aspire to a literary rather than an academic career. Voltaire's prose style — witty, epigrammatic, and distinguished by the well-turned sentence — seemed a worthy model for a sophisticated modern writer such as Krutch hoped to become.

As he completed his dissertation in Knoxville during the summer of 1920, Krutch also wrote an essay in the spirit of the man whose bust sat before him, taking the first tentative steps toward establishing himself as a man of letters. His topic itself was worthy of Voltaire: suicide considered as an art. "In no department of human activity," he began drolly, "is our decline from the grace of the ancients more evident than in that of suicide. It is not that people do not continue to take their own lives, but that they no longer do it exquisitely. We achieve our ends with devastating thoroughness, but with all of our effectiveness, we are crude. The polished gesture is no more. Our crass utilitarianism has destroyed all of the fine arts, including that of suicide, and we are no longer careful that no act of life shall be more becoming to us than the leaving of it." Recalling some of the great ancient practitioners of the art (Socrates, Petronius, and Cleopatra) and suggesting that contemporary life offered "an abundance of inducements to get away from it," Krutch called for the return of the golden age of suicide.[14]

"Threnody upon a Decadent Art" was, of course, little more

than an entertainment, an audition in which Krutch could display his verbal and intellectual cleverness. In its callow and calculated effort to shock and command attention, it was patently an apprentice piece, but it achieved its end. Shortly after he sent the essay to H.L. Mencken, who, along with George Jean Nathan, edited the *Smart Set*, Krutch received their acceptance ("Your essay amuses us") and a check for twenty dollars, his first payment for the writing he increasingly hoped might be his life's work.[15]

Beyond its clever virtuosity, however, his *Smart Set* essay also reveals the penchant for the ironic that marked, though never again so baldly, much of his writing during the 1920s. Irony, he said in 1922, is "the highest form of literary expression . . . . It alone can adequately suggest the complexity of life and indicate that the whole truth, composed of contradictory untruths, is too elaborate to be defined in a direct statement. . . . The ironist is a necessary Devil's Advocate to test our faith. . . . He must embrace a world of contradictions. He must proclaim in a riotous parody of Mohammed: 'There is no God, and I am his prophet.'"[16] For want of a more deeply felt attitude which was authentically his own, the ironic mode seemed useful to a young writer like Krutch, one who was starting out, eager to establish his intellectual sophistication and the stunningly modern character of his thought.

In Knoxville that same summer he also wrote another essay that he hoped might help launch his career, a "Defence of Book Reviewers." It too was clever and ironic; but Krutch took reviewing more seriously than suicide. It was, he sensed, an ideal literary activity for someone who (like himself) desired regular public exposure but lacked the time required for more ambitious performances. In this apologia for a genre in which he himself hoped soon to work, he explained the reviewer's function and suggested — as in his first undergraduate editorial — that, if he was serious about writing, he was hardly solemn.

The reviewer's work "is but the result of a passion, deep rooted in the human soul, for making books out of other books . . . . Few men can love books without wishing to increase their number." He went on to acknowledge that baser impulses played a part as well: "Journalistic criticism may also be thought of as having its origin in a passion yet more deeply rooted than the one just referred to — in the

33

passion, that is, for food and clothing. Book reviewing is . . . another one of those strange ways—like putting your head in a circus lion's mouth or selling false mustaches on Broadway—which men have found to make a living."[17] Even as an undergraduate Krutch had been wise to the ways of literary life, and he perhaps foresaw that much of his own reviewing would be occasioned by the latter passion.

Krutch sent off his amiable "Defence" to Henry Seidel Canby, who edited the *Book Review* of the New York *Evening Post* (soon to become its distinguished weekly supplement, the *Literary Review*, and later, when Canby and most of his staff left the *Post*, the *Saturday Review of Literature*). Canby not only accepted the essay, which he published that July on the front page of the *Book Review*, but he also invited Krutch to practice the profession he had drolly defended. Later that summer Krutch's first professional book review appeared, on a study of nineteenth-century thought. By the time the *Literary Review* began publication in mid-September, he was one of Canby's regular contributors.

Krutch and the *Literary Review* prospered together. Recognized as one of the most distinguished such publications of its day, the journal soon enjoyed a national circulation of nearly 10,000. Krutch was delighted to be appearing regularly along with such other reviewers as Kenneth Burke, Malcolm Cowley, Ford Madox Ford, H.L. Mencken, Ezra Pound, John Crowe Ransom, and Edmund Wilson. Within a year he had written nine lengthy and prominently placed reviews, primarily on recent fiction and on the Restoration and eighteenth-century England of his graduate specialization. By the time the *Literary Review* had metamorphosed into the *Saturday Review of Literature* in the summer of 1924, his contributions totaled some three dozen review essays. The "Defence" written in Knoxville had opened a door through which he was taking his first steps toward a career as a man of letters.

❧ Having completed his dissertation and having made a modest but encouraging beginning in his literary career, Krutch left Knoxville in late August 1920 for his new position at Brooklyn Polytechnic. He was hardly enthusiastic about returning to the classroom, but if teach he must in order to support himself, he was happy at least to have a job in New York, the nation's literary marketplace. He was gratified as well to be among the Columbia friends who appreciated — and by their admiration encouraged — the witty sophistication he was trying to develop. Most especially he was grateful to be able to continue his conversations with Mark Van Doren, who would be teaching at Columbia.

With Van Doren he rented a spacious apartment in Greenwich Village, a location which recommended itself not only for its equidistance from Brooklyn and Morningside Heights but also for its growing status as the literary and artistic center of the city — indeed, of the nation. Throughout the twenties they remained Villagers in address, but neither Krutch nor Van Doren partook of the careless, hedonistic life which was celebrated there. In hours stolen from teaching (and, presently, from courtship) each was working hard to fashion for himself a literary reputation, Van Doren as a poet and Krutch as a critic. They had neither the time nor — any more than in Paris — the inclination for bohemian frivolities.

Krutch would have preferred to be teaching, like Van Doren and several of his other friends, at Columbia. But his inauspicious debut in the classroom there had not gone unremarked, and he was not offered a position. Instead, he would be teaching engineers in Brooklyn. His second attempt at teaching was hardly more successful than his first; present fears fed on the knowledge of past failures, and he remained wholly incapable of generating the sort of discussion which might bring his classes to life. His students found circuits and bridges far more exciting than the poems and stories he assigned; and, failing to elicit any response from them, Krutch resorted to a routine of lecture and recitation which was as dreary for him as it was for his captive audience. The perfunctory "themes" required in the freshman course which constituted the greater part of his load were resented equally by the young men who wrote them and by the aspiring young writer who had to read and correct them.

Occasionally — but rarely — he encountered an exceptional student who, like his instructor, was a misfit at a technical school, and with such a student he could discuss the modern literature which was even then becoming his preoccupation. But to most of his students

35

Krutch was a likeable but ineffectual teacher. The poetaster who commemorated each faculty member beneath his photograph in the 1922 student yearbook suggested fairly the magnitude of Krutch's impact at Brooklyn Polytechnic:

> His modern idea, to you may not be clear,
> But he'll offer you a smoke, whenever you're broke.

Even for the most enthusiastic and skillful teacher, the job would have been far from ideal. Krutch soon began to chafe under the burden of teaching sixteen hours of class a week (some at night), reading papers, conferring with students, and discharging the other chores expected of a young faculty member in a small college. He was disheartened as well to be confirmed in his suspicion that teaching, and especially the leading of discussions, was not one of his gifts. The knowledge of his failure and the recognition that he was, for the moment, pursuing a career for which he was ill suited preyed upon him. It can hardly have been coincidental that Krutch then began suffering from migraine headaches—the first of a series of ailments, real and imagined, that dogged him throughout his none-too-healthy life.

His restiveness at Brooklyn Polytechnic was, of course, amplified by his knowledge that his duties there distracted him from pursuing the literary career where his future might lie. On weekends he was writing as many reviews as time and energy allowed. He also wrote one witty, autobiographical essay about education which reflected his frustration as a teacher. "Every year hundreds of students are called upon to admire beauties which they have no organs to perceive; and rare wines are forced across palates which cannot taste," he said. "In my class of engineers there is perhaps a larger percent of unfit than in a group of ordinary college students." But he recalled that he had himself once been an aspiring mathematician to whom the joys of art were suddenly revealed, and he comforted himself with the hope, however faint, that some of his students might enjoy a similar revelation. "Probably [the college] is wise in requiring that they shall all offer themselves to books for the sake of the man here and there who will be exposed to some work which will open eyes that might otherwise have remained shut. For his sake, the ninety and nine will have to sacrifice many hours in utter boredom."[18] And so too their teacher.

Its having provided him the material for that essay was perhaps the greatest fruit of his four years' labor at Brooklyn Polytechnic.

   Almost incidentally, in the course of his plaint over teaching, Krutch wrote: "I may teach certain facts concerning the history of literature, I may enforce reading requirements and exact summaries, but I cannot teach anyone to love. I may give you the dimensions of my mistress's eyebrows, and the number of her teeth, but to you she will remain a woman and no amount of exposition can prove her a goddess."[19] Though the yoking of literary love and human love was perhaps a bit forced, in its context the remark seemed apt enough. The mistress, though, was more than a figure of speech fabricated to amplify Krutch's point. In fact, by the time the essay appeared in the spring of 1923, he had already made her his bride.

   Two years younger than Krutch, Marcelle Leguia had been born in the small French Basque village of Hendaye. Several years later her family had moved to Paris, where she lived until, shortly before the outbreak of the War, she traveled to Boston to visit a sister who had married an American. With travel home precluded by the War, she remained in Boston and patriotically enrolled in a nursing course at Massachusetts General Hospital. After completing that program and a further course in public health nursing, she went in the summer of 1920 to New York, to become a visiting nurse for the Henry Street Settlement.

   One evening that Christmastime, Krutch met Marcelle in a Village restaurant. Several years earlier, as a graduate student, he had fallen "'seriously in love' for the first time" with a contralto who was perfecting her Italian at Columbia.[29] She had gone off to Europe to continue her musical studies, and Krutch, twenty-seven and still a bachelor, was impatient to find a wife. On first meeting Marcelle he resolved, with an instinct that proved entirely sound, that she should be that wife.

   During the winter and spring their relationship flourished, and by the summer—when he was on vacation—they were together nearly every evening for theater, concerts, films, or dinner with friends like Mark Van Doren and his intended, Dorothy Graffe. In a few months, however, Marcelle was due to depart for France to work in a public health program sponsored by the Rockefeller Foundation; Krutch feared that she might vanish from his life, as had the contralto before her. By early 1922 she had resigned her position in France to return to New York, and particularly to Joe. In February 1923, they were married, and that summer they took a belated honeymoon to France and Italy.

Though the couple made their home in Greenwich Village, several blocks from the apartment Krutch had shared with Van Doren, their life was hardly typical of that popularly associated with the Village of the twenties. He was a conscientious teacher and an aspiring writer, and she was a professional woman who worked first in an infant care program of the New York Diet Kitchen and then, for nearly a decade, as a nurse in the morning clinic at Hunter College. Meanwhile, she gladly accepted the peculiar office of the literary wife, making it her function to maintain a household where Krutch could devote himself, undistracted, to his writing. Marcelle's dedication was complete, and domestic responsibilities became a creative activity hardly less satisfying for her than writing was for him. By the mid-1930s, however, when they had a home in Connecticut as well as an apartment in New York, she abandoned her career as a nurse in order to devote all of her considerable energies to her husband and his many needs.

Even allowing for the incentives of love, devoting oneself wholly to Krutch must occasionally have been trying. His deep insecurity was often manifested in his shyness and reserve toward strangers; occasionally it was transformed into a childish petulance when he felt he was being denied the admiring attention he craved. Generally preoccupied with the writing and thinking he took to be his calling, he thoughtlessly — often selfishly — expected others to attend on his behalf to the practicalities of life. The care that his mother and even his older brother Charles had lavished on him well beyond his teens had come to seem his due. In Marcelle he found someone who tacitly accepted his sense of himself. With a curious mixture of deep love and almost clinical detachment, she tirelessly ministered to his various needs.

Though she well understood how unreasonable her husband's

selfish demands could be, she also knew how necessary it was to meet them—especially in his increasingly frequent times of sickness. Marcelle was, in Mark Van Doren's words, "an earthly paragon of affection and devotion."[21] Joe demanded (indeed, deeply needed) no less. For nearly fifty years the Krutches were rarely apart for more than a few days at a time, and then generally because he was away lecturing. Sitting alone in railway stations, airports, or hotel rooms, he each day sent off a message on one of the preaddressed postal cards she had prepared for him. The magnitude of his dependency upon her then became clear, even to him.

Marcelle, for her part, thrived on the relationship, which at times seemed as much maternal as conjugal. From the beginning Krutch had insisted that he wanted no children. Doubtless his increasingly poor health and his dismay over the drift of contemporary affairs figured in his resolve. Moreover, Krutch was unwilling to share with any child Marcelle's loving attention. For her he became both the child she never had—to be picked up after and lovingly tended—as well as the patient she had earlier been trained to nurse.

The migraines that appeared soon after Krutch began teaching in Brooklyn were presently joined by a succession of fevers, catarrhs, weight losses, and other, often undiagnosable, symptoms of malaise. Through all of his illnesses, organic and psychosomatic, Marcelle was faithfully there, rubbing him, covering him, reading to him, bringing him juice and water, and proffering the unqualified attention he craved. If her care was physically as well as psychologically necessary to him, it is equally true that the assurance of such care played some part in reinforcing in Krutch the neurotic hypochondria which made him a chronic valetudinarian.

For all its apparent singularity, their relationship was one which all who knew them described as extraordinarily happy and beautiful. In almost every respect each was the antithesis of, and thus complemented, the other. He was tall, blond, and lean; she was shortish, dark-haired, and ample of build. He was serious, given to chronic worrying and not infrequently to an indistinct melancholia; she, on the other hand, was gay, ebullient, and unfailingly optimistic. Wary of strangers and covetous of his solitude, he was generally more comfortable with books and ideas—and eventually with animals—than

39

with people; she was gregarious, indefatigably social, and a generous hostess to even the most casual acquaintances. Where he was often sickly and frail, her feisty vitality seemed boundless. Above all, Marcelle, deeply intelligent but not broadly educated, neither was nor fancied herself the strenuous intellectual Krutch aspired to be. She rejoiced in, and by her very presence constantly reminded him of, the simple pleasures of the common life he tended to undervalue in his early quest for literary fame.

While Joe strained to gain recognition as a sophisticated writer and thinker, Marcelle provided a foundation of security and conventionality. Not the least of her gifts was the bracing middlebrow counterpoise she provided to his own disingenuous efforts to become a highbrow. Nearly every day he read to her what he had written during hours closeted in his study; eventually she became his image of the kind of reader he sought to address: *l'homme moyen sensuel*. Much of his best writing after the 1920s might well have been dedicated to her, as was *The Twelve Seasons*, the first of his nature books: "For Marcelle, who will be found between the lines."

≈§ "Most writers," Krutch remarked in 1924, "begin with a love of words — with the desire to say something rather than with something to say."[22] He spoke from personal experience. Increasingly certain of his failure as a teacher, he sought ever more anxiously to make writing his career. But he lacked both a subject and, given his academic responsibilities, the time for the kind of extended performance which might truly establish his reputation. For such a man the book review proved an ideal genre. Offering a ready-made subject, it was also sufficiently modest in compass to allow a writer of Krutch's facility to execute it in a weekend's time. While teaching at Brooklyn Polytechnic, he was also honing his literary skills — and discovering a subject for later, more ambitious efforts — as a reviewer. Many of his review-essays were appearing in the *Literary Review*; still more were published in another of the most distinguished weeklies of the day, the *Nation*.

Like many of his early opportunities, the invitation to contribute to the *Nation* was due to the generosity of a Van Doren. In 1920

Carl Van Doren became the magazine's literary editor, and he invited his brother Mark as well as Krutch to write occasional reviews. With that invitation began an association with the *Nation* which spanned more than three decades and led to Krutch's publication there of nearly two thousand book reviews, drama reviews, essays, and editorials.

He made an unremarkable debut in summer 1920 with a review of one of those books that appear regularly to announce that "Shakespeare's" plays were in fact written by someone else. As a novice who eagerly seized any opportunity to write for publication, Krutch did not cavil at the titles offered him. Initially they were a sorry lot: generally novels that no one more senior cared to review, and miscellaneous volumes of nonfiction ranging from *Dramatic Publication in England, 1580–1648* to *A History of Prostitution.* Within four years, however, he had become a fixture on the *Nation's* review pages, where he published some sixty review-essays, each 1,000 to 1,500 words long, as well as several dozen "Books in Brief" paragraphs.

Even the most facile writers would have found taxing such prodigious quantities of reviewing as Krutch undertook while also holding a full-time job. The sacrifice of sleep to writing took its toll on his health; and the pressure under which he worked was occasionally obvious, as when he discussed in the *Literary Review* the very books he was that week also commenting upon, somewhat differently, in the *Nation.* But he was intoxicated by the joy of writing, and his effort seemed richly justified by the broad national exposure he was gaining.

After several years as a literary journalist, Krutch possessed a no more exaggerated sense of the permanent importance of reviewing than he had when, at the beginning, he wrote his "Defence" of the occupation. The reviewer cannot "possibly hope by a whole lifetime of devoted labor to win either in money or fame the recompense which is reserved for the author of the most transitory popular novel or play."[23] Indeed, no literary genre was more transitory than the reviewer's. "Each issue to which he has the troublesome happiness to contribute," he wrote in 1929, "seems to enshrine in all the eternity of type the latest of his lucubrations, but each is, as a matter of fact, swept away the next day, or the next week, or the next month. And the more popular the contributor, the more regularly he fills an allotted space, the more acutely he must realize the Sisyphean curse resting upon his labors."[24] Nevertheless, reviewing was the activity in which, almost willy-nilly, Krutch found himself engaged. He lavished on his essays all the care of a young man eager to establish himself as a writer. From the beginning, his lean and clear prose was a perfect instrument of efficient yet civilized communication. With their delicate balance, their aptness in phrase and figure, and their eminent readability, his sentences seemed each to have been elegantly though effortlessly crafted. What he wanted to say was said clearly, though rarely simplistically; forcefully, but never belligerently. His paragraphs, deftly paced and enlivened by the witty locution or thought, seduced the reader gracefully through his argument. Described in his prose, even the dullest book enjoyed a certain liveliness.

From the beginning Krutch also understood the peculiar requirements of the journalistic review. Both the *Literary Review* and the *Nation* were journals of wide general circulation whose readers were not so much literary as, in the broadest sense, literate. Especially in the *Nation*, where the focus was on social and political matters and the reviews were relegated to the back of the magazine, it was essential that—apart from the importance of the works he was discussing—his reviews be engaging in themselves. Thus, around even the slightest book he sought to construct a significant essay of interest to a civilized reader. But if he sought in his reviews to go beyond summary and evaluation, to reflect on a book's art and thought, he realized as well that the reviewer had a reportorial duty both to his reader and to the author of the book under consideration. He assumed no license to make the review merely an excuse for writing an essay in which he could display his own brilliance.

Criticism, he wrote in 1922, is "an attempt to penetrate into the soul of a work and to discover what the author meant, how sincerely and passionately he meant it, and, finally, how true and important is his meaning."[25] As a reluctant English professor whose reviewing diet was largely one of literary mediocrity, he resisted the tendency of many academic critics whose vision is so singlemindedly on the masterpieces of the past that they dismiss out of hand the imperfect products of the present. He likewise resisted the seasoned periodical reviewer's glib, uncritical acceptance of the inevitable inadequacy

42

of much that was contemporary. He judged honestly, by his own standards.

Krutch's reviews, however, showed a distinct uncertainty concerning those standards. A young man eager to make his mark as a sophisticated critic in the early 1920s, he understood the strategic value of adding his voice to the chorus of respected critics who eagerly welcomed the experimental works of literary modernism then appearing. "The story of art," he wrote in an early review, "like the story of morals and the story of science, is the story of the breakers of tablets, and the business of the writer is not to be constantly afraid of overstepping the limits set by his material." Instead, Krutch continued in the current idiom, "he should do all in his power to break through them, for every really important piece of writing is, in some sense, a crashing through the limits of what it was formerly believed possible to make words say and readers understand."[26]

Different standards and a contrary sensibility were evident in several other reviews, however. His tastes were innately those of Knoxville, though they sought to encompass those of Greenwich Village. Occasionally his reviews betray an impatience with the drift of much modern fiction and his preference for the realism, vividness of character, and traditional moral perspective generally associated with the art of the eighteenth and nineteenth centuries, rather than the dawning twentieth. Reviewing two novels published in 1924, Krutch registered his dissent from the canons of contemporary literary fashion and suggested his own, more conventional preferences:

> Both of the writers under discussion are intensely occupied with "style"; both produce "pure literature" without any implications for life; and hence their books will be hailed as among the important events of the season by that group of critics to whom whatever literature touches life as it is lived seems always a little vulgar. But to me, I confess, it seems that a literature so "pure" is somewhat anemic, and that really great books do come home to men's bosoms and concern themselves with their affairs.[27]

It was not only the formal experimentalism of modern literature with which Krutch was uneasy. He was, by his own description, a "critic of the ideas in current fiction,"[28] and in that capacity he be-

43

gan even in his earliest reviews to describe the constellation of attitudes he would later define as the "modern temper." Here again he showed more the basic conservatism than the modern sophistication of his temperament. He was made uneasy by the evidence of many recent books that traditional values had lost their power, and that many of the most sensitive and articulate writers of the day were embarked on a clumsy, desperate, almost frenetic search for new values and principles with which to replace the old. "The greatest enemy to his art which the contemporary novelist has to fight," he said, "is the too complacent sense of his modernity and the feeling that his principal duty is to demonstrate it."[29]

In the writing of D.H. Lawrence and Aldous Huxley, among others, Krutch pointed to evidence of the spiritual malaise of the moderns. Lawrence, he wrote, "is a genuinely tortured spirit and no mere player at disillusion and despair." He was, in fact, "the best example of that drifting rudderless state of mind, without settled aims, beliefs, or standards, of which this age is so proud." Lawrence, Krutch suggested, was a product of the critical spirit of the times: "Like the rest of us he has enthusiastically destroyed illusions in the hope of arriving at truth, but having torn away the veils he is not sure that there is anything to see. . . . He is the most interesting and the most unsatisfactory of novelists writing today."[30] The "us" is telling: while criticizing Lawrence's art, Krutch was associating himself with the critical spirit that lay behind it.

Huxley, too, was symptomatic of the modern turn of mind. Discussing *Leda and Other Poems* in one of his earliest reviews, Krutch wrote: "he has learned to pray before he learned to scoff and his cynicism is the result not of impotence but of the consciousness of futile power . . . ." His remarks on one of Huxley's poems are typical of the philosophical (indeed, moral) analysis of contemporary literature to which, from the beginning, Krutch as a reviewer frequently turned:

> The poem is simply the maddest and most revealing cross-section of a vagrant mind of the most modern type. It gets you nowhere because the super-skeptical author doubts that there is any where to be gotten. Mental attitude follows mental attitude, only to crumble before self-criticism. Cynicism chases out romance, then cynicism, conscious of its own futility, vanishes before the determination to seize

the day, and that determination fades before the realization that there is nothing to seize. Futility contemplates itself and goes out: Yet the poem is significant because it accurately reproduces a modern dilemma. The destructive criticism culminating in Freudianism and the new psychology has opened abyss below abyss, and the spirit plunges headlong.[31]

From the beginning, Krutch contemplated the abyss with less equanimity than did many of his contemporaries.

In a 1924 *Nation* symposium on "New Morals for Old," he returned to the image of the abyss. As he did frequently in his book reviews, he looked in his essay, "Modern Love and Modern Fiction," to imaginative literature for evidence of the intellectual temper of the day. Preoccupied by the corrosive influence of the critical mind, many authors, he said, treated love as though it were a mere matter of sex, and thus debased a vital human value. But he proposed no simple alternative to the "modern dilemma." There could be no honest escape from the recognition of "man's ironic predicament between gorilla and angel, a predicament typified by the fact that as he grows critical he realizes that love is at once sublime and obscene and that only by walking a spiritual tight-rope above the abyss can he be said to live at all in any true sense."[32] During the twenties Krutch was walking a similarly thin line between his desire to establish his sophistication as an exponent of the currently fashionable modernism and his temperamental resistance to that movement.

Krutch's frenetic activity as a reviewer during the early 1920s was part of his effort—increasingly urgent, as he grew more and more unhappy with teaching—to write himself free from the classroom. By spring 1924, he had succeeded. Ludwig Lewisohn, who had been the *Nation*'s distinguished drama critic for five years, suddenly vacated the post to live in Europe. Krutch, by then a familiar figure on the pages and in the offices of the magazine, seemed an obvious replacement, and the editor and publisher Oswald Garrison Villard invited him to join the *Nation* staff full-time.

Krutch was not long in accepting. He was happy to be able once again to frequent the theater with the luxury of press credentials, something he had not enjoyed since his youth in Knoxville; to have his own weekly column in a distinguished journal; to enjoy the prospect of more time to pursue other writing more ambitious than reviews; and, above all, to put his teaching career in the past. He would be listed on the masthead as "Associate Editor," and would be expected to produce a weekly drama column during the season, to contribute occasional book reviews and editorials on cultural topics, and to attend the Thursday morning editorial meetings. The starting salary—to be supplemented with payments for essays, book reviews, and editorials—was sixty-five dollars a week. It was, he wrote Villard in accepting the offer, an "eminently satisfactory" arrangement.

His earnings from the *Nation*, combined with Marcelle's salary as a nurse, would of course be adequate to provide for their modest needs. But Krutch was ambitious to achieve something greater than subsistence; he was eager for fame as well, and the wealth that might accompany it. He knew that to achieve those he would need to write a proper book. He remained, however, a writer largely without a subject—until a subject (and a contract) were presented to him, again through the good offices of a Van Doren. Carl Van Doren had heard that Alfred A. Knopf was eager to publish a book on Edgar Allan Poe. He suggested Krutch, Knopf agreed, and Krutch eagerly accepted.

Ironically, just a few months after he taught his last classes in Brooklyn, his dissertation was published, and the academic Krutch was finally legitimized with the Ph.D. he no longer needed. Having left the academy—permanently, he imagined—he was at last a professional man of letters.

3.

❦ TO THE PALACE OF REPUTATION

Having during the previous four years established a national reputation as a book reviewer, having just been appointed drama critic of one of America's most distinguished periodicals, and looking forward to writing his first nonacademic book, Krutch in 1924 was uncharacteristically optimistic about the prospects for his literary career. Two years earlier he had drawn on his own experience in remarking that "the great majority of reading Americans do not come from 'literary homes' and an interest in literature is with them not even a generation old. It is not wholly a misfortune for us," he added, "that literature has not lost for us the zest of a new discovery."[1] New readers and new markets were appearing hand in hand. Looking back on the twenties two decades later, Krutch said it was an "age which believed . . . that nothing is more important than those activities of the mind and spirit which literature represents." Notwithstanding the materialism and catchpenny opportunism of the day, "an unusually large section of the public believed that literature was worth taking seriously. . . . Anyone who had ever written a book — almost anyone who had ever thought he might like to write a book — was eagerly listened to by all sorts of audiences."[2]

In 1926 Krutch observed, "There is probably no country in the world where the writing of a book confers as much distinction as it does in America."[3] He was happy to be embarking upon his career at such a moment, when the kind of work in which he was engaged seemed especially timely. "No literary phenomenon of the last two decades," he wrote in 1928, "has been more striking than the increased interest in literary criticism, as indicated by the growth of literary journalism."[4] As a critic and, shortly, a literary biographer, Krutch would be a middleman between authors and readers in this national cultural and intellectual awakening.

"Even though the writer whose field is scholarship or criticism still has a difficult time making a living," he wrote in 1927, "his struggle is less long and desperate than it has been at any time since he came to depend upon the public rather than the patron, and as for the writer who has the good fortune actually to catch the public fancy, his financial rewards are such that not only artists of the past but its Maecenases as well might envy him."[5] Krutch was hopeful that he might soon enjoy those rewards himself. But the very wealth of opportunity awaiting the new writer in the 1920s was a mixed blessing —especially for someone like Krutch, who was more eager to be successful than to enjoy any *particular* kind of success, and who was perhaps too ready, in the spirit of the day, to measure success by wealth. Though he might be spared some of the hardships of his Grub Street predecessors, the young writer might be distracted from doing his best work, devoting himself instead to ephemeral projects which lacked in genuine challenge what they promised in instant public recognition and financial reward. In 1926 Krutch itemized some of those possible distractions: advertising, consulting, editing, and teaching. The writer's dilemma, he said, was that "the way to a comparatively easy and pleasant livelihood is opened up to him, but the livelihood carries as a condition the necessity of abandoning an undivided effort to write the things he most wants to write."[6]

That dilemma was Krutch's as well. The promising literary career on which he had embarked was, for all that, not precisely one of his own making. He had, almost by chance, fallen into book reviewing, drama criticism, and now a biography of Poe. He was writing to meet the demands of whatever market presented itself, and he had not yet deliberately fashioned for himself any identity more distinct than that of the man of letters. His apparently happy task was not that of finding something to write or someone to publish him, but of choosing among the wealth of possibilities. He seized them almost indiscriminately. One opportunity brought another; work led to more work. By the end of the decade his literary life had accelerated furiously—still largely without any deliberate direction by him—as he enjoyed increasingly the success and reputation he craved.

It was, of course, the *Nation* which provided the focus for Krutch's literary work in the late 1920s. As associate editor, he attended the weekly editorial conference and Villard's occasional luncheons for eminent men of politics and letters; but his was not an "office job." During the season he attended the theater several times a week, and in his Village flat he composed not only his column of a thousand words or so on the week's most interesting opening, but his other *Nation* contributions as well. He continued to review books, and between the beginning of his full-time association with the magazine and the end of the decade he produced more than a hundred review essays, most often on new fiction.

He was also expected to help fill the several pages of unsigned editorial comment which appeared in the *Nation* each week. Generally he wrote about books, authors, the theater, artistic censorship, and other cultural topics; if an author's death was to be commemorated, an important new work of scholarship welcomed, the award of a literary prize recognized, or another instance of censorship condemned, Krutch would be assigned the task. Some of his editorials, however, were distinctly less momentous, and in many of them he commented ironically on some of the harmless perversities of the American scene: the lurid contents of *Screenland* magazine; the prospect of the American Legion's holding its convention in Paris; a dispute as to whether a Brooklyn girl aged twelve had been, as claimed, the author of two popular volumes of poetry; the arrest on drunk-driving charges of the son of a Virginia Anti-Saloon League official; and the publication by the YMCA of a handbook on "The Sex Life of Youth" which solemnly announced that "sexual intercourse is the only means by which human beings can be created."

During his first five years on the *Nation* board he wrote more than a hundred such editorial columns, as well as several dozen briefer editorial paragraphs. Frequently his work appeared as many as four times in a single issue: a drama review, a book review, and a couple of editorial contributions. For a less ambitious writer, the *Nation* would have been a full-time job, but Krutch also contributed occasionally to the new *Saturday Review of Literature*, which had succeeded the *Literary Review*, and to the New York *Herald Tribune Books* supplement, edited by Irita Van Doren. Indeed, he would write for nearly anyone who would print (and pay) him. His thirst for work and for the various kinds of rewards it brought was apparently insatiable. During the first five years of his full-time literary career he published two books and nearly five hundred items in periodicals. For the literary journalist, quantity is one measure of achievement, and Krutch was proud of his.

Obviously, he wrote rapidly, but composition was hardly effortless. Writing for him was not merely a means of earning a living; it was also an act of communication, of exhibition, of self-display. Krutch's shyness when confronted by strangers face to face — his fear that he mightn't shine, mightn't be accepted — found its counterpart in the anxiety with which he approached each new essay. As he closeted himself in his cluttered study each morning to pound away clumsily on his typewriter, chain smoking and surrounded by scribbled notes and aborted paragraphs, it was not self-expression he sought so much as the admiration of his readers. Dr. Johnson, he remarked some years later, "spoke for many when he said: 'I allow that you may have some pleasure from writing, after it is over, if you have written well; but you don't go willingly to it again.'"[7]

In the 1920s, however, writing was but one of many kinds of activity which offered income if not reputation to the ambitious man of letters; and Krutch was nothing if not ambitious. At the New School for Social Research he lectured occasionally on literary topics, and he participated frequently in public dinner discussions sponsored by the *Nation* on topics ranging from "Censorship of the Stage" to "Is Man a Machine?" He also resumed, part-time, the teaching he so disliked. On Mondays he traveled to Poughkeepsie to conduct a seminar in "Advanced Creative Writing" at Vassar (a course "in the practice and theory of criticism, the purpose of which is to aid students of some proficiency who are seriously interested in the writing of criticism"). Thursday afternoons he taught a course in "Dramatic Criticism" at the Columbia Journalism School ("training in the writing of critical reviews of dramatic productions of various types"). He was at least pleased now to have, instead of captive freshmen, older students who had elected his courses and who flattered him with their eagerness to learn the secrets of his literary success.

Indeed, Krutch had by the late 1920s become an important literary figure in New York. Publishers invited him to euphemistically described "teas" held to mark the appearance of a new book; though he disliked crowds and had little taste for Prohibition "tea," he frequently attended in order to see and be seen. Dreiser, perhaps reciprocating Krutch's kindness in having described *An American Tragedy* as "the greatest American novel of our generation," included him among those regularly invited to his fashionable Thursday evening salons. O'Neill wrote to tell Krutch that he was "one of the very few critics whose verdict I look forward to and take seriously. . . . I want to talk to you about my plans for future work," he said, urging the Krutches to visit him in France. "I feel talking to you would be immensely stimulating to me."[8]

In 1926, just a few months after the beginning of the Book-of-the-Month Club, the Literary Guild was established. Krutch became part of that enterprise as well, when Carl Van Doren invited him to join the selection committee. The book clubs, like new magazines such as the *Saturday Review of Literature* and *Reader's Digest*, both of which appeared in the twenties, were designed for that "great majority of reading Americans who do not come from 'literary homes.'" Krutch welcomed not only the potential profit from his association with the Guild, but also the opportunity to become an arbiter of taste more powerful than any mere reviewer or critic.

"The fellowship of books is more real than the mere gregariousness of a public assembly," he wrote enthusiastically in the first issue of the Guild's monthly, *Wings*. The Guild's members would be "united by a common love of reading and by a common taste for the best that contemporary literature affords. Membership in the Guild will make them part of an important movement. It will give them a sense of sharing a series of important experiences with a group of like minded people and it will enable them, in their discussions, to meet upon a common ground."[9] Through the fulsome puffery of his manifesto one can see Krutch's genuine sympathy with this popular, essentially middlebrow enterprise in which he was engaged, while at the same time he was elsewhere trying to establish himself as a literary highbrow.

The Guild prospered, and within two years the monthly reading (or at least book collecting) of more than 70,000 subscribers was guided by Krutch and his fellow editors. The hours he spent reading manuscripts, conferring about the monthly selections, and writing blurbs for *Wings* were part of the burgeoning career in which Krutch found himself engaged.

New York in the 1920s was all that the young man from Knoxville, recently graduated from Columbia, and ambitious for a literary career had imagined it might be. Even if some of the novelty had worn off, he had lost none of the enthusiasm for the city that he had felt years ago on his first childhood visit. Now, as a man of letters, he valued the various kinds of opportunities which were nowhere else available so plentifully.

Marcelle, however, took less pleasure in urban living. Her idea of the good life could be lived more nearly in the small Basque village where she had spent her childhood than in Paris, Boston, or New York, to which she later found herself exiled; and she desired to recapture that life. Because she had early understood the expedient of proposing an idea to Krutch so that he could fancy it had been his own, shortly after their marriage she began "exploring" with him the possibility of their finding a country place to which they might occasionally retreat from the bustle of New York. Her motivation was partly selfish, but with the shrewd intuitive understanding which rendered her so ideal a wife, she also sensed, long before her husband did, how he might thrive apart from city pavements. The migraine headaches he had experienced while teaching in Brooklyn were soon joined by a variety of other chronic ailments which defied the diagnosis or treatment of the numerous physicians he consulted. A nurse as well as a wife, Marcelle recognized that some respite from his exhausting New York schedule might prove beneficial.

Krutch was not readily convinced. Though he had enjoyed visits with Marcelle to the weekend homes of friends, he doubted that he would find such a life congenial himself. As Lewis Gannett recalled, "He felt that the lush vegetable growth of the country was stifling; he was eloquent in proclaiming the superiority of civilized to wild life."[10] Nevertheless, in 1925 Joe acceded to Marcelle's urgings that they try out a summer of country living, and he agreed to rent a farmhouse in Cornwall, Connecticut, near one that Mark and Dorothy Van Doren had purchased two years before.

Several hours by car from New York, Cornwall was in the northwest corner of Connecticut, on the southern hills of the Berkshires. Attractive valleys, meadows, and small lakes dotted the low, wooded slopes that dominated the landscape; lovely eighteenth-century farmhouses and barns, even then mostly abandoned, suggested the bygone pastoral New England. Yet Krutch was hardly enthusiastic when he moved there to spend the summer. He consoled himself with the thought that if he soon tired of the landscape, as he anticipated, he would at least enjoy the company of the Van Dorens and other summering New York literati. Moreover, he had his Poe book to divert him from the tedium of country life.

As the summer passed, however, Krutch was delighted to discover how easily his writing on Poe progressed while he was away from some of the grosser distractions of the city, how much Marcelle relished keeping house in the country, and how his beloved pet cat Minou (whom he had rescued the previous winter from the streets of Manhattan) reveled in the freedom of the fields. Not least of all, Krutch was pleasantly surprised to find that he himself was enjoying his summer holiday. Strolling through the countryside as eagerly as he had earlier walked the streets of New York, he took unexpected pleasure in fresh air, country greenery, and various nonhuman fellow creatures. Before returning to New York that fall, he and Marcelle decided to buy a country place of their own. With the assistance of Krutch's mother, who had recently inherited her late husband's estate, they purchased a small old house in a mountain meadow several miles from the one they had been renting.

During the next three years, at the end of the theater season and, when possible, on weekends, the Krutches returned to Cornwall with ever greater enthusiasm. While Marcelle tended her large vegetable garden, Joe roamed delightedly among the meadows and hills. His childhood interest in science, largely suppressed during his headlong rush to literary fame, recurred. Carrying on his walks guidebooks to the birds and plants of the region, he discovered in flora and fauna a fascination he had lately imagined to exist only in books and plays. He began studying the sensitive plant, *Mimosa pudica*; as his Cornwall neighbor Lewis Gannett recalled, "He spent many hours on his stomach in his garden, with an alarm clock by his side, testing whether the sensitive plant, which closes its leaflets at a touch and reopens them shortly afterward, was human enough to become progressively tired, and slow in reaction."[11]

As his experiments with *Mimosa pudica* suggest, science, rather than nature, initially engaged him in Cornwall. He was still largely deaf to the sense of poetry which distinguishes the nature lover from the merely interested observer—a poetry which his nearby friend Mark Van Doren was endeavoring to capture in verse. Krutch came to Cornwall more to escape the city than to explore the world of nature; but gradually he was also discovering that in the untamed, unpaved universe of Cornwall could be found experiences, feelings, even lessons elsewhere unobtainable. Several sentences in a review he wrote during his second summer there suggest that discovery:

> We have gained much by freeing ourselves to some extent from nature, by being no longer so intimately a part of her as once we were; but we have lost something too. We have specialized our consciousness so that if it has modes unknown to the more primitive, it is no longer so intensely aware of the total process of living, so joyously participant in the mere vital surge of universal life. The crops which nourish us grow where we do not see or feel them grow; we are heated in winter and fanned in summer so that the very seasons are half remote; and thus we have become creatures apart, no longer in step with the procession from which we have turned aside.[12]

❮❯ Though he came to love the natural beauty of Cornwall, Krutch also took pleasure in the company of a number of his *Nation* colleagues who summered there: Oswald Garrison Villard, the editor; Freda Kirchwey, the managing editor; Lewis Gannett, an associate editor; and Mark and Dorothy Van Doren, who were not only the Krutches' closest friends but also his *Nation* associates, he being part-time literary editor and she a full-time member of the editorial staff. That these *Nation* colleagues should have desired to be near one another even during their holidays bespeaks the warm feelings among the magazine's staff then.

Krutch, though never an expansively social man, happily shared in the camaraderie that characterized life at the *Nation*. The young men and women who worked there were proud of their association with what was generally considered America's leading weekly of fact and opinion. They were committed to the liberal mission of the magazine, and they were devoted to each other even when, as Gannett wrote at the time, they frequently disagreed: "They don't like the same plays; they don't like the same books; they have differing degrees of like and dislike for the British and the bankers and the babies, and different ideas upon the way to make clam chowder and apple pie. They are always expressing disapproval of each other's clothes and suggesting improvements in the management of each other's homes and the education of each other's children."[13] Yet the wrangling among the strong-minded young intellectuals on the staff was amiable and assumed a deep mutual respect. At that time they were all, Krutch recalled, "a happy family."[14]

Presiding as a genial *pater familias* was Villard. Fully twenty years older than most of his staff and a millionaire, he took a personal interest in the affairs of his employees and generously meted out advice on stocks, real estate, and other practicalities. "I am hurt that you and Joe did not consult me before selling your lovely house," he wrote Marcelle in 1930. "Please, please do remember to call upon me for advice hereafter whenever anything like that comes up. I think I can give both you and Joe sound business advice in view of my now great age and long experience. Certainly I would advise you as I would my own wife and daughter."[15]

Villard frequently collected his staff for lunch at the exclusive Railroad Club to meet — and be met by — such people as British Labor party members, D.H. Lawrence, Sinclair Lewis, the Bishop of Oxford, Nehru, and two Negro girls who described their lives in the Deep South. His generous interest in the continuing education of his writers also led to their occasionally being sent abroad. Under his patronage Gannett traveled from China across Turkestan to Russia and Western Europe; and in 1928 Villard sent the Krutches on a grand tour of the theatrical capitals of Europe and Russia.

Villard's great enthusiasm for Russia in the 1920s was one among many signs of the liberalism which marked the *Nation* under his editorship. From its liberal perspective, it became a vigilant critic of contemporary affairs, denouncing threats to academic freedom, denials of civil liberties, discrimination against Jews and Negroes, the oppression of the labor movement, the disappearance of a competitive and free press, the growth of big business, miscarriages of justice like the Sacco and Vanzetti trial, U.S. foreign policy in Central America, and British policy in Ireland and India. For Villard and his staff, the Progressive movement was still alive. "We were at bottom fundamentally optimistic, and we were gay crusaders," Krutch wrote, recalling the *Nation* staff in that decade. "We thought we knew what Liberalism was and we were confident both that it would triumph and that, by triumphing, it would create a better world."[16]

Though Krutch was fundamentally apolitical, and though his *Nation* writing was largely concerned with arts and letters, he was happy to be part of that enterprise. Insofar as he had political opinions, they were liberal, and, challenged by the radicalism of the 1930s, his liberalism would be confirmed. But during the twenties, he was especially pleased to be associated with a forward-thinking, liberal journal like the *Nation*. Liberalism was an essential attribute of the sophisticated, modern thinker Krutch was trying to become. As an editor of the *Nation* he was proud to show that he had transcended the provinciality of his Knoxville youth.

In 1925 he had an opportunity to make that announcement even more explicitly. The Scopes trial was scheduled to take place that summer in Dayton, Tennessee; Villard invited Krutch to serve as the *Nation*'s correspondent, and to provide a native son's account of events there. Krutch seized the opportunity both to establish his credentials as a *Nation* liberal and, as an urban sophisticate, to condescend toward the narrow village mentality he was happy to think he had shaken off. At the end of June he put aside the nearly completed manuscript of the Poe book and left Cornwall for Dayton.

The trial of John Scopes for violating a recent law prohibiting the teaching of evolution in the public schools was precisely the kind of event the *Nation* delighted in viewing with alarm. The trial would concern an important issue of civil liberties, for the Tennessee statute in question, involving a serious abridgment of academic freedom, was of a piece with the many other legislative and governmental prohibitions so prevalent in post-War America and so odious to the journal.

In the unsigned editorials he had been writing during the past several months—indeed, in his undergraduate writing as well—Krutch expressed his own distaste for this illiberal drift of affairs. "Never during the hundred years just past has the right of dissent been attacked in America from so many different quarters as in our decade," he wrote in November 1924. "Never before have suppressions figured so frequently in the news of the day or been accepted so complacently. A book disappears from the shelves of a public library, a theatrical manager modifies or withdraws a play, and the process of censorship comes to be, by mere repetition, accepted as a normal process."[17] In principle, all censorship was noxious to Krutch. But his specialty was cultural affairs, and several months later he asked a rhetorical question which he answered in many of his *Nation* editorials through the 1920s: "Shall the artist write with his eye upon the good and the intelligent, or shall he assume that his first responsibility is to that imbecile minority which may possibly, according to the censor, find in a perverted vision of a work a natural food for its corrupted mind?"[18] Artistic freedom was, of course, not the issue in Dayton, but Krutch saw the trial there as another test of the forces of darkness against the forces of light in America.

At the same time, the Scopes trial promised to be good entertainment. To the *Nation* liberals, the law at issue seemed so ludicrous, the principals so colorful, and the setting so appropriate that it was difficult to take the proceedings too solemnly. With his "terrified traditionalism" and his "thunder against evolution," William Jennings Bryan, who would be prosecuting, had long been a butt of *Nation* fun.[19] And shortly after Krutch joined the staff the magazine had begun paying special attention to affairs in Tennessee. Commenting editorially on the efforts of the head of the Knoxville chapter of the Daughters of the American Revolution to prevent the performance of W. Somerset Maugham's *Rain*, Krutch wrote, "Tennessee has a

State university so pure or so cowardly that when the governor signed the anti-evolution bill not one professor dared protest. From such a center, radiating 'not light but rather darkness visible,' the super-censor might well be expected."[20] As the *Nation*'s correspondent there, he would elaborate upon that theme.

By the time he arrived in Dayton a week before the trial was to begin, the town was "already in a state of excited bewilderment and almost of shock at the discovery that it had been selected as the site of an Armageddon."[21] "What one saw there," he recalled, "was perhaps one-tenth dangerous fanaticism and one-tenth genuine intellectual debate, but all the rest was circus, jape, and at least moderately clean fun."[22] In writing his dispatches Krutch looked forward to having some fun as well.

He was clear as to who the heroes and villains were at Dayton. Against the defense attorney, Clarence Darrow (a man of "unquestionable greatness"), were arrayed Bryan (who had been "driven from politics and journalism because of obvious incompetence, become ballyhoo for boom-town real estate in his search for lucrative employment, and forced into religion as the only quasi-intellectual field in which mental backwardness and complete insensibility to ideas can be used as an advantage") and the State Fathers of Tennessee (whose "courteous drawl" could be "so disarming to those who do not know with what inflexible obstinacy it can give utterance to the blackest prejudices").[23]

For Krutch there were, of course, serious implications to the trial. It was "a symptom of the vast gulf which lies between the two halves of our population." "In the centers of population men have gone on assuming certain bodies of knowledge and certain points of view without realizing that they were living in a different world from that inhabited by a considerable portion of their fellow-citizens, and they have been unconscious of the danger which threatened them at the inevitable moment when the two worlds should come into conflict." In Tennessee such a moment had arrived. "The mob is up," he wrote; "it has tasted blood and smelled smoke."[24]

As a "reformed" provincial, Krutch was remarkably tolerant of that Tennessee mob. "There is no state of the Union, no country of the world, which does not have communities as simple-minded as this one," he acknowledged. He reserved his fury for those who might —even in Tennessee—be expected to resist the mob's power: "If Tennessee has become the laughing-stock of the world it is not because she has her villages which are a half-century behind the centers of world thought but rather because among her sons who know better there is scarcely one who has the courage to stand up for what he thinks and knows. . . ."

Talking with teachers and administrators at the university and with family friends in Knoxville during a brief visit to his mother before the trial, he had been reassured that reasonable, educated people there recognized the absurdity of both the anti-evolution legislation and the prosecution of Scopes. But cowardice prevailed over principle. Krutch took obvious pleasure in describing the mentality he was proud to show he had overcome: "The legislator is afraid of some fundamentalist hid in the mountains; the president is afraid of the legislature; the faculty is afraid of the president; and the newspaper editor is afraid of someone who is afraid of someone who is afraid of someone else. . . . In Tennessee bigotry is militant and sincere; intelligence is timid and hypocritical, and in that fact lies the explanation of the sorry role which she is playing in contemporary history."[25] When Lewis Gannett received the dispatch back in New York, he gave it the title, hardly more provocative than Krutch's essay, "Tennessee: Where Cowards Rule."

Those paragraphs, like much of Krutch's writing from Dayton, were partly an expression of his conscientious distaste for illiberal thought and action, wherever found and in whatever form. He had written similarly before, and in the following decade he would have further occasion to express his liberalism when, in an age of Marxist fanaticism, it was even less fashionable. But the incendiary rhetoric characteristic of Krutch's Dayton dispatches further reveals the pleasure he took in demonstrating his superiority by condescending toward his native state. Writing about the Scopes trial he had an opportunity, greater than that offered by any of his unsigned editorials or book and drama reviews, to display his sophistication and publicly repudiate his own Tennessee past.

The New York *Times* was doubtless correct in surmising that "Tennessee: Where Cowards Rule" had been written "with the genial intention of 'giving pain.'" It was also correct, in a lengthy discussion of the article on its editorial page, in speculating that "if any of [Tennessee's] bolder sons see Mr. Krutch's article, we shall hear more about it and him."[26] That very day the Knoxville *Sentinel* devoted an editorial to the recent work of a New York journalist whom it never deigned to name. But Krutch's dispatches were by then the topic of lively conversation in Knoxville, especially among family friends. There was no mistaking "the native son character" who had returned home "with the ambition to shine and stink in the public prints by muck-raking his native land."

The *Sentinel* was not surprised that the trial had brought to Tennessee "the journalistic muck-rakers, the literary high-brows and know-it-alls, the agnostics, atheists, free-thinkers, free-lovers, socialists, communists, syndicalists, psychoanalysts and what not." (To have been numbered in some of those ranks — and especially the second — must have given Krutch great pleasure.) The editorial insisted that it was unnecessary to defend Tennessee from the "dirt-daubing" of the likes of Krutch; it was sufficient to explain that his "delectable methods" have been "developed and acquired in the putrescent atmosphere and reeking environs of Manhattan's moral and physical slums." The *Sentinel*'s valediction augured well for the success of the kind of career Krutch was trying to fashion for himself there:

> We wish this native son to know that we are not proud of him in view of his odious exploits. Knoxville will not reserve for him any niche in their future halls of fame and enroll his name among the sons to whom they will point with pride. We presume that he was born for some good purpose. There is nothing in nature or creation that is without design. The humble tumble-bug serves a purpose in the wondrous plan. But we do not envy him his job or covet his company.[27]

Krutch was doubtless well pleased by the *succès de scandale* of his Dayton dispatches. He had written partly to shine, to display his rhetorical gifts, and to gain attention, and he had unmistakably achieved at least the latter goal. His mother, however, was less pleased. After experimenting with several literary signatures, Krutch had adopted the full middle name *Wood*, largely to cheer his recently widowed mother, who was proud to associate her son's growing literary reputation with her own family name. (In addition, one imagines, he enjoyed the nice wit in yoking *Wood* with the frequent mispronunciation and misspelling of his surname as *Crutch*.) But now, having achieved her desired identification with her son's literary fame, she discovered that, in Knoxville at least, she partook of infamy instead.

Mrs. Krutch was deeply hurt both by her son's attack on Tennessee and by the *Sentinel*'s attack on her son. Still dutiful, Krutch interrupted his stay in Dayton to return to Knoxville to comfort, as best he could, his disconsolate mother. However, for a young writer eager to establish himself, even a mother's grief was a small price to pay for such attention as his articles had brought him.

When the festivities in Dayton had concluded and he had returned to Cornwall, Krutch again took up the Poe biography which he had been working on fitfully for more than a year and which he had promised to deliver that fall. Poe was not precisely the subject Krutch would have (or had) himself chosen for his first book. When he accepted the publisher's contract, he knew little of Poe's life or works, and he realized that he would be writing the book from scratch. But he felt that Poe was a nearly perfect subject for a popular critical biography, and he sought to achieve something of the success — even the *succès de scandale* — that he had won with his recent dispatches from Dayton.

To the largest part of the public, Krutch remarked in the 1940s, Poe was "probably *the* American classic. . . . In families which do not own more than three books, other than casual contemporary strays, one is almost certain to be Poe's poems or stories." Both Poe's writings and his life enjoyed a popular fascination on which Krutch hoped to capitalize in his book. "In the first place, his writings are sensational enough to make, inevitably, some sort of impression on even the dullest of sensibilities; in the second place, Poe himself fulfills more perfectly than any other well known writer the vulgar idea of what the personality and career of a great artist ought to be."[28] Preparing the market which he hoped awaited this, his first book for a general readership, Krutch wrote anonymously in a 1924 *Nation* editorial that the "mystery" of Poe "will never be fully solved until his

personality is more carefully studied by someone capable of understanding the malady of the soul from which he suffered."[29] That was,
of course, Krutch's very goal.

As he worked on the book between his reviewing, lecturing,
and teaching duties during 1924–25, Krutch found that the more he
read by and about Poe, the less sympathetic his subject became. Poe's
life seemed less that of a great artist wronged by his society than that
of a mean-spirited, childish, egocentric, hypocritical, spiteful, dis-
honest man whose "venomous pride, envy, and malice led him to dis-
honorable acts which no palliation can do more than excuse."[30] Poe's
works likewise left little for a critic of Krutch's taste to admire. As a
reviewer of contemporary fiction he had been demanding realism,
but now he recognized that there was "not, in the ordinary sense, one
iota of observation or touch of reality in any story or poem which
[Poe] produced." Whereas Krutch felt that literature should be relevant to life, in Poe he found "a complete absence of human interest
which results from the fact that they contain no observations of real
character or manners and touch normal experience at no point."
"Nearly all the things which ordinarily give value to a piece of literature are absent from Poe's work," he concluded. "The whole realm of
moral ideas is excluded . . . ; no characters are created, no social
problems presented, and no normal psychology exemplified."[31]

As a biographer, Krutch abjured the "abysmal sentimentality"
current among the "American cult" of Poe enthusiasts who uncritically excused his life and venerated his works. But Krutch was then
happy to be at odds with popular middlebrow taste, and thus to display the independence of his highbrow literary judgment. After the
manner of Lytton Strachey, who had recently achieved such success
with his *Eminent Victorians*, Krutch's book would be an exercise in
literary debunking. Early in the book he pointed proudly to his refusal to avail himself "even to a legitimate extent of the biographer's
privilege by virtue of which he may defend his hero and palliate the
less admirable aspects of his career and character."[32] His biographical
task, as he saw it, was not to provide panegyric, but to explain the
dynamics of a career as curious as Poe's. Here, too, he could draw
upon one of the fashionable literary movements of the day: psychoanalytic criticism. As a biographical and critical tool, psychology was

hardly novel in 1925 — and all the less so in reference to Poe. But while most of the earlier psychological studies of Poe had been simplistically genetic or neurological, Krutch seized eagerly on the newer Freudianism which lately had attracted the attention of those sophisticated young intellectuals among whom he was eager to number himself.

Three years earlier, in a review more sober than the present book, Krutch, who was then still an uneasy academic, had cautioned that "the new psychology in general and Freudianism in particular is . . . . a science and not a religion. Its hypotheses, like those of every new science, are probably more or less wrong, and it needs the most rigid testing. Yet it has, unfortunately, acquired far too many disciples who have accepted it as a new religion, and they have gone about unlocking all doors with this universal key, babbling of sublimation and repression as one once babbled of original sin and salvation by grace."[33] As he prepared his book, however, Krutch concluded that Poe was "the first of the great neurotics of literature."[34]

Edgar Allan Poe: A Study in Genius was in part a declaration, just a year after the book publication of his dissertation, of Krutch's independence from academic scholarship. Employing Freudian insights for which literature professors then had little patience, and dismissing the "silliness of those who would detach Poe, of all authors, from his work," he wrote as a man of letters rather than as a scholar.[35] Like Strachey, whose work he admired, Krutch felt free to be selective in adducing evidence, speculative in drawing inferences, and tendentious in framing his argument if in the end he could produce a book which — whatever its contribution to the understanding of Poe — was a work of art itself.

To Krutch, Poe was "a psychopathic case," "a man inexplicable by the laws of normal psychology." His account of Poe's life was simple — not to say, simplistic. Adopted when his mother died, before he was three, into the aristocratic Virginia universe of the Allans, and then unceremoniously rejected, Poe sought compensation by escaping into a world of fantasy, hoping to achieve as a writer the social success of which he had been deprived in Richmond. "The real world would have none of him," Krutch explained, and Poe flew "into the world where dreams count as facts and where, also, alas, shadowy horrors become no less real than shadowy triumphs."[36]

"This strange world of his imagination was the only one in which Poe could dwell, and he never left it once it had been found." That strange world, however, was narrowly circumscribed by his perverted sexuality, a state likely caused by the "baneful fascination" exercised over his mind by "the memory of his mother which made him see in sickness one of the necessary elements of the highest beauty" and which "stood between him and any normal fruition of love."[37] "The key to his morbidity," Krutch suggested, may be found in the "complete sexlessness" of Poe's writings. "That sense of melancholy, foreboding, and horror which, even though its exact meaning is disputed, is generally recognized as the usual accompaniment of deeply inhibited sexual desires, made his life one long misery, and a similar cloud of horror hung over his stories."[38]

According to Krutch, Poe's entire life, including much of his fiction, was "a struggle, conducted with all the cunning of the unconsciousness, against a realization of the psychic impotence of his sexual nature" as well as "against a realization of the mental instability to which the first gave rise." As he had earlier fled reality by creating an apparently irrational universe of fantasy, Poe later fled from fantasy to reason; recognizing that he was going insane, he created ratiocinative tales ostensibly founded on pure logic. "Poe, to whom life was perpetual, half understood torture . . . found a mode of escape by occupying himself with ingenuities which have the property of completely occupying the intellect without either engaging the passions or serving to remind one at any point of a world full of human dissonances."[39] The tales of ratiocination, then, like the tales of fantasy, were Poe's efforts to cope with his own neurosis. Indeed, his critical theory itself was merely a justification of his literary practice—an achievement, in Krutch's view, of a man "whose genius consisted, perhaps, in the possession to an extraordinary degree of the faculty of rationalization, which is one of the distinguishing characteristics of all neurotics."[40]

At the end of his study Krutch announced magisterially, "We have, then, traced Poe's art to an abnormal condition of the nerves and his critical ideas to a rationalized defence of the limitations of his own taste." Having torn him from his context in the Anglo-American literary tradition, Krutch had portrayed Poe as a writer *sui generis.* "His works," Krutch insisted, "bear no conceivable relation . . . to the life of any people, and it is impossible to account for them on the basis of any social or intellectual tendencies or as the expression of the spirit of any age."[41] His imagination was "outside his control" and had "mastered him." The notion of literary creation advanced by Krutch seemed almost calculated to titillate the common reader's mythical concept of the artist. "Instead of being deliberately invented," Krutch said, Poe's "stories and poems invented themselves." Ultimately, in fact, they were not his work at all, but the products of his neurosis: "The forces which wrecked his life," Krutch insisted, "were those which wrote his works."[42]

Even as he was writing, Krutch was surely aware of the excesses to which the steamroller of his argument had taken him. "The fallacy of origins, that species of false logic by which a thing is identified with its ultimate source, is nowhere more dangerous than in the realm of art," he noted toward the end of the book.[43] But Krutch was apparently so taken with the literary effect he achieved in employing that fallacy that he forged on, largely without qualification, in order not to compromise the artful coherence of his specious interpretation. He later recanted some of the grosser "absurdity" of his argument when he remarked that he had "neglected to ask why, if all geniuses are neurotic, all neurotics are not geniuses."[44] Still, at the time he hoped—as he had in his essays from Dayton—that the road of excess would lead to the palace of wisdom, or at least of reputation. He was not disappointed.

The reservations of academic critics counted for little with him, considering the nearly unanimous enthusiasm with which reviewers for the popular press greeted the book. H.L. Mencken, who had earlier published a chapter in the *American Mercury*, welcomed the volume in the *Nation* as "the most intelligent and convincing account of Poe ever written."[45] James Rorty in the *New Masses* described it as "one of the best critical volumes of recent years"[46]; Edmund Wilson in the *New Republic* said it was "the ablest and the most important of recent American writings about Poe"[47]; and the New York *Times* hailed it as "a model for a readable and yet professional application of modern psychology."[48] Even critics popularly associated with the conservative New Humanist movement were generous in their praise.

65

Reviewing the book in the *Saturday Review of Literature*, Norman Foerster allowed that, "As books go, this is an extremely interesting and able book."[49] And Stuart Sherman, somewhat lapsed from his earlier New Humanist militancy, described it in the New York *Herald Tribune Books* as "a brilliantly illuminating" work which "marks the definite arrival of a fresh and candid mind with modern psychological equipment, lively curiosity, critical objectivity and a singularly lucid, persuasive exposition."[50]

Fifty years later, in the light of the greater sophistication both of psychoanalytic thought and its application to literature and biography, it is difficult to wax so enthusiastic. Unlike the more restrained biographies of Johnson and Thoreau which Krutch would write two decades later, *Poe* can hardly be said to be a standard work on its subject. Nevertheless, the book was a bold early effort to apply psychoanalytic insights to literary biography, and Krutch was hardly more reductive than other contemporary practitioners of Freudian criticism. Moreover, *Poe* had clearly achieved Krutch's more immediate end: to announce, in his first extended literary performance, the arrival of a clever and sophisticated new writer and thinker. The book's sales were rather less impressive than the reviews; in straining to employ the latest critical tools, he had apparently overshot that general readership he had also aimed to win. For the moment, however, Krutch was content with the approbation of the fashionable critics of the day, and he was happy to feel that he had been accepted as an important young American man of letters.

He also well understood the evanescence of such celebrity as he then enjoyed. In a *Nation* editorial written shortly after he delivered the manuscript, he had observed: "We are . . . a nation of enthusiasts and we are so eager for heroes that we make them overnight. We set up the exultant cry 'A genius at last!' and then, next year, we find him out. . . . Writers leap into fame and disappear into obscurity."[51] His further challenge was to ensure that such a fate would not become his.

4.

☙ THE MODERN TEMPER

In the flush of his success with *Poe*, Krutch in early 1926 could almost imagine that he had arrived as a writer, although in more sober moments he recognized that to most people he was still that lesser creature, a reviewer. Even as he basked in the admiring notices of *Poe*, he knew that another such major performance was necessary for him to consolidate his reputation. But his crowded schedule of lecturing, teaching, editorializing, and reviewing left precious little time for him even to contemplate the subject of, let alone to write, that next book. Nor did he have the energy. He was exhausted from the frenetic pace he had set for himself in the early 1920s, and even his periodic retreats to Cornwall were insufficient fully to restore his health. His migraines became more frequent and acute, and they were presently joined by fevers, attacks of faintness, and weight loss. For the moment, then, he was content merely to carry on with his work at the *Nation* and, when time and energy allowed, to write an occasional review or essay for some other publication. But even as a reviewer he was—at first unwittingly, then deliberately—gathering material for his next major performance. Reading books, seeing plays, and writing reviews, he was marshaling insights and publishing notes toward *The Modern Temper*, the most important of his works.

By the time Krutch became the *Nation* drama critic in the fall of 1924, some of the spirit of the modern drama that he had encountered during the past decade in New York's small experimental theater groups had found its way to the Broadway stage. He missed the opening weeks of the new season while he recovered from yet another illness (appendicitis), but when he finally took his seat on the aisle he enjoyed, in rapid succession, *What Price Glory?*, *Desire under the Elms*, and *They Knew What They Wanted.* In those new works by American playwrights he found cause to believe that he was about to witness a renaissance on the Broadway stage. "Never before," he recalled, "had so much radically new talent been popping up here and there in the American theater. Such a beginning seemed to hold out the possibility that a real golden age of the drama was not far away."[1] It was, he said, "an era of novelty and adventure when it was possible to hope that next week might reveal something nearer true greatness than anything that had yet appeared."[2]

Not even that remarkable 1924–25 season, however, could sustain the splendor of its early months. Many of the 230 openings demonstrated how far the producers' demands for new plays outstripped the playwrights' capacity to bring forth masterpieces. Krutch confessed in June, "During the nine months just past the professional playgoers must have suffered many days and even whole weeks of boredom and discouragement."[3] The theatrical world, like the literary world generally, was booming during the late twenties, and as quantity increased, average quality declined. During 1927–28 the 80 operating theaters in New York saw some 280 new productions, with 11 openings on the evening of December 27 alone. Judged by its average product, the success of even the best of seasons was hardly unqualified. "Yet in the realm of art," Krutch remarked after his second season, "averages are always low, for art is a phenomenal thing in which only the exception counts; and the critic, with his carefully cultivated power of forgetting, remembers only those things which are worth remembering."[4]

The prospect of someday feasting on memories of the best plays he had seen might well have comforted him as he made his way home after another dreary opening, but as a reviewer Krutch was more immediately responsible for filling his weekly column of 1,000 to 1,500 words. In his drama criticism, as in his book reviews, his challenge was to write memorably even on works little worth remembering.

He could not alone hope to offer in the *Nation* a comprehensive account of the activity of the New York stage; there were too many openings and too few evenings. Nor, in a political weekly where the books and arts pages were sent to the typesetter first, could he hope to achieve in his reviews the timeliness of the daily papers. So Krutch adopted in his drama columns, as he had in his book reviews, "an 'intellectual' approach."[5] While also providing much of the information essential in any proper review, he sought further to become a critic of ideas and to interpret for his readers such general propositions as were suggested by the themes or forms of the plays he saw.

From among the week's offerings he generally made one play the focus of his review-essay. Before even mentioning that play, he frequently began his column with a discussion of some topic it suggested. Even when (as was not infrequently the case) the play offered little evidence of art or intelligence, he seized upon some issue, philosophical or artistic, suggested there, developing it deftly in a paragraph or two. Thus Krutch's early reviews of long-forgotten plays remain interesting for their brief, cameo-like essays on such theatrical topics as farce, expressionism, melodrama, tragedy, burlesque, acting, or public taste, or on such themes as fatherhood, war, youth and age, psychoanalysis, bastardy, pastoralism, or science and faith. A revival of an older play often occasioned Krutch's succinct estimate of the playwright's talent and his times, as well as of the current production. To readers seeking only the "news" of Broadway, such discussions doubtless seemed gratuitous. But for most of Krutch's readers they constituted the distinctive excellence of his reviews. However banal the play, he had some intelligent thoughts—occasionally on banality itself.

In his drama reviews, as in his earliest book reviews, Krutch approached contemporary works with special interest in their depiction of the "particular emphasis, temper and mood" of the times.[6] The reviewer of current literature is, in part, properly a cultural historian "concerned with the meaning and significance of works to those who produce them and to those for whom they are produced; he sees them as expressions of the spirit of his times and he judges them as such. The concern of our writers with national life is direct and eager; their chief occupation is with the experiment which we are at present making in the art of living."[7]

Krutch was little interested in the external aspects of that

69

experiment—the flappers and other such phenomena that were so much a part of the popular image of the decade. Instead, he was concerned primarily with what he had described as early as 1920, in one of his very first book reviews, as "a modern dilemma." "Destructive criticism," he had written then, "opened abyss below abyss, and the spirit plunges headlong."[8] In the ensuing years, as he read scores of books and attended hundreds of plays in his professional capacity, the nature of that dilemma became ever clearer; indeed, the modern dilemma became his own. In many of his reviews Krutch described the causes of that headlong plunge of the spirit and his uneasiness over the new intellectual dispensation in which he found himself.

Though the texts for his remarks were the works of novelists and playwrights, he knew, if only from his own recent ruminations, that the critical tendency and sense of spiritual loss were not unique to them. He felt certain that their works mirrored as well as created a broader intellectual climate, and that the germ of skepticism infected many who never read a book or saw a play. "The life of nine hundred and ninety-nine out of a thousand persons," he declared, "is a series of meaningless actions controlled by no principle either inside or outside themselves, and leading to no conclusion either satisfactory to them or edifying to those who watch them." In the epidemic of disillusionment, Krutch felt, the shopgirl felt in her own way as lost as the latest product of the best education.

The skepticism which rendered contemporary man so unhappy was a product of the same scientific spirit which had brought so many creature comforts. Thanks to it, Krutch acknowledged, "we know more than any age ever knew before of the events which take place around us," although "we are also less sure than any that we can understand them."[9] In the characters created by an Ibsen or Joyce ("these figures of the dawn") one was struck by "so much intelligence and so little wisdom. They threw off the prejudices of a century and they thought their way with brilliant clarity through the maze which passion and prejudice create, but they forgot in their enthusiasm that no man can make of himself a wholly rational animal."[10] For Krutch, the modern dilemma was the apparent inevitability of the attempt, yet the impossibility of the achievement. Seeking to fashion himself into a sophisticated modern thinker, he too had been trying to throw off the prejudices of his provincial background. Finding, however, that he had no new values with which to replace the traditional ones he felt he must reject, he found that his spirit too was plunging into the abyss.

For Krutch, it seemed clear that the scientific spirit was fundamental to the destructive criticism characteristic of modern thought. Given his own youthful interest in science, he was perhaps especially vulnerable to the modernist skepticism to which he yielded during the 1920s. But even as he tried to make that modern spirit his own, he was uneasy over the cost of the effort: "Whoever pours the solvent of thought upon the visible world will find it melting away."[11] The relentless questioning, analyzing, and criticizing of science had infected all of man's thinking, but man's feelings rebelled.

It was, Krutch said, "the testimony of contemporary letters" that there was "a widening gulf between current modes of thinking and current modes of feeling. While science has approached existence from one angle, emotion and to some extent art have approached it from another and older angle, so that many people, at once sensitive and intelligent . . . suffer from a sort of permanent split in the soul which prevents their achieving a stable and harmonious life."[12] He traced the spiritual discontent felt by his contemporaries and himself to "the commonplace fact that the intellect of man adjusts itself much more readily than do his emotions to all the changes which go on in the world he inhabits."

> Science, if it has not created a new world, has at least destroyed the old, and to many at least it seems that we do nothing except wander, emotionally, among the ruins. Mentally it may not be difficult to grasp the fact that God is dead and that with Him has passed away a whole universe of emotional realities, but the Soul — and the very necessity for employing this word is a sufficient indication of the inadequacy of our adjustment to a godless universe — demands without being able to find something satisfactory to herself in the meaningless world of which science describes the disjointed fragments. The mind leaps, and leaps perhaps with a sort of joy, through the immensities of space, but the spirit, frightened and cold in the vast emptiness, longs to have once more above its head that inverted bowl beyond which may lie whatever paradise its desires create.[13]

It is significant that, while Krutch was trying to establish himself as one of the advanced thinkers of his day, he should also be resorting to such old-fashioned notions as *spirit, soul,* and *wisdom.* The "split in the soul" he described was his own as well. He was torn during the 1920s between, on the one hand, his genuine respect for science and his desire to make the currently fashionable modern skepticism his own; and, on the other hand, his deeply conservative temperament, shaped in Knoxville, which craved stability, the comfort of traditional values, and commonsense belief, rather than labored doubt.

His stubborn conservatism was reflected in his reaction not only to the ideas in modern literature, but also to the forms in which they were expressed. Instead of the realistic amplitude of the great novels of the past, he found only a wordy intellectualism. "There is nothing which reveals more clearly the most characteristic defect of modern fiction," he said, "than the fact that the chief theme — even the chief substance — of most contemporary novels is easily reduced to intellectual terms."[14] The growing subjectivity of contemporary literature and its preoccupation with abstractions was, for Krutch, symptomatic of the skeptical tenor of the age. "It is," he said, "merely the result of the development of the human mind which has proceeded step by step away from the observations of the senses and, trying to get behind them, has hoped vainly at each step that it has at last found the ultimate meaning of things."

Contemporary thought might, he suggested, be compared with the process of a man opening a nest of Chinese boxes: "We lift each lid in the hope that we have at last come to the end, but there is always an inner box to be investigated. Perhaps we shall some day realize that the ingenuity of the force which created the universe is, unlike the ingenuity of the Chinese, entirely without limit, and realizing that the number of boxes is infinite, we shall regret despairingly that we did not rest content with the picture on the outermost lid."[15] Action was no less worthy a literary subject than reflection, and man's life in the world no less compelling than his tortured soliloquies with himself. Krutch regretted many contemporary writers' impatience with the outermost lid of existence. "As their criticism penetrates deeper and deeper," he said, "as they proceed from disillusion to disillusion, they come upon those dissonances which no manipulation can resolve, and . . . they feel in them rather than in the details of time or place the real materials of philosophy and art."[16]

The way in which that disillusionment and unresolved dissonance enfeebled literature was pointed up, for him, by the appearance on Broadway of a revival of *Hamlet* and two new American plays "essentially tragic in their feeling." The contrast exemplified "how far are our days from deserving that adjective 'spacious' so fittingly bestowed upon the days of the great Elizabeth." It was a long way, he said, from the palace at Elsinore to the Harlem flat which furnished the scene of Patrick Kearney's *A Man's Man*, and from "the imperious lust of the most seeming-virtuous queen to the petty schemes of the selfish wife" bitterly depicted in George Kelly's *Craig's Wife*. "But it is the way which the modern mind has come, gradually losing its grandiose vision and becoming more and more absorbed in the trivialities among which it has its being. . . . We have our tragic sense of life, bitterer, perhaps, than that of any other age, but it is less a sense that man fails greatly, like Hamlet, than that, without grandeur or greatness, he fails in meanness of spirit and triviality of circumstance."[17]

In such asides, scattered throughout his reviews, Krutch was manifestly moving toward some more complete definition of that "modern mind" and some fuller expression of his own reaction to the primary coinage of the day's intellectual and spiritual currency. But a sentence or two here and a paragraph or two there hardly allowed him the necessary scope to build upon the insights and to pursue the speculations which had so distinguished his reviews. To marshal his thoughts in an essay—for at the moment, he thought of nothing more ambitious than that—would require more time than he could find in his hectic New York schedule. In Cornwall that summer he knew he would have that time. And in the case of that essay, as often in his career, Krutch's resolve to write was sealed when a publisher expressed interest in purchasing the finished work.

In the spring of 1926, shortly after the publication of *Poe*, Irita Van Doren had suggested to Ellery Sedgwick, editor of the *Atlantic Monthly*, that he might solicit a contribution from Krutch. Sedg-

73

wick's letter found Krutch empty handed; he would never be one to allow his writing to age in a drawer. Krutch responded to the invitation by saying that he had lately been preoccupied by a number of related issues which might well constitute the basis of an appropriate *Atlantic* piece, and he promised to have something to Sedgwick by midsummer. As soon as the theater season ended and he arrived in Cornwall, he set to work on "The Modern Temper," the essay toward which he had been writing notes in many of his reviews.

"It is one of Freud's quaint conceits," Krutch began aphoristically, "that the child in its mother's womb is the happiest of living creatures." Even as an infant he is content that the universe which fulfills his every need and responds to his every wish is one with his heart's desires. Presently, however, the child discovers with enraged surprise that there are wills other than his own and physical circumstances that cannot be surmounted by any human will. "Only after the passage of many years does he become aware of the full extent of his predicament in the midst of a world which is in very few respects what he would wish it to be."[18]

Thus, too, a civilization passes from its innocent youth to its disillusioned maturity. "As civilization grows older, it too has more and more facts thrust upon its consciousness and is compelled to abandon one after another, quite as the child does, certain illusions which have been dear to it." Confronted by the facts of science, modern man found himself dispossessed of such sustaining illusions as mythology, religion, philosophy, and ethics. Even "man's most fundamental myth," that there is "a moral order to the world," seemed shattered. Ethics, Krutch allowed, may be "imaginary things"; yet "it is extremely doubtful if man can live well, either spiritually or physically, without the belief that they are somehow real."

In place of the warm human comforts of poetry, mythology, and religion, science offered only the cold knowledge of nature. But to Krutch at the time it seemed a sterile knowledge, meaningless to man. "Nature's purpose, if purpose she can be said to have, is no purpose of his and is not understandable in his terms. Her desire merely to live and to propagate in innumerable forms, her ruthless indifference to his values, and the blindness of her irresistible will strike terror to his soul." Man's rational investigations reveal only "a world which his emotions cannot comprehend." Bereft of the beliefs which science has effectively undermined, man finds himself "more and more alone in a universe to which he is completely alien."

Some men, Krutch recognized, have welcomed the new dispensation: scientists, of course ("to whom the test tube and its contents are all-sufficient") and captains of industry ("to whom the acquirement of wealth and power seems to constitute a life in which no lack can be perceived"). But to one of Krutch's mind—"the robust but serious mind which is searching for some terms upon which it may live"—it was no more possible to welcome the new age than to return to the old. "Refuge in the monotonous repetition of once living creeds" or belief in "the formulae of the flabby pseudo-religions in which the modern world is so prolific" were options only for "weak and uninstructed intelligences." To the dilemma of the modern temper he offered no solution, only the dour prediction that "There impends for the human spirit either extinction or a readjustment more stupendous than any made before."

The devoted reader of Krutch's reviews would have recognized in his essay an orchestration of many of the themes he had touched upon earlier. Indeed, his argument was hardly novel. Most of the ideas he presented there had long been current in a tradition of modernist imaginative and philosophical literature which can be traced back at least as far as the writings of Dostoevsky and Nietzsche, and which found another famous formulation in Freud's *Future of an Illusion*, published shortly after Krutch's essay. "The Modern Temper" was remarkable, then, less for its stunning originality than for the powerful eloquence with which Krutch had brought together some of the leading ideas of at least one variety of that "temper." As he could not in the scope of any single review, he revealed in his essay both his profound understanding of the drift of contemporary thought and the agony of a man of "robust but serious mind." As in his recent book on Poe, he was eager to shine, to advance his reputation as a fashionably sophisticated thinker, and to gain the attention a young writer covets. If he had perhaps oversimplified the modern dilemma and strained to display the exquisite sensitivity of his feelings, he had written (as in *Poe*) partly to achieve a certain literary effect. As he mailed the essay late in July 1926 — "stamps enclosed" — he was uncertain of Sedgwick's reaction.

His apprehension was understandable. The *Atlantic Monthly* under Sedgwick remained largely a product of the genteel New England tradition and was addressed more to middlebrow captains of industry and devout believers than to anguished highbrow thinkers like Krutch. The beginning of Sedgwick's response was hardly encouraging. "God help you," he wrote, "for your creed never will." He regretted that Krutch's argument led "directly away from the enthusiasm and ferment which are at the bases of the creeds that work." He continued, however, by confessing that "What I think about your beliefs no whit affects my satisfaction at having so able a piece of work." And he accepted the article "with pleasure."[19]

When it appeared in February 1927 — along with some of the *Atlantic*'s more typical fare: an inspiring "Story of Conversion" and a helpful essay entitled "Teach Us to Pray" — Krutch received the attention he had sought. Ministers wrote to say that he misrepresented religion; scientists, that he misunderstood science; and a lady who said that she had subscribed to the magazine for most of her eighty-four years, to regret that space in "our best-beloved magazine should be given over to Professor Krutch's brilliant intellectual gymnastics which would seem to prove nothing unless it be that there is nothing to prove. What good," she asked, "does that do?"

Few readers wrote to say that they shared Krutch's ideas, but one, from Walla Walla, Washington, thanked the *Atlantic* for publishing the article "because it illustrates finely how far the mind may go when it has cut loose from all philosophical moorings. I hope we may have more by the same writer." Sedgwick agreed. The editor was no less pleased than the author by the controversy the essay had generated, and he invited Krutch to contribute further essays on the same theme. When he returned to Cornwall in June 1927, after another year's reviewing, Krutch resumed the argument begun in "The Modern Temper."

That first essay had set forth in general terms the tension between humanism and science — between man's emotional attachment to that universe of mythology, philosophy, religion, and art, which nurtured his sense of value; and man's intellectual attraction to the rationalism of science, which seemed effectively to deny all that humanism asserted. In the two following essays, written during the summer of 1927, Krutch considered the possibility of man's resolving the dilemma by committing himself wholly to either humanism or science.

Even as he was beginning to achieve in Cornwall that understanding of the human significance of nature which would provide the inspiration for many of his later books, Krutch insisted that "Nature reveals herself as extraordinarily fertile and ingenious in devising *means*, but she has no *ends* which the human mind has been able to discover or comprehend." Impelled by "her inscrutable appetite for mere life in itself," Nature, according to his Darwinian understanding, is concerned with the welfare of the species rather than with that of the individual. The ant, who has perfected the social virtues and has merged his own interests completely with those of his kind, has demonstrated a capacity for survival far greater than man's. "In the eyes of Nature he has made a much greater success in life." But man could never be satisfied with the "peaceful security" of the ant. Humanism, he wrote in his second essay, is concerned with "those qualities, characteristics, and powers which distinguish the human being from the rest of animate nature" and separate him from, rather than bind him to, his community: individualism, skepticism, irony, and the power of dispassionate analysis. "Minds which are keener and wills which are stronger than the average" resist the antlike conformity nature demands. In Nature's scheme, however, the artist and philosopher are not, "in the most fundamental or necessary sense, useful or productive." Preoccupied with his critical intelligence, the humanist relies for physical survival on the efforts of those more blindly acceptant of Nature's demands.

"The Paradox of Humanism" was its enmity to "those natural impulses which have made the human animal possible" and its tendency "to paralyze natural impulse by criticizing natural aims." Intellectual virtues are thus biological vices; the more human man becomes, the less fit he is to survive. There were, Krutch feared, limits to Nature's tolerance of man's unnatural humanism. "A choice must ultimately be made between a stable, essentially animal existence and

77

the dangerous — ultimately fatal — life of the society which starts out in pursuit of purely human values."

If humanism was biologically inexpedient, Nature and her disciple, science, were humanly unsatisfying. In "The Disillusion with the Laboratory" Krutch observed, "Science has always promised two things not necessarily related — an increase first in our powers, second in our happiness or wisdom, and we have come to realize that it is the first and less important of the two promises which it has kept most abundantly." The fruits of science, especially social science, were bitter to human taste. Scrutinizing man's humanist beliefs enfeebled them. "In the laboratory," Krutch wrote, "there can be found no trace of the soul . . . no sign of the will . . . and no evidence of the existence of any such thing as morality except customs. . . ." The light science casts upon the nature of man "is not adapted to our eyes and is not anything by which we can see."

Intellectually, Krutch realized that "the universe with which science deals is the real universe," even though emotionally he was convinced that "the belief in God, however ill founded, has been more important in the life of man than the germ theory of decay, however true the latter may be." If man could not survive by a thoroughgoing commitment to humanism, neither could he cast his lot wholly with science. "The most important part of our lives — our sensations, emotions, desires, and aspirations — takes place in a universe of illusions which science can attenuate or destroy, but which it is powerless to enrich." Man was thus left clinging precariously to his humanity, "because it is the thing which we recognize as ourselves, and if it is lost, then all that counts for us is lost with it."

Love was, of course, one manifestation of that humanity. In his third essay that summer, "Love — or the Life and Death of a Value," Krutch examined an instance of science's having "humbled our dignity and clipped the wings of our aspirations." In those same Victorian decades when the expectations of progress through science were so high, imagination had been enlisted in the service of Nature and had made of a mere biological act "not merely one of the things which make life worth while, but *the* thing which justifies or makes it meaningful." Soon, however, rationalists like Havelock Ellis, "eager to clarify an illusion," turned their analytic attention to love; "and the result, which now seems as though it might have been foretold, was to destroy that illusion." With the taboos of sex challenged by the cold light of scientific reason and its physiology subjected to the rude investigations previously reserved for other, less sublime biological processes, the illusion of love was "stripped of the mystical penumbra in whose shadow its transcendental value seemed real, though hid." With his greater understanding of love, man had won the right to indulge in it more freely. But "in the course of the very process of winning the right to love," Krutch said, "love itself has been deprived of its value. . . . If love has come to be less often a sin it has come also to be less often a supreme privilege."

In modern literature, he observed, "love is at times only a sort of obscene joke . . . which turns quickly bitter upon the tongue, for a great and gratifying illusion has passed away, leaving the need for it still there." "Nor," he said, "is human life so rich in values as to justify us in surrendering any one of them complacently."

> A color has faded from our palette, a whole range of effects dropped out of our symphony. . . . We are carried one step nearer to that state in which existence is seen as a vast emptiness which the imagination can no longer people with fascinating illusions. . . . We have grown used . . . to a Godless universe, but we are not yet accustomed to one which is loveless as well, and only when we have so become shall we realize what atheism really means.

As he wrote those essays on humanism, science, and love in Cornwall during the summer of 1927, Krutch was obviously warming to his theme. He had, as in the concluding sentences of his essay on love, pulled out all the rhetorical stops. The more he wrote, the more he discovered he had to say. One essay now had become four; and he knew that he had not yet exhausted the literary possibilities of his exploration of the modern temper. At Sedgwick's invitation he had embarked upon that exploration, and Sedgwick's enthusiastic reception of these three new efforts encouraged him further. "I am tremendously indebted to you for this series," the *Atlantic* editor wrote after receiving the essay on love. "It has stirred me and must create silent and serious debate in many minds and hearts. I cannot say that your articles enliven my evenings, but they certainly stimulate them.

You are following a most interesting theme relentlessly and with cumulative effect."[21]

When they appeared in the *Atlantic* in December 1927 and March and August 1928, the essays elicited from readers more of the lively responses that had greeted "The Modern Temper." Krutch, too, knew that his articles had a cumulative effect. Indeed, he sensed that, without having quite intended to do so, he had written several chapters of a book which might be a worthy successor to *Poe*.

꿿 Though his reviewing of books and plays continued to provide Krutch with a fund of new insights on various aspects of the modern temper, he had little hope of being able to carry on with his writing when he returned to New York in the fall. He made notes on points to be covered and outlined possible chapters, but he was resigned to postponing further writing on the book until he returned to Cornwall the following summer. As it turned out, however, that summer was not to be spent in Cornwall. The *Nation* had offered to send Krutch on a late spring tour of the theatrical capitals of Europe, culminating in several weeks in Moscow; and the Krutches decided to stay on in Paris for the summer of 1928. They sailed in April and, after several days in Berlin, left by train for Moscow — traveling over such "flat, cold, empty, depressing country" that they felt they were "rapidly approaching the very end of the habitable globe." Moscow, however, he wrote to Villard, was "certainly one of the most fascinating places I have ever seen." Once there, he interviewed a number of prominent figures (including Eisenstein, several writers, and the commissar for education) and, with the aid of an interpreter, made his rounds of the theaters and cinemas. To Villard, then an enthusiast of the Soviets, Krutch reported himself "very much impressed by the progress that has been made and by the apparent efficiency with which the government is functioning."[22]

By the time he reached Vienna and wrote more candidly to Mark Van Doren, Krutch's enthusiasm was rather more qualified. Though "in comfort and other things" the Russians were "still a long way behind," he noted that they were "really advancing" and he was "very much amazed to find Communism actually working as an every day commonplace affair." He should, he said, "not be at all surprised if it were really the government of the future." Nevertheless, it was not a prospect in which Krutch rejoiced. "There is too damn much regulation in Moscow," he wrote. "You must get visas to go in, visas to stay, visas to go out, and permits for every move you want to make. . . . I as you know am dilletanty enough to prefer the present (perhaps the past) to the future and I am not heroic enough to care for a revolutionary society. For my own pleasure I could exchange a little of the hope in Moscow for a little comfort and luxury."23

Although in the 1930s, when he wrote further about Russia, Krutch would recall the surfeit of regulation he found during his visit there, in 1928 he was especially struck by the contrast between the "hope" he discovered among the people he met in Moscow and the despair he had recently been describing in his essays on the modern temper. This, too, he would incorporate into his book. But as he traveled from Vienna to Paris, his thoughts were less on that book than on the drama dispatches he would be writing for the *Nation* and, when they were completed, the carefree summer he would enjoy in France before a new Broadway season called him back to New York.

When he arrived in Paris, however, he found a cable from Harcourt Brace announcing their desire to publish his book and inquiring when they could expect the completed manuscript. Ever quickened by a publisher's interest, Krutch resolved to devote the summer to *The Modern Temper* and promised the manuscript by August. By now a seasoned literary journalist, Krutch was inspired rather than intimidated by deadlines. Foregoing the Parisian holiday he had hoped to enjoy, he closeted himself each morning in an improvised garret study and emerged, generally by lunch time, with another thousand or so of the 30,000 words he calculated would be needed to fill out the series of essays—and the book.

The first of the four essays he wrote that summer came especially easily. Watching and writing about dramatic tragedy, he had frequently remarked upon the way in which the tragic spirit, like the mystique of love he had discussed earlier, had withered in the insalubrious climate of contemporary skepticism. What was once a noble form of art and a heroic vision of life was now, he said in one of his most famous essays, merely "The Tragic Fallacy."

Tragedy had begun among peoples like those of Periclean Greece or Elizabethan England, who were "fully aware of the calamities of life [but were] nevertheless serenely confident in the greatness of man, whose mighty passions and supreme fortitude are revealed when one of those calamities overtakes him." Founded upon belief in "human dignity," "the importance of human passions," and "the amplitude of human life," genuine tragedy is "an affirmation of faith in life, a declaration that even if God is not in his Heaven, then at least Man is in his world." The modern age, however, patently lacked the vigorous faith of a Sophocles or a Shakespeare. "Distrusting its thought, despising its passions, realizing its impotent unimportance in the universe, it can tell itself no stories except those which make it still more acutely aware of its trivial miseries." *Ghosts* was an exemplary text of our times, just as *Hamlet* was of its own. "The journey from Elsinore to Skien," Krutch said, "is precisely the journey which the human spirit has made, exchanging in the process princes for invalids and gods for disease."

To the modern mind, the confident faith of earlier centuries may seem little more than a sentimental fallacy of an immature civilization, Krutch acknowledged. "But fallacy though it is, upon its existence depends not merely the writing of tragedy but the existence of that religious feeling of which tragedy is an expression and by means of which a people aware of the dissonances of life manages nevertheless to hear them as harmony." "The death of tragedy," he concluded, "is, like the death of love, one of those emotional fatalities as the result of which the human as distinguished from the natural world grows more and more a desert."

In retrospect, the image is not without irony. Ultimately Krutch would find in the desert of the American Southwest precisely that spiritual peace which modernism seemed to deny. But for him at that time, as several years earlier for T.S. Eliot, the desert seemed an apt image for the spiritual drought that afflicted so many of his contemporaries. Desperate for relief, some had fled to art and others (by then including Eliot himself) to religion. In the two essays to which he next turned his hand, Krutch examined those alternatives.

The first, "Life, Art and Peace," considered aestheticism—the attempt of those men who, convinced of the bankruptcy of tradi-

82

tional precepts of religion and morality, tried to lead their lives as though they were works of art. It was, Krutch said, a popular modern assumption that "life has no purpose fixed by a power outside of life (as distinguished from such purpose as the individual may be able to choose or believe in for himself)," and that thus "there is no more any such thing as *the* good life than there is any such thing as *the* good work of art, although of course, there may be various good lives just as there are various good works of art." Each man's life could be ordered, like a work of art, simply according to "the rules of his own being." Such aestheticism was the ultimate extension of the asocial, individualistic humanism Krutch had discussed earlier. For the man who sought to make his life merely a work of art, success would be judged "not by considering the end which he proposes but merely by the extent to which he is successful in his effort to achieve that end." With its "inclusive tolerance" such aestheticism would be powerless to deny that "the life led by the great monster is as truly the good life as that led by the great saint."

The fallacy of aestheticism, Krutch pointed out, was that of confusing two discrete universes: the imaginary world created by the artist in his works, and the real, contingent world of nature in which he lives and over which he lacks complete control. "No society organized upon such principles could possibly last," he said. "Nature would not tolerate a humanism so complete and would wipe out the animals who dared try to exist upon principles so completely antithetical to those necessary for animal survival." The artist can, at best, hope to achieve in his imaginary universe a certain peace, a temporary refuge from the disorder of the natural universe. Art, Krutch concluded, furnishes "a means by which life may be contemplated, but not a means by which it may be lived."

Like art, metaphysics offered a peaceful refuge for the contemplation of reality. However, as Krutch argued in the third of that summer's essays, "The Phantom of Certitude," metaphysics was hardly more helpful than art as a guide to conduct. Krutch had never been attracted to aestheticism, but he did long for that religious feeling by means of which, as he had written in his essay on tragedy, "a people aware of the dissonances of life manages nevertheless to hear them as harmony." If, at age twelve, he had rejected what he had been taught in Sunday school when the bishop led him to Herbert Spencer, he had still retained the basically religious need for the spiritual stability that comes of seeing a greater order and meaning to the universe than science appears to allow. Emotionally, he was attracted to religion, but intellectually (as a self-consciously "robust but serious mind" infected with the modern belief that "the universe with which science deals is the real universe") he could not accept a metaphysics which denied natural realities and scientific revelations while suggesting that "certain 'human' truths may exist quite independently of the scientific truths which cannot contradict them because the two occupy completely separate realms."

Permitting no external test of the adequacy of its theories, metaphysics, he said, sought to "re-establish a liberty to believe whatever one happens to want to believe." Using pure logic, the metaphysician tries to establish "a serviceable code." But Krutch was unable to accept the argument of the "metaphysical moralist," which he described as follows: "It is admitted that moral and spiritual certitudes are useful both to the individual and to society. Science has failed to furnish either, but logic is capable of supplying both. Take what she has to offer, live by the principles she proclaims *as though* they were true, and you will discover that they either *are* true or at least, what is really the same thing, that they will work *as though they were*." Ultimately, the effect was to try to make life an art; metaphysics, he suggested, was an aestheticism whose materials were logic. Both failed, however, in dismissing too readily the reality of nature revealed by science.

A metaphysics that had conclusively argued that the sun revolved around the earth was not one Krutch could accept; nor could he escape the suspicion that "metaphysics may be, after all, only the art of being sure of something that is not so and logic only the art of going wrong with confidence." Insisting on its complete divorce from science, concentrating on what might be rather than what is, surrendering (as Krutch felt it had) any pretension to establish truths of reference, "metaphysics, which promised so much, thus ends by confirming the very despair which it set out to combat." That despair, which Krutch himself had come to feel, seemed the inevitable lot of any thoughtful man.

Recently, however, while in Russia, he had observed a nation of hope. Philosophically untroubled and dedicated to the achievement of material ends, the Soviets appeared free from the despair he had been describing and wholly and gladly absorbed in the "processes of life for their own sake." Drawing now on his recent travels as he had drawn earlier on contemporary books and plays, Krutch considered in the "Conclusion" to his book the possibility that, in a creed like communism, men and women like himself might find the sense of purpose that the modern temper seemed to deny.

A young race, historically isolated from "the successive and debilitating stages" of European culture, the Russians remained innocent of "any problem more subtle than those involved in the production and distribution of wealth" — and thus devoted themselves to the immediate necessities of living, with complete faith in the ultimate importance of those necessities. "Communism assumes that nothing is really important except those things upon which the welfare of the race depends." Still enjoying the primitive vitality that European man had lost, the Russian, as described by Krutch, resembled the ant (which, he earlier had noted, had made a success of life as judged by Nature's standards). The Communist philosophy, he remarked, "comes nearer than any other to that unformulated one by which an animal lives."

In the context of his argument in *The Modern Temper*, the comparison was not wholly unfavorable. Indeed, Krutch saw the "fundamental optimism" of the Russians as a function of their living according to Nature, rather than adopting a decadent humanism. "If Russia or the Russian spirit conquers Europe," he said, "it will not be with the bomb of the anarchist but with the vitality of the young barbarian who may destroy many things but who destroys them only that he may begin over again." Seen through Nature's eyes, there was justice in such a conquest: "Such calamities are calamitous only from the point of view of a humanism which values the complexity of its feelings and the subtlety of its intellect far more than Nature does. To her they are merely the reassertion of her right to recapture her own world, merely the process by which she repeoples the earth with creatures simple enough to live joyously there."

The natural primitivism of the Russian spirit, however, was

not one that Krutch could embrace. "Its hopes are no hopes in which we can have any part," he said. "Skepticism has entered too deeply into our souls ever to be replaced by faith, and we can never forget the things which the new barbarians will never need to have known." As with aestheticism and metaphysics, communism ultimately provided no satisfactory refuge from a world "in which an unresolvable discord is the fundamental fact." In that world of discord Krutch and his fellow spirits "must continue to live, and for us wisdom must consist, not in searching for a means of escape which does not exist but in making such peace with it as we may." Man could at least take "a certain defiant satisfaction" in having "discovered the trick which has been played upon us" and in knowing "that whatever else we may be we are no longer dupes." "Ours is a lost cause and there is no place for us in the natural universe," he concluded, not a little melodramatically. "But we are not, for all that, sorry to be human. We should rather die as men than live as animals."

❦ In *The Modern Temper* Krutch had displayed the same talents of selection, summary, and interpretation employed so successfully in his reviews. Drawing upon nearly a decade of reviewing, he sought to offer a synoptic account of a frame of mind then defining itself as modern—the convictions, and above all the doubts, of men who were "haunted by ghosts from a dead world" (the world of humanistic values) and "not yet at home in [their] own" (the natural world revealed by value-blind science).[24] In his essays Krutch hoped to present a document of the contemporary spirit as memorable as Eliot's recent diagnosis in *The Waste Land*. Moreover, he sought, like Eliot, to present himself as a representative figure of that modernism. Krutch's new book was to reinforce his reputation, gained with the publication of *Poe*, as a literary intellectual of consequence. The melodramatic and foreboding conclusion was of a piece with the mood Krutch artfully sought to create throughout. Indeed, there was a certain joyous energy in the cumulative movement of his bleak chronicle of disillusionment. Like a Byronic hero, he seemed almost to glory in his melancholy, and the pose he struck was characteristic of the modernist's commitment to the ineluctably problematic nature of human life. For men without faith, strenuous sincerity and stoic resignation seemed sufficient in themselves. Krutch was doubtless thinking of his essays on modernism when he remarked some years later: "The pessimism of the young is defiant, anxious to confess or even exaggerate its ostensible gloom, and so exuberant as to reveal the fact that it regards its ability to face up to the awful truth as more than enough to compensate for the awfulness of that truth."[25]

Notwithstanding the exaggeration of his gloom to achieve his desired effect, the despair Krutch portrayed in *The Modern Temper* was unmistakably his own. He subtitled the book "A Study and a Confession," and he acknowledged in the foreword that the apparent objectivity of his "study" of contemporary thought was colored by the subjectivity of a more personal "confession." The book grew, he said, "out of an effort to understand myself," and though he assumed there was "something characteristic" about his conclusions, he acknowledged that he had "no mandate to speak for anyone but myself and obviously there are many different tempers existing side by side today."[26]

Krutch's despair was compounded of many elements, most of them philosophical but some simply physiological. His illnesses during the late 1920s became increasingly chronic; as he tried with less and less strength to achieve more and more of a reputation, his health declined and his anxiety grew. But no more than *The Waste Land* (written by the sickly Eliot in Lausanne) was *The Modern Temper* merely a product of its author's physical exhaustion. Krutch's despair, like Eliot's, was fundamentally spiritual — the despair of a man who wants and needs to believe, but cannot.

When he prepared his notice for the 1926 *Who's Who in America*, Krutch gratuitously described himself as "Agnostic." He could have simply left blank the space beside "Religion," but he remained eager to display his sophistication and to assert his independence from the provincial background his biography revealed. His attitude was, in fact, agnostic, and he was unable to embrace — as one imagines he might have liked — the complete atheism of some of his free-thinking contemporaries. His scientific background, his effort to become an advanced thinker, and his exacting, skeptical intelligence drew him one way, and he repudiated religion. But the experiences of his

87

Knoxville youth had shaped his character even more fundamentally, and they drew him with equal strength in the opposite direction. His inner, emotional self craved such certitude and consolation as religion offered—the sense, however illusory, of a discernible meaning and purpose to life. He sensed that wisdom, or at least happiness, began with the capacity for feeling and faith. Nevertheless, the Sunday school dogma he had known in Knoxville had immunized him from any further participation in organized religion, and he could not conscientiously deny that the wisdom (or at least the knowledge) of modern civilization grew less from the mysteries of orthodox faith than from the rationalism of scientific doubt.

Although Krutch dearly wanted to be numbered among the advanced thinkers of his day, his temperamental conservatism made him feel that the material progress wrought by science was perhaps not worth the loss of the humanist tradition which brought such spiritual comfort. Just as he had described the ways in which science had demythologized—and thus enfeebled—such humanly precious notions as religion, love, and tragedy, Krutch sought in *The Modern Temper* to demythologize science and to show it as the distinctly mixed blessing he recognized it to be. His effort to strip from science the mantle of virtue it popularly wore was a reflection of the conservatism he would manifest even more explicitly in his attacks upon technology, thirty years later, in his social criticism.

His effort also was a characteristically romantic one, and beyond the insistent modernism of *The Modern Temper* it is not difficult to see the transcendental cravings of the romantic. "Intellectually," he remarked at one point, "we may find romantic people and romantic literature only ridiculous. . . ."[27] But the qualifying adverb is telling. Emotionally, romantic values and attitudes attracted him. Like the earlier romantics rebelling against the rationalism of the Enlightenment, he was made restless by a modern scientific rationalism that had estranged men like himself from effective belief in any spiritual universe which admitted room for value as well as fact. Unable to reconcile himself to the spiritual dispossession he described in *The Modern Temper*, he yearned to see man in the context of some divine or transcendental continuum and as a part of (rather than apart from) Nature.

To move beyond the despair he described, he would need to discover a means of reuniting man with a universe of value from which modern positivism had separated him, and to discover a way of revivifying the natural world that science seemed to have robbed of concreteness, vitality, and human significance. Even as he was composing his essays, Krutch was beginning such an effort of discovery in Cornwall. While it would be two decades before, in the first of his nature essays, he would announce his success, even in the late 1920s he must have seen the possibility of some passage beyond the spiritual paralysis of *The Modern Temper*. Significantly, no such hope was offered in the pages of that book, for if it was a study of the intellectual climate of the age and a confession of Krutch's own mood, it was also written as a work of art. To suggest some passage beyond modernism would have been to compromise the effect of unmitigated despair which Krutch the artist strove to achieve as fully as philosophical precision, historical accuracy, or autobiographical truth.

Intellectually appraised, the book is hardly unexceptionable. The analysis frequently proceeds from unexamined assumptions; terms like *humanism* and *Nature* are assigned narrowly stipulative definitions; complex ideas like *love* and *tragedy* are reified and treated as absolutes unaffected by developments in social and intellectual history; and the simplistic either/or is consistently preferred to the more subtle, but less dramatic, both/and. If not from his reviewing of recent literature, then at least from his happy marriage, Krutch surely knew that love was not universally dead. If only from his undergraduate courses, he knew that science was more than the humanist's bugaboo: that it was also, in part, a benign force which helped man to control his physical environment, and that for many it was a richly creative enterprise with charms and beauties not unlike those of art. If only from his holiday explorations in Cornwall, he knew that nature was not wholly without human meaning. And he knew as well—to cite but two final matters—that metaphysics was something other than the mere caricature he had portrayed it, and that his was hardly the first generation to experience such disillusionment as he described.

Because *The Modern Temper* was conceived more as a work of art than as a treatise in philosophy or social history, its appeal was rhetorical as well as intellectual. As in his earlier psychoanalytic biography of Poe, Krutch was trying out certain ideas for literary effect and was pursuing them as far as his wit and eloquence would allow; he again deliberately followed the road of excess, trusting that it would lead to the palace of reputation. The kind of reputation he sought was clear. With no little pride, he wrote his publisher that "the book is of course a distinctly high-brow one."

At the same time that Krutch was hoping to consolidate his reputation as a highbrow, he was happy to contemplate the possible achievement of commercial success by shocking the middlebrow public with his strident doubt. As he explained to his publisher, "I have a feeling that it can be made not only to get a good deal of critical attention but to go over to the general public if it is handled right: There is enough controversial material in it to get a lot of people of one kind or another excited and we must see to it that it comes to the attention of the Catholic priesthood and [other] people . . . who will denounce it with excellent results I think."[28] Some years earlier he had sought to shock that "general public" by debunking Poe's reputation. "As many who have risen to fame and fortune through the practice of shocking the public know," he had written in an early review, "there is a right time to say the wrong thing."[29] With great material prosperity and glib optimism being enjoyed by many people in the 1920s, the time seemed ripe for Krutch's expression of spiritual pessimism.

The nearly unanimously favorable reviews that greeted *The Modern Temper* in spring 1929 seemed to vindicate Krutch's hopes of enhancing his reputation. In a front-page review in the New York *Herald Tribune Books* Irwin Edman described it as "a terrifyingly honest book, a singularly penetrating statement of the impasse in which a mind both sensitive and honest finds itself. . . . Mr. Krutch is that rare thing in any age, and particularly in our own, a mind so fine in its intellectual texture and structure, humane in its sympathies and highly engaging in its expression. He and his book belong in the congenial tradition of genuinely philosophical literature."[30] Van Wyck Brooks described *The Modern Temper* as "one of the most comprehensive statements of the modern point of view that has appeared in recent years. . . . [It] will add greatly to Mr. Krutch's reputation as a thinker and as a writer." Lewis Mumford called the book "a lyric of despair"[32]; Reinhold Niebuhr found it "tremendously worth reading"[33]; and Bertrand Russell said it was "profoundly interesting and very penetrating in its analysis."[34]

Shortly it appeared on the *Herald Tribune*'s best-seller list, and it was clearly one of the most important books of the season. Preachers and lecturers cited it, students and teachers discussed it, and even the New Humanists, then making their desperate last stand, drew attention to it with their angry denunciation of Krutch's defeatism. Granville Hicks's estimate that *The Modern Temper* was "likely to become one of the crucial documents of his generation" seemed just.[35] In fact, it did assume that status. When Frederick Lewis Allen published his immensely popular history of the 1920s, *Only Yesterday* (1931), he turned primarily to Krutch's book as the authoritative source for understanding the disillusionment of the decade. Through Allen's redaction (still widely read today), through frequent discussions in scholarly studies of the twenties, and through continued reference to and assignment of the book in college courses, *The Modern Temper* has become a touchstone for the understanding of the decade, and Krutch himself has become a famous figure of the period. His being invited, shortly after the book appeared, to contribute to *Living Philosophies*, one of the published symposia so popular then, was a token of the celebrity he enjoyed. Naturally he took pleasure in being thus included, along with such other eminent writers and thinkers as Irving Babbitt, John Dewey, Theodore Dreiser, Albert Einstein, H.L. Mencken, Lewis Mumford, George Jean Nathan, Bertrand Russell, Beatrice Webb, and H.G. Wells.

However, the wealth Krutch also sought proved elusive. The time was, in fact, not ripe for his saturnine book. Several months after publication of *The Modern Temper*, the stock market crash brought a sudden end to the optimism Krutch had so powerfully debunked. With the economic debacle of the fall, Christmas book-givers on whose purchases he had relied were disinclined to present their friends with Krutch's ruminations. The book was too gloomy and philosophical for a generation which found, at the beginning of the Depression, little charm in Krutch's despair and craved instead more hopeful sentiments and more practical solutions to immediate problems.

Eager to do what he could to advance the book's sales, Krutch set out early in 1930 on an exhausting five-week midwinter promotional tour. Through much of the previous year he had been confined to bed with various illnesses, and for three months that spring he had been forced to abandon even his routine work on the *Nation*. That he should have roused himself from his sickbed for the tour bespeaks the urgency with which he desired the wealth that eluded him, along with the reputation he already enjoyed.

Addressing almost any willing audience — college students, temple sisterhoods, book and play discussion groups, and some of the informal *Nation* clubs which had formed in various places — he stopped in more than a dozen cities and towns between New York and Los Angeles. Although the enthusiastic audiences which greeted him all spoke admiringly of *The Modern Temper*, Krutch was unsatisfied by mere praise. "So many people tell me they have read [it]," he wrote from Chicago, "that I am forced to conclude either that there are an awful lot of liars in the world or that the five or six thousand copies sold so far must be worn to shreds by now."[36] For a professional man of letters like Krutch, sales were as important as admiration.

The mere *succès d'estime* of *The Modern Temper* was, for Krutch, not the only casualty of the 1929 Crash. He had lost his savings as well. With their two salaries and modest expenses, Marcelle and he had, since their marriage, been able to make regular investments in stocks; by 1929 their portfolio was worth, on paper at least, well over $50,000. As he lay in his sickbed during the early part of that year and contemplated the prospects (and subsequently the glowing reviews) of his new book, he hoped that he might shortly be able to resign his post at the *Nation* and support himself solely by the income from his investments and the sales of whatever essays or books he chose to write. The Crash put an abrupt end to those hopes. For Krutch, the philosophical disillusionment he had recently described became unexpectedly concrete. For the first time since beginning his career, he wondered whether he would in fact ever achieve not only the recognition but also the wealth which he had imagined awaited the successful writer.

5.

REASSESSING PRIORITIES

Krutch's disappointment over the commercial failure of *The Modern Temper* and the loss of his savings was somewhat relieved when he learned that he had been awarded a Guggenheim Fellowship and would be able to take leave of his work at the *Nation* for at least a year. As soon as the Broadway season ended in June 1930, he and Marcelle sailed for France. During the next fifteen months he hoped to regain his health and, free from the interruption of his many activities in New York, complete two books he had had in mind for several years. Both volumes would show that, even as he was so exquisitely confessing his disillusionment, Krutch recognized the possibility of passage beyond the despairing resignation of modernism.

The first, *Five Masters: A Study in the Mutations of the Novel*, was in fact nearly complete even before he departed. The chapter on Boccaccio had appeared in the *Atlantic Monthly* that spring, the Richardson chapter was scheduled for publication there that summer, and the Cervantes and Stendhal essays had also been written. All that remained by the time Krutch arrived in France was the chapter on Proust. After several weeks' research in Paris and a summer's writing in Hendaye (the Basque town where Marcelle had been born), it too was completed.

In tone as well as substance, *Five Masters* departed markedly from Krutch's two earlier books. Its critical approach was as modest as that of *Edgar Allan Poe* had been pretentious; its style as amiable as that of *The Modern Temper* had been urgent; and its argument as understated as that of both books had been exaggerated. The dazzling pronouncements and the studied effort to shock and establish himself as "distinctly high-brow" were wholly absent. Having found that past efforts had brought only a *succès d'estime*, Krutch now seemed less eager to associate himself with the literary and intellectual avant-garde than to present a series of elegantly written essays which, after the manner of the Literary Guild, would introduce the lives and works of five important novelists to that "great majority of reading Americans who do not come from 'literary homes.'"

His essays were informed by extensive research and serious thought, but he wore his scholarship and critical sophistication lightly. Deftly combining material drawn from their letters, journals, and biographies with extensive quotations from their writing, Krutch sought to offer the general reader a popular account of the lives and works of his masters. Around the same time he had begun rereading, for the first time since graduate school, Boswell and Johnson; and his latest effort corresponded to Dr. Johnson's in the *Lives of the Poets*. Indeed, what he later remarked of Johnson's *Lives* could be said of Krutch's *Five Masters* as well: it seems "to have been written more nearly con amore than any of his previous work."[1] In the imagined worlds of earlier fiction he had found respite from the contemporary world of modernist despair.

One can well understand the *TLS* reviewer's conclusion that "We have here an amiable amateur in criticism who has passed some leisure hours agreeably and not unprofitably in the company of some great authors."[2] Krutch clearly sought to lead his readers to do as he had done. But *Five Masters* is deceptively genial, and the essays are more than mere adventures among the masters and their masterpieces. Read as a sequel to *The Modern Temper*, it illuminates not only the works and authors criticized, but also the critic himself.

For Richardson, Krutch had the least sympathy. As in *Poe*, he took a certain pleasure in patronizing a widely popular writer. Richardson's was an "essentially vulgar" soul. He "thought what others thought in their most commonplace moments; he was not Bobus but Bobissimus."[3] The souls of his other masters, however, seemed to Krutch more refined and thus of greater interest. Boccaccio's was torn between "the promises and threats of a dogmatic church versus the insistent demands of rebellious flesh"; Cervantes', between the

94

claims of the humanist ideals of the imagination and an often contradictory world of fact; and Stendhal's, between "enthusiasm for the
beauties of nature and the ineffable ecstasies of love" on the one hand
and "a cool detachment and a cautious common sense" on the other.[4]
Krutch well understood the anguish of such divided souls. In his essays
— and especially in his discussion of Proust — he demonstrated how
such men could cope with their intellectual and spiritual quandaries
and, through art, find peace and comfort.

Krutch's description of Proust was strikingly reminiscent of his
own recent self-portrait in *The Modern Temper*. "Sceptical of their
faiths, cold to their enthusiasms, [and] incapable of taking part in their
labors," Proust found the world of his contemporaries unsatisfactory.
Unable to "share the aims and opinions of his fellows," he had either
to "give a new meaning to life or rest content with finding it forever
meaningless." He was, like the earnest modern thinker Krutch had
described, "faced with the task of creating a world out of the ruin into
which an accustomed world had been thrown by the decay of the
principles upon which it had rested"; as an artist, he had to find "the
means of rescuing something from the flux, of establishing in the eternity of art the experiences which he had undergone or observed."[5]

Believing in "the sufficiency of the senses — at least as furnishers
of the material which contemplation might transform," Proust found
life "still absorbingly, still amazingly, interesting." He was able to see
beyond the apparent anarchy of his world by virtue of his discovery of
"a kind of memory not identical with the ordinary sort: a vision of
the eternity in which even the most completely forgotten experience
had already taken its place." As an artist he learned "the secret of ex-
tracting the permanent and the significant from the transitory and
the trivial."[6] Writing *The Remembrance of Things Past*, Proust not
only found a personal satisfaction he failed to find as a participant in
the world of affairs, but also achieved "certain qualities (like charm,
and order, and peace) which seemed to have departed forever from
modern literature." The book was, Krutch said, "one of the most
beautiful . . . most accomplished . . . most perfect formal designs
ever achieved by a writer of prose fiction."[7]

Each of the essays of *Five Masters* remains a valuable
biographical-critical introduction to the author it considers. "Proust"

was, moreover, significant as one of the earliest studies of the entire *Remembrance*—only three years after the final volume had appeared, and before the complete work had been translated into English or Proust's importance had been widely recognized in America. Krutch's choice of Proust as the last of his masters was partly, no doubt, a sign of his continued desire, even while writing for the general reader, to be associated with the most current intellectual and artistic movements. His having been chosen by Random House to write the introduction to its 1932 edition of the complete *Remembrance* betokens his achievement.

But *Five Masters*, and especially the Proust essay, also provides a telling footnote to the argument of the book with which Krutch had just won such acclaim as an advanced thinker. His essays on the novel suggested, as *The Modern Temper* never had, that confusion and disillusionment were experiences hardly unique to the first quarter of the twentieth century, and that other souls had been torn and other spirits striken with anguish like his own. Moreover, the examples of Boccaccio, Cervantes, Stendhal, and Proust showed that art offered a fruitful way of dealing with, if not wholly escaping, such intellectual and spiritual dilemmas as characterized modernism. Dismissing aestheticism, Krutch had written in that previous book that art does "furnish a means by which life may be contemplated, but not a means by which it may be lived."[8] Concentrating on the second part of that statement, he had not pursued the implications of the first; to have done so would, of course, have been to compromise the hopelessness he had sought to dramatize.

Though the point was never insisted upon in the book (there was neither an introduction nor a conclusion), *Five Masters* demonstrated that the contemplation of life that art afforded made life more bearable—that one might respond to a great sense of confusion by creating a great work of art and thus achieve some issue from such despair as others before Krutch and his generation had felt. Those essays in practical criticism were in fact prolegomena to the extended essay in theoretical criticism to which Krutch turned in the fall of 1930, after he left Hendaye and moved to Cap d' Antibes, along the Mediterranean. In *Experience and Art: Some Aspects of the Esthetics of Literature* he brought together the premises of *The Modern Temper* and the counterevidence of *Five Masters*, arguing explicitly that art, broadly understood, offered a hope beyond the hopelessness he had recently described.

Like *Five Masters, Experience and Art* was a modest book directed less toward the specialist than at the general reader who, Krutch hoped, might welcome a gracefully written, nontechnical discussion of the nature of art. The book made no pretension "to the dignity or completeness of a treatise. It grew," he said, "simply and informally out of my experiences with various works of art and represents only an effort to understand these experiences more fully by relating them both to one another and to the more general experience of living."⁹

The description here of life in the realm of nature echoed that in *The Modern Temper*. "Most of the events which take place in [nature] are as emotionally unsatisfactory as they are intellectually incomprehensible," he wrote. "They do not seem either directed toward any rational end or calculated to provoke any unified emotion, and we are tempted to conclude that if any power directs them, then that power must be alien to both our feelings and our understanding." *Experience* he defined as man's perception of that world, and it inevitably shares nature's deficiencies by being insufficient both in quantity (limited as man is by time and place) and in quality (since man fails to discern any order or pattern in the phenomena around him). The function of *art*, Krutch concluded, "is to supply the defects, both quantitative and qualitative, of our experience with nature."¹⁰

Realistic fiction, adventure stories, and tales of exotic lands are among the types of literary art which offer readers an opportunity vicariously to extend their range or quantity of experience. But art's far more important function, he insisted, is to enrich the quality of life. "The artist selects and classifies what nature mingles in a hideous confusion and in so doing he is, in one of his many ways, adapting the universe to our minds by presenting it in an order which our emotions can follow." Art then "satisfies one of the most fundamental of human desires—the desire for oneness and harmony." Art in general and literature in particular "minister . . . to man's need for permanence, to his need to escape from the endless succession of mere phenomena."¹¹ But art, according to Krutch's understanding, is neither the childish wish fulfillment of a Cinderella story, nor "merely the art

97

of producing illusion," nor any "simple escape from the realm of our experience into a more pleasing realm of undisciplined fancy." Like other arts, such as philosophy or religion, literature can be judged "not only by the beauty of its pattern, but also by the extent to which it has been able to include within this pleasing pattern some considerable portion of the crude stuff of experience."[12]

Around such principles Krutch built his further discussion of comedy and tragedy; the ways in which art influences behavior; and the responsibility of the critic. Perhaps the most personally telling pages of *Experience and Art* were those in which Krutch called explicitly for an art and a philosophy which would mitigate, if not wholly resolve, the anguished dilemma of modernism. He continued to feel that the modern world was essentially uncongenial to the human spirit. "We cannot completely identify ourselves with the representatives of the present," he wrote. "The world of speed and power and exactitude in which they live is a world which still exists only upon the periphery of the consciousness." As earlier in his reviews, he lamented that modern literature reflected the modern confusion. "It is — like ourselves — doubtful, divided, eclectic and experimental. . . . It has given us no self-justifying image because its creators have achieved no self-justifying vision." And he continued to deny that such a vision could be achieved by following "those eccentric converts to fifth century paganism, thirteenth century Catholicism, and seventeenth century Anglicanism, who propose to live and write as though they were in the heyday of the culture they have chosen. . . . There is no golden age of faith, of simplicity, or of ignorance to which we can return."[13]

Significantly, where in 1929 he had concluded his similar diagnosis with little better than a plaintive sigh, he now ended with a bracing challenge. He called for — and now felt possible — the development of a philosophy and, based upon it, an art which would order the fragmented experience of his times as the masters of previous ages had given form to the experiences of theirs:

> What we long for is the ability to function in this complicated world
> as easily and freely as others seem to have functioned in a simpler one;
> to find life, not merely exciting, but satisfactory and meaningful as

well. We want to see it whole but we also want to see it all. . . . We want a philosophy which is more than merely cold and reasonable, a philosophy whose ultimate expression is one of those works of art which seem not only to sum up but also to justify a civilization.[14]

Just whence such a philosophy might come, he neither said nor knew. Nevertheless, he had at least gone beyond the passive resignation of *The Modern Temper* to affirm the humanism he had earlier dismissed as bankrupt; to suggest that skepticism and its consequent confusion should not be ends in themselves, but could instead inspire the creative imagination; and to insist that art is a worthier mark of man's humanity than the heroic despair of modernism. Writing to Ellery Sedgwick, Krutch said: "The subject [of *Experience and Art*] is one which appears at first sight to be somewhat narrower than that of The Modern Temper, but actually the two books are closely related and supplement one another. In a sense this one is a statement of what I *do* believe. . . . Though the subject is ostensibly the aesthetics of literature I think I make it clear from the beginning that what I am really talking about is Civilization."[15]

However, Krutch's highly abstract, philosophical concern for civilization was rather remote from the intensely practical concerns of the early 1930s. While most Americans were preoccupied with questions of politics and economics, and while Marxist criticism was becoming the literary fashion, his book almost wholly lacked immediate social significance and barely suggested the role of literature as an instrument of social change. For the first time he had difficulty finding a publisher, and when *Experience and Art* was finally published in the fall of 1932, at the nadir of the Depression, it enjoyed sales even more meager than had *Five Masters*, published two years earlier.

"I am rather distressed over the fact that there seems to be a wide spread lack of interest in *Experience and Art*," Krutch wrote Mark Van Doren early in 1933. "I don't feel I've done all I can for the world, but it really ought to show more eagerness."[16] Having set aside his desire to appear "distinctly high-brow," Krutch had hoped with his books on art to achieve among general readers the popular success which had eluded him with *Poe* and *The Modern Temper*. But again he had failed, and his dismay was compounded by his recognition that the newly fashionable intellectual and artistic attitudes of the 1930s were none he could honestly affect as his own. The world's lack of eagerness for his writing in the early thirties was matched by, and in large part caused, Krutch's own growing indifference to the kind of literary career toward which he had been aspiring during the previous decade. If he could look forward to neither the admiration of the arbiters of highbrow taste nor extensive sales among general readers, he could nevertheless enjoy the luxury of speaking his mind on the art and thought of the day. At least for the moment, he resigned himself to more modest ambitions for his career and looked elsewhere for the satisfaction he failed to find as a writer.

Writing *Experience and Art* on the fashionable Côte d'Azur, Krutch had been physically and intellectually distant from the preoccupations of America at the beginning of the Depression. However, he had made an unexpected return visit to America in the midst of his writing, because the year in France, during which he hoped to recuperate from nearly a decade of ill health, had instead seen a serious worsening of his condition. His fevers and migraines became even more frequent, and during the late fall his weight suddenly dropped from his normal 170 to less than 130 pounds. In December 1930, he decided to consult a specialist in Baltimore; after six weeks of insulin therapy and nearly total rest, his weight returned to a not unhealthy 150 pounds. In the Johns Hopkins Hospital he seemed to have had the worst of his illness resolved, though for the rest of his life he would continue to be preoccupied with his health. Still, no more in Baltimore than in France had he been in touch with the realities of contemporary America. Krutch had of course shared in the losses of the Crash, and had been disappointed that *The Modern Temper* had not achieved the stunning commercial success for which he had hoped. But as he was writing *Experience and Art*, assured of his position on the *Nation* when he returned to the States that fall, he still believed that America would richly support writers of the kind he sought to be.

In a 1931 essay, written in France, Krutch compared America favorably to France, commenting particularly on the greater openness of American life, its lack of cultural parochialism, the willingness of Americans to engage in "perpetual self-criticism," and the promising circumstances for art in a country like America, "where wealth and power and ease are to be found in most abundance."[17] The United States to which he and Marcelle returned in September, 1931, however, was much transformed from the America they had left. The bracingly critical attitude of the Young Intellectuals of the 1920s was being replaced by the dogmatic rhetoric of the Left; prosperity had yielded to widespread poverty and unemployment; and writers who only a few years before had insisted on the autonomy of the artist were now demanding the art become a servant of the promised social revolution.

The new realities were at once apparent to Krutch when he resumed his weekly drama column for the *Nation*. Not only were the Broadway openings fewer in number than when he had left, but the quality was also inferior. "Whenever audiences shrink," he remarked, "it becomes more and more necessary to strike somewhere near the common denominator of a very large group, and the common denominator of a very large group is found in some form or another of skilful mediocrity."[18] It was not so much the banality of some productions which upset him as the pretensions of many others. Returning from France, he discovered that, virtually overnight, the stage had become political. Many dramatists were selling their artistic birthrights for a mess of Marxism. The art of the political stage was not the kind for which Krutch had recently called in *Experience and Art* — one which would not only "sum up but also . . . justify a civilization." During a decade when politics impinged upon nearly every area of American intellectual life, Krutch as a critic and essayist for the *Nation* courageously took his minority stand and announced what he truly believed.

It was with little joy that Krutch entered the thickets of political controversy in the 1930s, and with still less that he dissented from the intellectual and artistic movements of the day. Unlike his previous political pronouncements (his writing on Prohibition and his dispatches from Dayton), his dissent sprang now from deeply felt conviction, rather than from any desire to shock and thereby further his reputation. Indeed, a measure of his sincerity was his willingness to jeopardize his hard-earned reputation as an advanced and sophisticated thinker by criticizing the newly fashionable political theater and the radical enthusiasms behind it.

From his earliest writing it was clear that Krutch's ideas about art differed greatly from those which lay behind the new political drama. In his dissertation he had shown his distaste for the enlistment of literature in the service of moral reform, noting, "Very few imaginative writers in whose minds the desire to give moral instruction was always uppermost have ever produced great literature."[19] During the 1920s he had frequently returned to that theme. "Metaphysicians do not usually write good drama," he had remarked in 1926; "A passion is, dramatically at least, more interesting than an idea and a fact more impressive than a moral," he said the following year. In 1928, reporting on his travels to Russia, he dismissed Eisenstein's theories about the purely instrumental function of art as "futuristic dilettantism."[20]

By the time he returned from France to resume his reviewing, his principles had not changed. The political drama which he now increasingly encountered seemed to him less the work of artists than the product of sociologists more concerned with causes than with human beings. The great conflicts which he felt gave drama universal significance—those of man with himself or with fate—were largely absent from the social protest plays which saw life simplistically in political and economic terms. He felt most such plays were no more successful dramatically than mediocre melodrama.

Indeed, even as propaganda Krutch found the plays disappointing. "Great propaganda must manage in some way to hold even those who do not want to hear," he said. "Doubtless the drama of social forces must deal with generalities; but if it is to do this effectively, then it must do it so clearly that the human beings involved will seem to us more than merely colorless individuals."[21] The failure of many political plays of the 1930s was due to the radical playwright's assumption of an artistically untenable role. Inheriting a closed and dogmatic ideological system, such a writer was, Krutch wrote in 1935, "at the periphery, not the center, of 'the movement'—a mere appendage to an intellectual development whose main front is the economic principle." Worse yet,

> this ready-made system is so distressingly complete that, granted the desire for orthodoxy which seems to be usually his, he is limited to the task of devising fables which will illustrate with almost mechanical accuracy the principles laid down in sacred writings. It is not, I think, unfair to say that most of the Marxist plays so far written in America tend to exhibit the defects inherent in this narrow conception of the playwright's business. On the intellectual side they are less efforts to discover what aperçus the artist can add to the dialectician's formal scheme than attempts to devise puppet shows in the course of which stock figures, generalized almost to the point of allegory, are made to move precisely as the laws of the dialectician require that they should. On the emotional side, they tend to confine themselves to obvious appeals to partisan spirit and to indulge in red-flag waving of a sort which George M. Cohan might have approved of if Mr. Cohan had been a Communist.[22]

Predictably, Krutch's expressions of these reservations were ill received by the playwrights and Left theater groups, who had hoped for rather warmer support from the *Nation*. The conservatism of his critical principles and his apparent blindness to the artistic needs of the thirties were not calculated to endear him to the vocal new masses of radical intellectuals. But Krutch was unapologetic. "If to be capable of thinking a play bad even though it does attempt to express radical social ideas is to be a bourgeois decadent," he told the League for Industrial Democracy, "then that is what I am."[23]

For Krutch, the issue was ill defined by his opponents as one of "art for art's sake" versus "art for humanity's sake." "The question," he argued in a 1935 *Nation* editorial, "is not whether art should exist for humanity, but what it is that art can do for the humanity to which it so obviously belongs."[24] To defend "Art for art's sake," he said in another editorial the following year, was to defend the position, no less valid then than a decade earlier, "that the aesthetic emotion can be a self-justifying pleasure, good in itself, not because it leads to something else. . . . One of the justifications of a good society may . . . be that it produces good art," he continued. "Uselessness and valuelessness are not the same things. Of all the goods men may pursue and of all the blessings they may hope to gain, the joy of art is the one which least often fails them, which is there when the others have eluded their grasp."[25]

Many readers must have been surprised—indeed, disappointed—to find the *Nation*'s editorial column extolling "the joy of art" at a time when so many of the goods necessary for mere subsistence were beyond the reach of millions. Krutch never doubted that the Depression would pass; he feared, however, that their preoccupation with the means of politics and economics might lead men to lose sight of more basic ends. Twenty years earlier, as an undergraduate editorialist, he had insisted that "The cultivation of the appreciation of beauty is distinctly utilitarian because it produces happiness, the only ultimate end of any useful thing." He was no more now than then a mere aesthete. Rather, he was registering his dissatisfaction with the political vision of the 1930s, which he felt was, in its way, as narrow as the East Tennessee utilitarianism he had known as a youth.

While debating with Edmund Wilson the question "Is Politics Ruining Art?," Krutch demurred from the commonplace that, because of the crisis of the Depression,

> it is the duty of all men, whatever their training or capacities, to drop whatever task they may be best fitted to perform in order to turn themselves instanter into amateur politicians. No reasonable man would deny the gravity of the present situation and no decent one would be inclined merely to wash his hands. But for all that it is still not entirely clear that the philosopher should cease from philosophizing or the poet from counting his syllables. "Business as usual" is a slogan not wholly base if by "business" is meant all those human activities which make life worth living in even an imperfect world.[26]

Wilson's generally respectful but impassioned response defined the distance which separated Krutch from those of his contemporaries who had eagerly embraced the politics of the Left: "What Mr. Krutch is really defending is not merely his right to ply his literary trade . . . ; it is rather his right to persist in a state of mind which is becoming common among American critics and which is breeding at least as much intemperance as the opposite state of mind it combats. This state of mind—Mr. Krutch's state of mind—may be called politicophobia." Wilson accused Krutch of "exaggerating the political activities in which other writers have lately been engaging"; of "getting to sound like adolescent boys in provincial American towns who have just gotten hold of Arthur Symons"; of denying the validity of "the Marxist theory of classes"; and of demonstrating a general unwillingness "to look to the political theory of the Marxists for the intellectual seriousness and vitality which have gone out of the politics of the dominating class even in its liberal phases."[27] The debate with Wilson was, of course, concerned with a larger issue than the nominal question of politics and art. If Krutch suffered from "politicophobia," it was because he believed that the demands of politics (at least of the Marxist variety then prevalent) were incompatible with his greater responsibilities as an intellectul. The acrimonious debates of the 1930s were leading him to define, more clearly than before, just what those responsibilities were, and what his politics were to be, if politics he must have.

Krutch's indifference to politics at the outset of the 1930s had persisted through six years' service on the *Nation*'s editorial board. He was, he said, "never very politically minded," and he accepted "almost without even superficial examination the political opinions I was presumed to have."[28] Notwithstanding the conservatism of his Knoxville background, Krutch found the liberalism of Villard's *Nation* in the 1920s congenial; the liberal and the conservative both prefer evolutionary to revolutionary change, and both have a respect for individual liberty often absent in the radical. But toward party politics, as toward religion, Krutch had remained agnostic. The 1930–31 *Who's Who* which thus described his religious preference omitted any indication of political affiliation.

During the 1920s Krutch had been content to concentrate on his writing, leaving politics to the politicians and economics to the economists. Like most of his literary contemporaries, he felt it was occupation enough to be a craftsman manipulating words and ideas as his inspiration prompted. The question of "responsibility" was scarcely raised, for it was widely agreed that the writer's responsibility was simply to write well.

In the 1930s, however, few things were so simple. "Art for art's sake" was now widely condemned—often by the same writers who had only recently argued loudly for that principle. Art, it was insisted, must contribute to the reconstruction of a decadent capitalist society discredited by the economic chaos of the Depression. For many writers who gladly accepted the call, the new decade of socialist or Communist faith offered a sense of purpose they had lacked during a previous decade of studied doubt.

In many respects Krutch would seem to have been a ripe candidate for the conversion experience so many of his contemporaries enjoyed. Though Marcelle's job and his own post at the *Nation* meant that the Krutches were not in financial straits, they too had suffered in the Crash. Moreover, the despair of *The Modern Temper* was precisely that man lacked a faith in which he could passionately believe and a sense of purpose which would give life meaning. But even while writing that book he had insisted that the hopes of the Soviet experiment "are no hopes in which we can have any part." As he wrote Mark Van Doren in 1928, he was "not heroic enough to care for a revolutionary society." Any momentary impulse to jump aboard the Marxist bandwagon was overcome by Krutch's fundamentally conservative appreciation of stability and tradition, the bourgeois legacy of his Knoxville background, and his respect, as a liberal, for individual liberty.

Just as he was unwilling to exchange old literary and dramatic values for new ones, he was unwilling to exchange the traditional role of the writer and thinker for the new role proposed in the thirties. During the first decade of his career he had enjoyed "the privilege, and it did seem to us a very fine thing—this right to disregard everything except the immediate fact or the isolated aperçu which we seemed to have got hold of, and to set it down for what it was worth."[29] He observed that intellectuals had now become tacticians; ideas and facts were evaluated according to their "practical effect" in achieving some political end. "The present generation," Krutch wrote in 1933, "no longer believes whole-heartedly in dispassionate study.

. . . Many of its thinkers are saying that the day of 'the open mind' is past."[30] He was unwilling to accept the inevitability of its passing, and he came to feel a new sense of responsibility, as a writer, to see that it did not.

Krutch was convinced that the ivory tower of disinterested intellectual pursuit had, in fact, a useful function: "Towers are not . . . built to be shut up in; they are built to be looked out from, and they afford a perspective from which it is sometimes possible to get a truer view of things than any to be obtained in the midst of battle. Your genuine philosopher is not averse to towers, but he uses them for their legitimate purpose, and when the smoke has cleared away, civilization is generally glad to know that someone was perched upon that point of vantage."[31] During the thirties Krutch sat in his tower overlooking the political and ideological skirmishes of the day and sent down several dispatches reporting his reactions to the scene below. In his own way, he was exercising what he saw to be his social responsibility as a writer. A rather lonely liberal in a radical age, he courageously sought to defend some of those same humanist values whose continued relevance he had doubted as a strenuous modernist only a few years before.

Like his essays on the modern temper, Krutch's writings on the revolutionary temper of the 1930s were both a study and a confession. To his study he brought many of the same talents and attitudes which had distinguished his earlier book: an ability to summarize the drift of contemporary thought, a tendency to examine the implications of those ideas, and an inclination to measure the advance represented by the new against the loss of the old. As in *The Modern Temper*, Krutch was restive when confronted by the apparently inevitable transition from one spiritual and intellectual dispensation to another. In the 1930s he felt he was witnessing a transition hardly less fundamental than the one he had described earlier.

Marxism was, in some respects, merely another symptom — a translation into concrete political terms — of the scientism he had described in the 20s; it too seemed to undermine, when it did not explicitly attack, the traditional values he cherished. His essays in the thirties were, in part, a poignant confession of his bewilderment, but they were more than that. In the twenties he had felt helpless to resist the scientific revolution; he could at best lament it. The Communist revolution, however, seemed — to him at least — hardly inevitable. He wrote now not merely to lament, but also to oppose.

His most comprehensive discussion of communism appeared in a series of six essays published in *Harper's* and the *Nation* between 1932 and 1934, collected in *Was Europe a Success?* The question posed in that title was rhetorical, and Krutch's answer was clearly, if cautiously, affirmative. While the Depression alone offered abundant evidence of the need for various kinds of reform in Western society, Krutch insisted that, however worthy the ends of the reformers, the means need not be so radical as the Communists implied. The rhetoric of the Left precluded the free discussion of issues which was then especially needful; the revolution Marx had predicted three-quarters of a century before was no more inevitable now than then; life in a new, revolutionary society might be far less attractive than in the old decadent one; and "bourgeois" European civilization embodied many values which should not be forfeited casually.

Krutch was not, he acknowledged, "economically minded," and he wrote not as a specialist but as a moralist, a "mere detached observer of human nature" who might be able to provide a useful perspective on important, but often overlooked, implications of contemporary enthusiasms. His attitude, he declared, was "sceptically humanistic."[32]

In the early 1930s, he felt much as a cultivated Greek or Roman must have felt in the early days of Christianity when he "discovered with amazement that his most intimate friends were turning, one by one, to the strange new delusion. . . . I, too," he said, "have now witnessed the process of conversion. I, too, have now found myself faced with friends whose mental processes have come, over night, to be quite incomprehensible and to whose vocabularies have suddenly been added words obviously rich with meanings which elude all my efforts to comprehend them."[33]

"The world certainly needs to be saved," he acknowledged, "but it is less evident that it needs to be Saved." Krutch was willing to be convinced, but not converted. Even in this new age of faith he stubbornly continued to regard "the Communist State with the same detachment we employ when we consider the virtues or defects exhibited by monarchy, fascism, democracy. . . . We must insist upon the right to value some things which have no bearing upon either production or distribution," he said, "and we turn aside from the economist because he proclaims—in too familiar an accent—'thou shalt have no other God but me.'"[34]

For Krutch, the term "Europe" usefully summarized "the whole complex of institutions, traditions, and standards of value" too readily dismissed by the Marxist. "Humanity as Europe knows it cannot be imagined apart from the social order which Europe has created, the sensibilities which European art has developed, and the realm of thought which European philosophy has set in order." A defense of Europe, then, was not "a defense of the *status quo* in our political or economic affairs" or a suggestion "that ours is the justest society which we can hope to attain." Rather, it was a brief for those non-economic attributes without which a revolutionary society, however just, would hardly be worth having.[35]

Krutch acknowledged the price at which the achievements of Europe had been bought: slavery, imperialism, military pride, nationalism, bigotry, and an arrogant sense of class superiority, to name a few. Nevertheless, he remained convinced that the European man "realized more of his potentialities than did the man developed in any other portion of the globe"; that "European thought and European art are superior to all others"; that "the European man has been the most successful in exploring that realm of consciousness which appears to be exclusively human"; that of all societies the European has been the most humane; and that "no other culture we know anything about seems . . . to exhibit a comparable richness or variety or to favor the existence of so flexible a creature."[36]

While the radical Marxist critique seemed to attack the very foundations of Western society, Krutch argued that some values were so central to European civilization that "they must be left to the European man in order that he may still be recognizably himself." Krutch cited, among those values: "a sense of the reality, the worth, and the sacredness of the individual"; belief in the "importance of something which has been variously defined but always called 'freedom' for this same individual"; "the tendency to profess a desire to see the privileges of freedom and individuality extended to a larger and larger portion of the community"; "the tendency to regard differentiation and variety as desirable in themselves"; and the disposition "to assume that all excellences are arranged in a hierarchy, the uppermost levels of which are not only inaccessible to most but barely if at all even visible to the best and most excellent of men."[37]

For a liberal thinker like Krutch, engaged in political controversy, a central principle of European civilization was "the privilege of making free intellectual judgments, of discriminating between the true and the false, the just and the unjust, or the right and the wrong, upon some basis other than a purely partisan one." He acknowledged that "European man neither consistently pursued the ends which these characteristics imply nor achieved them by any means completely when they were pursued."[38] Many of them appeared only during the Renaissance, and all were obscured at times by contrary tendencies. Nonetheless, they were, he felt, the ideals toward which European civilization aspired—and they were ideals which Soviet leaders and their American enthusiasts seemed to honor in neither theory nor practice.

Much of his discussion was devoted to examining auguries of the revolutionary future which could be seen in present realities. The tracts of the American Marxists, he said, "lack all those secondary virtues which are commonly implied when we speak of anything or anyone as 'civilized.' The thinking and the writing are dogmatic, harsh, and intolerant. They are full of an intense and burning hatred for that urbanity, detachment, and sense of fair play which make thinking amiable." Although Soviet art likewise offered little cause for enthusiasm, on it he was willing to suspend final judgment: "Its uncritical enthusiasms, its quasi-religious faith, its utilitarian emphasis, its stress on the common denominator, and its impatience with refinements perceptible only to cultivated sensibilities are merely the defects characteristic of thought and expression in any crude society."[39]

He found it less easy to excuse the political repression of that society. Even as a visitor in Moscow in 1928 he had observed and experienced "too damn much regulation." Now he proposed that "the prominent part played by the secret police, the ferocious suppression of all non-conformist thought, and the habit of resorting to decrees of exile or execution on the slightest provocation look suspiciously like survivals from the only form of government which the Russians have ever known."[40] Krutch acknowledged that "the average Russian is better off than he was under the Tzar and that he regards the future with ardent hope. But," he added pointedly, "we never had a Tzar." The Russian experiment offered precious little cause to believe that life in a post-revolutionary America would be better than even during the darkest days of what one still hoped would be a temporary Depression. "It is odd," Krutch noted, "that the only government which has the good of its citizen at heart should also be the only one (except for fascist Italy and Nazi Germany) which finds it necessary to prevent him from escaping from its jurisdiction. . . . Surely it is an odd Utopia which finds it necessary to lock its citizens in every night."[41]

There as elsewhere in his essays about Marxism, American and Russian, Krutch was scoring points. In the manner of the day, he wrote as a polemicist (though far more gracefully than most), and it is initially as polemics that his essays should be read. His disregard of the economic realities of contemporary Europe and his partisan description of conditions in the Soviet Union in many ways resemble the Marxist's exaggeration of economics and his selective portrait of bourgeois European capitalism. Krutch's aplomb in briefly acknowledging Europe's failings seems, at times, quite as facile as that of the Communist apologist discussing circumstances in Stalinist Russia. Indeed, the very evocation of "Europe" was patently polemical, and Krutch well understood the intellectual inadequacy (as well as the rhetorical power) of such usage. In a 1928 review he had himself complained that "Any argument which is based upon the supposed existence of entities as . . . the Western mind must . . . end in something no better than the calling of names."[42]

But as a polemical summary of the main outlines of the liberal, anti-Communist position in the 1930s, *Was Europe a Success?* was a work of considerable power. Albert Einstein said the essays "must make a great impression on thoughtful people," and Aldous Huxley found them "admirable. . . . For condensed statement and judicious commentary they could not be bettered."[43] Malcolm Cowley's acerbic comments are perhaps a still greater tribute to Krutch's success; the book was, Cowley said, "the most effective, the best written, and therefore the most dangerous defense of the old order that has appeared during the five years since writers came down from their ivory towers and began mixing in politics."[44]

The book has significance beyond that of a document of the political disputes of the 1930s. Seen in the context of Krutch's career, it marks a striking passage beyond the studied doubt of *The Modern Temper*. Though he described his attitude as "sceptically humanistic," the humanism shone through far more clearly than the skepticism. His earlier nostalgia for the old spiritual and intellectual order had, in the crucible of the decade's debates, matured into a faith. He could now go beyond lamenting the passing of that order in order to defend its continued relevance.

Was Europe a Success? also marks—even more explicitly than his two most recent books on art—a significant change in Krutch's image of himself as a writer. His essays on Communism constitute Krutch's unmistakable declaration of independence from what passed as advanced thought. If the same intellectual and cultural leaders who had lavished such praise on his writing in the twenties now dismissed him and his defense of liberal, "European" values as bourgeois and middlebrow, Krutch recognized that those values were more fundamentally his than the "distinctly high-brow" modernism he had uneasily embraced. In much of his subsequent writing he became a vigorous spokesman for those values, proclaimed himself more a humanist than a modernist, and in many ways unabashedly revealed himself to be less a free-thinking urban sophisticate than a conservative child of Knoxville.

The isolated evidence of his handful of essays during the 1930s might suggest that Krutch was a militant anti-Communist. In fact, those essays represent nearly the sum of his engagement in affairs of the day. "This, so it seems, is the extrovert's decade," he wrote in 1933. "Our typical heroes turn outward upon the world, not inward upon themselves, and their concern is with society, which must be made different from what it is before any personal happiness is possible."[45] Krutch himself, however, was turning inward—away from politics, and from his earlier frenzied quest for public recognition. "I realize that devices for detachment and escape play a large part in the scheme of my life," he wrote in his journal in the mid-1930s. "More insistently socially minded persons regard this as more than a merely contemptible weakness—to them it is I suppose a confession of failure. But I must admit that I know of no way of doing without them."

The stage for that inward life, the place to which he escaped, was the Redding, Connecticut, home that he and Marcelle had purchased in 1932. They had sold their house in Cornwall before leaving for France in 1930. Banking the proceeds from the sale until late 1932, they found that, thanks to the erosion of real estate prices during the Depression, they could afford a modest but comfortable old farmhouse, far more liveable than their home in Cornwall and set on a generous tract of land, surrounded by trees and a spacious lawn. At first they thought of making it only another weekend and summer home, though one which they might be able to visit more frequently since it was more accessible to New York City. Increasingly, however, Redding became their principal home, and their New York apartment became a mere *pied-à-terre* for those evenings when Krutch's reviewing kept him in the city.

Krutch was happy for the seclusion of Redding, for the absence there of even such literary society as Cornwall had afforded. Above all, he valued the presence in Redding of the society of natural things: the plants and gardens around the house; the birds who regularly visited their feeders; the wildlife which enjoyed the hospitality of their property; and the many domestic animals they kept, including at various times a crow, geese, fish, salamanders, a goat, and as many as fourteen cats. During the week Marcelle frequently remained in Redding to look after the menagerie while Krutch attended to his responsibilities in New York, impatient to return to friends far more precious than any of his professional colleagues.

The journal Krutch began keeping in the 1930s reflects his new priorities. References to the theater, to affairs at the *Nation*, to current events, and to his reading and writing are notable for their infrequency. "Read about three hours this morning as usual, and after lunch wrote review" is a typical entry. Domestic details are mentioned occasionally—the inconvenience of commuting, some work being done on the house, or a visit from friends like the Van Dorens. His valetudinarianism was obvious, with some distressing new complaint invariably appearing hard on the heels of the previous ailment's cure. Above all, as the journal makes clear, Krutch's consuming interest at the time was nature. References to his professional activities are far outnumbered by items about his pets, his garden, and the squirrels, newts, rabbits, butterflies, katydids, and wrens who made their homes around his. He became an attentive and meticulous observer of nature. In Redding he began to keep charts recording the fluctuations in temperature and the dates when spring flowers first bloomed, when leaves first appeared on trees, and when birds and other animals returned from their winter retreats. Early on he was listening for the spring peeper — the subject years later of his first nature essay. On April 7, 1933, he wrote in his journal: "Last night I heard the peeper. It is not cold." The entry is starkly matter-of-fact; Krutch had not yet found a suitable literary form in which to express his growing devotion to nature. It was still, in the 1930s, a largely private interest, his device for escape and detachment from a human world, and especially a literary world, which had for him largely gone sour. Though evident in his journal and known to his friends, his preoccupation with nature was rarely reflected in his public writing.

In the anonymity of the *Nation*'s editorial column Krutch did, however, in 1934 record his belief that there was world beyond politics, economics and literature: "No one totally ignorant of natural history has any right to call himself a modern. The difference between a person to whom a cockroach is merely a bug and one to whom it is *Blatta orientalis*, and thus a representative of one of the very oldest families of this earth, is the difference between one to whom man is a unique creature and one to whom he is merely the latest stage in nature's vast experiment with life."[46] To be "a modern" was no longer to feel apart from, but to be part of, nature.

Krutch was also reconsidering his earlier dismissal of science. Science, he acknowledged in a 1936 review, may well rob man of that feeling of spontaneous intimacy with nature that primitive man enjoyed. "But if we are less at home with nature, in this sense less intimate with other creatures, we have, and for the same reasons, a greater if dimmer sense of fellowship with them — more of a feeling that we are co-equals sprung from the same source and engaged, each in our own way, in the common adventure of living."[47]

In Redding Krutch was enjoying a fellowship with nature far greater than any possible fellowship in the politically charged New York literary world or at the *Nation*. Some years later, in his biography of Thoreau, he remarked: "The reader who does not respond to Thoreau's account of his social life in nature will not understand the solidest of the reasons why he found his life richly worth the living." During the thirties Krutch began to experience that social life himself. Even as he despaired of achieving the kind of literary career to which he had once aspired, he too "found his life richly worth the living."[48]

⁂ Upon returning from France in August 1930, Krutch was not long in recognizing that he was not likely to be one of the fashionable writers of the thirties as he had been during the twenties. Having seen *Five Masters* encounter only a tepid public response and *Experience and Art* languish some months for want of a publisher, and having no further projects in mind, he devoted himself increasingly to literary journalism and became more actively involved with the affairs of the *Nation*. In January 1933, he joined the four-member board of editors in which Oswald Garrison Villard vested the direction of the journal. That fall he became literary editor as well, responsible for the "Books and Arts" section. Those jobs, in addition to his drama reviewing, consumed nearly all of his now flagging literary energy, and he rarely contributed to other journals.

Although Krutch's fellow editors, whose interests were largely political, generally allowed him free rein with the back of the magazine, he inevitably found himself drawn into stormy controversy when the editors met each week to determine the content of the front. "For a short time," he recalled, "I assumed that all the staff members of *The Nation* were still loyal to the libertarian principles it had defended ever since my first connection with it." Presently he became "less and less comfortable there." On the Moscow purge trials, Roosevelt's court-packing scheme, and countless other issues, Krutch found that his was a distinctly minority voice among the editors. The earlier spirit of easy collegiality at the *Nation* had been replaced by an atmosphere of deadly earnestness and acrimonious dispute. "Never before," he said, "had I found myself so nearly surrounded by colleagues whom I knew to be enemies or, at least, certainly not to be trusted."[49]

Krutch was beleaguered from without as well; other radical intellectuals, also feeling that he displayed insufficient enthusiasm for the revolution, attacked his editorship of the *Nation*'s "Books and Arts" pages. In a long 1937 essay in the literary supplement of the *New Masses*, Granville Hicks charged that, with Krutch's assumption of the literary editorship, "the book-review section seceded from the rest of the magazine. . . . On the whole," Hicks said, "the *Nation* has remained true to its traditions. . . . The book-review section, on the other hand, has taken the wrong side on most issues, and it has not been fair." He objected that Krutch failed to invite "the party's spokesmen" to review books about Communism, and that "the Communist Party is never allowed to speak for itself. . . . Mr. Krutch's own war against Communism has been conducted in his dramatic criticism, in essays on literature, and even in political articles."[50] He suggested that *Nation* readers should resign their subscriptions if Krutch did not resign his editorship.

In fact, a few months before the appearance of Hicks's broadside, Krutch had resigned, in order to return to Columbia as a professor of English. His narrowly scholarly life had, of course, ended with the completion of his dissertation seventeen years before. But Nicholas Murray Butler, Columbia's president, had told the English department that he would like to see appointed a new faculty member who might represent the man of letters, rather than the specialist scholar then holding most appointments. As a member of the departmental committee charged with nominating a person for the new position, Mark Van Doren proposed Krutch. In spring 1937, Krutch accepted the offer.

Since leaving Brooklyn Polytechnic in 1924 to become the *Nation*'s drama critic and a professional man of letters, Krutch had continued teaching part-time—first at Vassar and the Columbia Journalism School, and then, since 1932, at Columbia's summer school, where he participated in English 200, "a series of lectures by distinguished authors and scholars on the outstanding movements of literature of the present day." Though his later efforts had been less onerous and more successful than those in Brooklyn, he had hardly discovered any new enthusiasm for teaching.

Several considerations figured in his decision to return to Columbia full-time. The professorship offered a salary higher than the *Nation*'s, the security of tenure, and the prospect of academic vacations in which to continue his nature study in Redding. Moreover, by the mid-1930s Krutch's literary career, begun so promisingly in the 1920s, seemed to have reached something of a dead end. He saw in it no immediate prospects of either happiness or success. Above all, he felt increasingly uncomfortable at the *Nation* and was happy to be able to escape the tensions and administrative responsibilities of his position there.

In August, 1937, Krutch resigned his literary editorship and his membership on the *Nation*'s board of editors, retaining only his post as drama critic—less, one imagines, because of his continued love of the theater than because he felt that, given the definition of his Columbia job, such activity was expected of him. In September he moved into his new office at Columbia—appropriately, next to Mark Van Doren's.

6.

Though Krutch was pleased by the honor of being appointed to a Columbia professorship, he took up his new responsibilities with several kinds of misgiving. He recognized that his acceptance of the position constituted tacit admission of at least temporary defeat in his attempt to earn his living wholly by his pen. He was uncertain about his ability to resume, after an interruption of nearly two decades, such scholarly writing as he felt he should once again pursue. Above all, he looked forward with little enthusiasm to returning full-time to the classroom. Though he knew teaching upper-class literature courses would be different from teaching freshman composition to engineers, and though he recognized that he now enjoyed a certain maturity (indeed, celebrity, as a writer and critic), he doubted he would feel any more comfortable or function much more effectively at Columbia than he had at Brooklyn Polytechnic.

By virtue both of his graduate training and his dozen years as a theater critic, Krutch was most obviously qualified to teach courses in the drama. From the beginning he offered two courses—one in modern drama, the other in English theater from Dryden to Sheridan —which he would give regularly during his sixteen years at Columbia. Although few conventional scholars could have been expected to lecture with more confidence on "dramatic literature from Ibsen to the present day, with special stress on American drama," Krutch approached his first classes wracked with self-doubt. His sense of awkwardness was evident at once. While lecturing he looked not at his

118

students, but sideways into the middle distance. When seated he tee-tered on the back legs of his cane chair, occasionally losing his balance and regaining it with a sudden great flailing of arms. When he took to his feet, it was to pace nervously back and forth across the plat-form, returning periodically to his desk to light a new cigarette, often before he had finished the last. Even after his first year the student yearbook remarked that his modern drama course was "characterized by his own nervous strides (no more than three paces in any direction from the desk)." Nevertheless, his enrollments grew, and his success as a lecturer was greater than he ever imagined—even though his ner-vous mannerisms persisted as he punctuated a paragraph by lighting another cigarette, or emphasized some point with a sudden halt in his pacing.

The popularity Krutch increasingly enjoyed was partly a func-tion of his sense that teaching was a kind of "reasonably high-class en-tertainment"; he sought to instruct and amuse his students in nearly equal measure. In the lectures which he conscientiously prepared and frequently revised, he aimed at something beyond the conventionally academic. References to the work of scholars and other critics were not wholly absent, but as some years before, when writing *Five Mas-ters*, Krutch was eager to share his enthusiasm for the works and writ-ers he was discussing; to offer sensible and considered judgments, if not brilliant new interpretations; and to make literary study no less humane than its subject, hearing about literature no less pleasant than reading it.

To some extent, he realized, teaching was a performance; and his readings from dramatic texts were delivered with impressive gusto and relish. Since he knew that many of his students were attracted to his courses because of his reputation as a practicing critic, he frequently interpolated into his lectures the news of a performance he had at-tended the previous evening. According to the 1947 yearbook, "No student in his modern drama class ever bothers to read the newspaper reviews of a play because, the morning after each opening, the Profes-sor gives his personal commentary on the new show, complete with hilarious re-enactments of key scenes."

Especially when discussing the modern American drama he had been reviewing since the mid-1920s, Krutch drew on his memories of the performed plays and the lore concerning actors and playwrights. For him, and for his students, drama was a living genre, and the playwrights, actors, set designers, and producers were as much a part of his subject as the texts of the plays themselves. Whatever the topic of his lecture, he could be trusted to have some apt and frequently amusing anecdote. In the slightly shy, slightly sly expression on his face when he concluded, one saw the delight he took in entertaining hundreds of young men with favorite stories previously shared only with small groups of friends. He delivered funny anecdotes so skillfully that some students came back a year later to hear a number of the same jokes a second time.

Part of Krutch's large student following at Columbia was due to his skill as an entertainer and—in the best sense of the word—a popularizer of literature. Undoubtedly, part was also due to his reputation as a notoriously easy grader. He was not, for all that, eager to curry favor with individual students. Indeed, one reason why his teaching at Columbia succeeded, whereas his previous such efforts had failed, was that the lecture format did not require continuous interaction with students. He was more comfortable in monologue than in dialogue, and though he was politely responsive when necessary— always ready to interrupt his lecture to recognize a hand which had been raised, however tentatively— he maintained an aloof, but never pompous, distance from his admiring students. Few were ever invited to his office, and fewer still had the temerity to appear uninvited. From the brusque, preoccupied way in which he strode into and, at the end of the hour, hastily left the lecture hall, students received the intended message.

With colleagues he also erected defenses against personal intimacy. Except for a few close friends—most of these, like Mark Van Doren, former graduate school classmates—he rarely saw his colleagues socially. At lunch he communicated largely by anecdote and quotation (both of which he had in apparently endless supply), and several of his former colleagues recall what seemed to be his touching helplessness in personal relations.

The appearance of remoteness is explained partly by Krutch's intense shyness, especially among strangers; partly by his feeling of uneasiness as a mere writer and critic in a community of distinguished scholars; and mostly by his desire to maintain the detachment which would permit him to pursue undistracted his new life in Redding. He deliberately remained on the periphery of the academic life, rarely contributing to discussions in department meetings, serving on few committees, and never directing a dissertation. Certain civic responsibilities were, however, inevitable. During his first five years there he served as chairman of the fiction jury for the Pulitzer prizes awarded by Columbia. Reading scores of novels, he sated once and for all his appetite for contemporary fiction. As his appointment to the Pulitzer juries suggests, Krutch was the department's resident critic — admired for his achievements, but generally somewhat removed from the narrowly scholarly work of most of his colleagues.

In fact, Krutch was a professor more in title than in spirit. He thought of himself less as an academic than as a writer who, for the moment at least, was once again teaching. For him, teaching was less a career than a means of supporting himself until he could again resume the full-time literary career which remained his deepest ambition. When, in 1938, he addressed the Modern Language Association and urged its members to take pride in the charge that they were devoted to the accumulation of "useless knowledge," he said: "The scholar is supposed to be a man who has renounced the world. But the world has very seldom seemed more eminently worthy of renouncing. The very reflections which were once leveled against you have turned into compliments."[1] Although the sentiments reveal something of the impulse behind Krutch's increasingly reclusive life in Redding, the use of the second-person pronoun is also telling. He did not presume to include himself among the scholar's ranks.

Krutch knew, however, that in his new position something at least approximating scholarship was expected of him. Because the luxurious vacations that were one attraction of the academic life were not intended merely for nature study in Redding, during the summer of 1938 Krutch dutifully set about producing a book such as he hoped might be appropriate. Given the courses he was teaching and his experience as a critic, no topic was more obvious than *The American Drama Since 1918*, a book which appeared late in 1939 with the modest subtitle, "An Informal History." Krutch was incapable of producing a truly tedious book, since even his most pedestrian ideas would be redeemed in part by the liveliness of his wit and the felicity of his prose. On balance, however, this may well rank as the least inspired of his many volumes. Not surprisingly, it bears many of the marks of a series of course lectures worked up none too enthusiastically into the kind of book he thought might appropriately come from a professor of literature. The voice was that of an articulate, unpedantic lecturer agreeably exhibiting his considerable knowledge of plays and playwrights as he leads a class of bright undergraduates through the history of modern drama. Like his lectures, Krutch's book assumed no special knowledge and refrained from ingenious interpretations and self-indulgent speculations. The book was partly historical, chronicling various tendencies in the drama since the Great War, describing the careers of various playwrights, and defining differences among them. It was also partly critical in its endeavor to estimate the importance of those writers, some still in midcareer.

As in his lectures, Krutch combined anecdote, biography, plot summary, speculation as to reasons for a play's success or failure in the theater, and occasional references to the actors and set designers who brought various works to the stage. Referring in its 300 pages to well over 200 plays, it represents at the very least a prodigious feat of memory (obviously assisted by some research) performed by a sensible, if not here dazzlingly profound, intelligence. Straining for sober respectability, however, it is so far from being tendentious that it ultimately lacks the interpretative framework necessary in a book, if not in a series of undergraduate lectures.

Throughout *The American Drama Since 1918* it was obvious that the subject was not one for which, in 1938, Krutch could generate much enthusiasm. After more than twelve years of professional theater-going, he was wearying of Broadway—all the more so because he had little sympathy with the most recent developments on the stage, the social protest drama to which he devoted nearly a fifth of his history. In fact, the book possessed a decidedly valedictory quality, demonstrating little of the energy which characterized his earlier writing on the drama, and conveying a sense that the greatness of at least one phase of the modern American theater had passed. He was able to muster kind words for Sidney Howard and George Kelly as realists; for Philip Barry, S.N. Behrman, George Kaufman, and

Young Joe with brother Charles' bicycle, Knoxville (c. 1897)

Krutch as an undergraduate (c. 1912)

Krutch (*l.*) with Mark Van Doren (c. 1920)

Joe with Marcelle, returning from France (1931)

Krutch recuperating from one of his numerous illnesses, with his favorite cat, Minou (late 1920s)

Krutch relaxing in yard of Redding, Connecticut, home (1930s)

Joe and Marcelle in yard of Redding, Connecticut, home (1940s)

The Krutch home in Redding, Connecticut (1940s)

128

Krutch lecturing at Columbia (1940s)

Krutch in Baja California (1960s)

Joe and Marcelle at South Rim, Grand Canyon (1960s)

Krutch taking notes in desert around Tucson (1960s)

The rear patio of Krutch's Tucson home, with mountains reflected in living room window (1960s)

Krutch with Kenneth Bechtel (*l.*) in Krutch's Tucson home (1960s)

Krutch with bobcat at Arizona-Sonora Desert Museum (1960s)

Robert Sherwood as comic writers; for Maxwell Anderson as a poetic dramatist; for Eugene O'Neill as a writer of tragedy; and even for John Howard Lawson, Clifford Odets, and Elmer Rice as playwrights of social criticism. But for Krutch, clearly, the most significant achievements of the recent American stage were well in the past, and for him the bloom had long since gone off the theater. The hopes of that first (1924–25) season, when he had reviewed in rapid succession the openings of *What Price Glory?, They Knew What They Wanted,* and *Desire Under the Elms,* had not been sustained. "Last week," he grumbled in a 1938 review, "was one of those—unfortunately not as rare as they might be—when even a drama critic was wisest if he spent most of his evenings at home with a good book."[2] Drama was now a topic about which Krutch prepared a weekly column for the *Nation,* which he lectured upon to undergraduates, and about which he dutifully wrote what he hoped would be at least a modestly serviceable, academically respectable book.

Until he retired from Columbia and moved to Tucson in 1952, Krutch continued reviewing plays for the *Nation.* It was an activity that he was often tempted to abandon, especially in the early 1940s, when he and Marcelle gave up their apartment in New York, made Redding their home, and he had to spend several nights a week in hotels during the theater season. More from force of habit than from love, he continued writing the column he had unexpectedly been offered in 1924.

By the 1940s Krutch's frustration was evident in his reviews. While he gladly welcomed the appearance of such promising new writers as Arthur Miller, Tennessee Williams, and Rodgers and Hammerstein, by and large he found that the new plays of the 1940s lacked even the misguided ambition of the previous decade's revolutionary political drama. His most thoughtful reviews were of those plays which provoked thought—most often, dramatic classics which producers were reviving in greater numbers to fill the vacuum created by the exodus of literary talent to radio and films.

Occasionally an especially outrageous play inspired Krutch to write an exuberant account of its banality, but generally his reviews became increasingly perfunctory and brief. "About the theater this week the less said the better," began a nine-line "review" of two new productions.[3] By the forties he had perfected the peremptory dismissal, and he was calling frequently upon epithets like "routine," "pretentiously empty and conventional," "a preposterous piece of romantic rubbish," "dreary and pedestrian," "flimsily artificial," "high-grade hokum," a "labored bit of pathos," and "a sleezy affair." "More and more of the new stage pieces," he said in 1944, "have the quality which one has learned to associate with popular magazines, with the movies, and with the soap operas rather than any which was characteristic of Broadway even when Broadway was at its worst."[4]

Reviewing *The Best Plays of 1943–44*, Krutch observed, "The new volume . . . finds the editor rather hard pressed to discover 'ten best' that are also 'ten good' plays."[5] Not even the Broadway audience escaped his scorn. Reviewing *Mister Roberts* in 1948, he wrote: "It comes as something of a shock to discover how perfectly a theatrical performance as crude, simple, and completely adolescent as this one is fits the taste of a metropolitan audience; to hear with what gales of deeply satisfied laughter that audience greets comic-strip situations; to overhear between the acts how eagerly it confesses that this is, at last, something about which it has no reservations."[6]

Given his growing impatience with Broadway, one wonders why Krutch continued his reviewing. In part, it was due to a kind of fellowship he valued as unique to the theater. "One participates not only in the play but also in the reactions of the audience," he wrote. "One senses as one can never sense while reading a book that one is sharing an experience. It is impossible to feel wholly isolated or completely alone."[7] The sharing was much like that he proposed as the goal of the Literary Guild. For a man who was hardly gregarious, it offered a kind of social life far preferable to publishers' receptions or academic dinner parties. Significantly, the fellowship he enjoyed in the darkened theater — like the fellowship he was coming to enjoy in nature — necessitated none of the intimate personal contact with people which he found so difficult.

Because of his shyness — and, he insisted, because he was eager to maintain his critical objectivity — Krutch mixed little with theatrical people. "The profession of playwright or actor does not seem to me any more romantic than the other artistic professions," he remarked. "In fact, temperament, grease paint, and dressing rooms tend to bore me."[8] Indeed, though he served for a year as president of the Drama Critics' Circle, he saw little even of his fellow critics. According to tradition, magazine reviewers attended the second, rather than the opening night of a new play; thus Krutch rarely encountered his counterparts from the daily press. Apart from the few meetings of the Drama Critics' Circle each year, the fraternity rarely fraternized.

Whatever glamor the theater had once held for him had long since vanished by the 1940s. When he had come to disdain even the fellowship of the audience, the theater offered, quite simply, a regular part-time job. As Columbia's resident man of letters, Krutch felt bound to continue his reviewing. As one who never felt financially secure, especially after the Crash, he welcomed the modest supplement to his academic salary. But above all he continued reviewing in order to keep his name before the public. His reputation as a reviewer had been well established in the 20s, and he was now capitalizing on that earlier renown. Each week his *Nation* reviews reached a wide and distinguished readership, and he hoped that, even while his other books and essays were few and far between, those journal readers would remember him when he resumed his now languishing literary career.

When Krutch began as the *Nation*'s drama critic in the 1920s, his weekly accounts of the New York stage were nearly works of art themselves. With their eloquent and thoughtful passages of philosophical and aesthetic speculation, they reflected his obvious effort (as in *The Modern Temper*, for which they were in a sense preparatory) to be "distinctly high-brow." While remaining faithful to his reportorial responsibility, he wanted also to display his literary and intellectual gifts in order to establish his own reputation. By the 1930s, however, his sense of himself and of his literary career had changed. He was now less eager to shine as a literary luminary or to associate himself with the advanced thinkers of the day. His ambitions for his column also grew more modest as he found the theater it chronicled less sympathetic. His weekly essays became more journalistic than artful, and he was content to produce works of use, rather than adornment. Though he began as a critic of the drama, he presently became a reviewer of plays. By 1943 he himself insisted upon the distinction: "The so-called drama critic is, most of the time, a reviewer rather than a critic," he said. "It is only as a reviewer that he can, as a rule, usefully employ his talents, however great they may be."[9] But, as he himself understood, even as a reviewer his role was limited. Though some plays may have run a few weeks longer thanks to his praise, none closed because of an unfavorable notice in the *Nation* two or three weeks after its opening. Indeed, many of his readers, spread across the country, were at best infrequent visitors to Broadway. His reviews, then, offered supplements to those appearing in the dailies—second opinions, for those readers in the city who valued Krutch's judgment; and accounts, for those in the provinces, of the week's activity on the New York stage.

The ideal review, Krutch felt, should contain at least three elements: the report of an item of news (that a play by this author featuring these actors was appearing at that theater and dealt with these situations); an impressionistic re-creation of the work itself, complete enough to entertain and convince the reader; and a judgment of the play's success. He followed the formula faithfully. If evaluation was the end of his effort, a complete and faithful report of the play was the means. Suggesting not only the content of the play but also the mood it created in him, he tried to give his reader "an indirect glimpse of what the experience of witnessing that performance would be like." Only then, he felt, would his estimate of the play's success be credible.[10]

In judging plays Krutch self-consciously resisted the temptation "to try each new offering by the highest artistic standards . . . to view everything from the aspect of eternity; to call nothing good which is not absolutely so."[11] Though he seized the occasion of an important new play or the revival of a classic to write as a serious student of drama, he generally wrote more warmly as an ordinary citizen who was happy to be diverted by a well-done, if slight, comedy or engaged by an effective melodrama. Even when he knew it lacked essential literary merit, he could applaud the ingratiating performance of an amusing, spirited, and original play. Whereas the critic might fairly demand art, Krutch, as a reviewer, was often content to settle for mere entertainment.

He had no procrustean critical bed upon which to force plays for analysis. The conclusions (or, more precisely, the absence of conclusions) in the two doctoral dissertations thus far written on the subject confirm what a careful reading of his *Nation* reviews suggests: that Krutch had various notions about the theater which he threw off rather casually from time to time, but no grand critical system which consistently informed his writing. In his reviews Krutch was both the Knoxville boy, whose sense of the theater had been formed on the lowbrow offerings of vaudeville houses, and the Columbia professor, whose standards had been refined by long exposure to the highbrow literary classics. His taste, incorporating both influences, was like that of most of his readers: middlebrow. What he said of George Jean Nathan might well be said of Krutch himself: "He never allows either his readers or himself to forget that 'pretty good' is no more than just that but neither does he prevent himself from taking his fun where he finds it."[12]

During the more than a quarter-century in which Krutch reviewed plays, and especially during the period between the appearance of *Was Europe a Success?* (1934) and that of *Samuel Johnson* (1944), it is likely that he was most popularly known as a drama critic. For most of those years, the *Nation* enjoyed a circulation greater than any of his books had thus far achieved, and with his reviews he continued to enjoy the broad readership he dearly wanted. But for Krutch reviewing, like teaching, was less a career than a sidelight to the literary vocation for which he remained eager.

By the end of his *Nation* days he had attended some 2,000 performances in his professional capacity and had written well over 500 reviews totaling hundreds of thousands of words. Though he devoted little attention there to the details of production, and though they are hardly comprehensive in recording the activity of the New York stage during those years, his reviews do offer a candid account of one man's reactions to the vicissitudes of the American theater. Generally he reacted with indulgent tolerance to the mediocrity it was his lot to witness week after week. Often (toward the end, frequently) he became angry and impatient, but occasionally he delighted to follow with enthusiasm the unfolding of an important new dramatic talent.

Quantitatively, his drama reviews constitute the greatest single part of Krutch's career as a writer. Qualitatively, however—when judged, that is, for their place in his total literary achievement—they figure as perhaps the least part. Of all his writing in a variety of genres, his drama reviewing was the most narrowly journalistic and thus the most ephemeral. Krutch himself surely recognized that fact. He was hardly reluctant to recycle his prose, and many of his books were collections of previously published essays. But unlike such fellow critics as Brooks Atkinson, John Mason Brown, and George Jean Nathan, Krutch never attempted to collect his reviews. On the one occasion when he appeared to—in 1928, to discharge a contractual commitment to Alfred Knopf before bringing out *The Modern Temper* with another house—he did so in the confident hope they would be rejected. And they were.

Like his frequent book reviews, his drama column was a sort of literary five-finger exercise on a subject neatly provided each week. But it was hardly more than the base above which appeared his more impressive achievements: especially *The Modern Temper*, and, during the 1940s, his biographies of Johnson and Thoreau. If the biographer may be permitted the indulgence of desiring his subject's career to have been other than it was, one might wish that Krutch had husbanded some of the considerable time and energy devoted to attending and reviewing the theater for use instead on some worthier, more permanent end. As he himself concluded in his autobiography, his reviewing was "respectable, though only occasionally 'significant,' work."[13]

His writing was most clearly "significant," and Krutch was himself most consistently a critic (rather than a reviewer), when he felt he had encountered works and authors of extraordinary talent. Had he no other achievement as a writer on the modern American drama, Krutch deserves to be remembered as the man who, perhaps more than any other, helped to establish Eugene O'Neill's literary standing. Beginning in the fall of 1924, when he reviewed *Desire under the Elms* during the opening weeks of his first season, Krutch wrote admiringly, though never dotingly, about O'Neill for nearly four decades. While he was a partisan of no author, Krutch's name will long be associated with O'Neill's. His body of writing, so consistently incisive and sympathetic in its exposition of the artist's aims, was instrumental in winning O'Neill recognition as the foremost playwright of his day.

O'Neill was, in fact, the only playwright with whom Krutch was more than casually acquainted. They first met in New York in 1927 and thereafter had a warm, if not close, relationship. Between their meetings over a number of years they exchanged letters (many now unfortunately lost), and according to O'Neill's biographers, Arthur and Barbara Gelb, Krutch "always remained O'Neill's favorite and most respected reviewer."[14] On at least one occasion, while working on *Strange Interlude*, O'Neill sent a draft of the play for Krutch's comments; on another, he invited the Krutches to visit him in France. And when in 1932 nine of O'Neill's plays, selected by the author, were published by the Modern Library, Krutch was chosen to contribute the biographical-critical introduction. "Let me take this opportunity to thank you for your Introduction to Nine Plays," O'Neill wrote him. "It says so much I'm so damned proud to have said — especially by you."[15]

Included in that volume was *Mourning Becomes Electra*, the most recently produced of his plays and the one Krutch to the end believed epitomized O'Neill's achievement as a playwright. Reviewing it in 1931, Krutch found there "a largeness of conception and a more than local or temporary significance which put to rest those doubts which usually arise when one is tempted to attribute a lasting greatness to any play of our generation. . . . It may," he said, "turn out to be the only permanent contribution yet made by the twentieth century to dramatic literature." Krutch was of course attracted by the dignity, honesty, and intense emotional conviction in O'Neill's plays; O'Neill came closer, Krutch felt, than any other American, closer perhaps even than any contemporary European, to capturing the tragic sense. However, he was also aware of O'Neill's defects. His one reservation about *Mourning Becomes Electra* was echoed frequently in his other writing about O'Neill's work: "To find in the play any lack at all one must compare it with the very greatest works of dramatic literature, but when one does compare it with 'Hamlet' or 'Macbeth' one realizes that it does lack just one thing and that thing is language — words as thrilling as the action which accompanies it."[16]

The play which inspired such praise was followed in the 1930s by two much slighter efforts: *Ah, Wilderness!* (1933) and *Days Without End* (1934). Twelve years passed before his next play, *The Iceman Cometh*, appeared; notwithstanding his receipt of the Nobel Prize, interest in O'Neill waned. Almost alone, Krutch continued to insist upon his importance. In *American Drama Since 1918* he devoted far more space to O'Neill than to any other writer. And when, in 1943, he was invited to write a chapter on American drama from 1915 to 1925 for the *Literary History of the United States*, Krutch agreed, devoting his essay exclusively to O'Neill. No more than in his reviews did Krutch, in these longer discussions, offer up unqualified praise of O'Neill. What he did offer was his considered judgment as a scholar and critic: "O'Neill is probably the most important playwright ever to arise in the United States."[17]

Shortly after O'Neill died in 1953, the playwright's widow invited Krutch to write his authorized biography. By then, however, Krutch had retired from New York to Tucson and lacked both the ready access to the materials and the enthusiasm for matters theatrical prerequisite to undertaking such a project. Though he was contributing various pieces to *Theatre Arts* and was writing admiring essays on the posthumous publication of O'Neill's plays, his real interests had long since moved elsewhere, and he declined the invitation which some years earlier he would eagerly have seized. "At sixty and more," he was discovering in Tucson, "one may stop going to the theater without losing anything absolutely indispensable to the good life."[18]

It was doubtless not only because of his reputation as a drama critic and his long association with the playwright's career, but also because of the reputation he by then enjoyed as a literary biographer that Krutch was invited to write O'Neill's life story. While teaching and reviewing in the 1940s, Krutch had also published two critical biographies—one on Samuel Johnson, the other on Henry David Thoreau—which were arguably the best such works yet written on their subjects and which remain two of the most substantial achievements of his entire career. His admiring studies of these men reveal the great influence they had had on his life and thinking during the 1930s. Moreover, each book was lavishly praised when it appeared,

141

thus serving to renew Krutch's reputation as an outstanding American man of letters.

While both books benefited from that modern form of literary patronage provided by the university, the preparation of *Samuel Johnson* was additionally facilitated by a sabbatical during 1943–44 (when Krutch also took leave of his *Nation* reviewing) and by the outbreak of World War II. Shortly after the publication in 1939 of his history of modern American drama, he had contracted to write the Johnson book when Mark Van Doren proposed the project to William Sloane, his editor at Henry Holt. At the outset Krutch worked fitfully on the book in whatever time remained after preparation of his Columbia lectures, his drama reviewing, his nature study, and the six-week trips to the southwest he and Marcelle had taken each summer since 1938. With the war, however, his travels were interrupted. His lectures had already been "worked up," and his students had dwindled to that small number either too old or too unfit to fight. Since his own contribution to the war effort was minimal — plane-spotting in Connecticut, and occasional work for the Office of War Information — he had, during the early 1940s, a welcome opportunity to concentrate on a project more ambitious than any he had yet attempted.

Though there had been little evidence of the fact in Krutch's writing during the thirties, Johnson had long been one of his favorite authors, and Van Doren knew it. For years, Boswell's *Life* had been Krutch's favorite bedtime reading; and Boswell had led him to Johnson's works themselves, where he delighted in both "a powerful mind and a powerful gift for expression."[19] Just as he had found the solace of nature in Redding, Krutch had found in Johnson a refreshing retreat from a world he found increasingly alien. In Johnson's life, works, and times he had discovered a sanity and grace absent from the politically charged intellectual world of the thirties, which lacked "all those . . . virtues which are commonly implied when we speak of anything or anyone as 'civilized.' "[20] Immersing himself in Johnson as he prepared his biography during a world war, Krutch was employing one of those "devices for detachment and escape" which he had realized "play a large part in the scheme of my life."

The Johnson book was not written merely for therapy. A major book was clearly due from Krutch, and he was eager that this be it.

While his Columbia colleagues had been producing works of distinguished scholarship, Krutch had been writing mere drama reviews and an undistinguished history of the American theater. Even while working on *Johnson*, he had been elevated to an endowed chair at Columbia, the Brander Matthews Professorship of Dramatic Literature, and he was determined at last to produce a volume worthy of his position. Moreover, since none of his subsequent books had received the great critical acclaim that had greeted *The Modern Temper* more than a decade earlier, he realized that a substantial work would be necessary if his popular reputation were not to become simply that of a periodical writer. To attempt again what Boswell had been thought to have accomplished once and for all was to venture boldly indeed. Krutch recognized that both his academic and his literary reputations required no less.

The recognition for which he was now eager, however, was distinctly different from that which he had sought with his previous biography, *Edgar Allan Poe*. The Johnson cult was hardly less numerous than the Poe cult he had earlier sought to scandalize, and Johnson's life offered no less material for another callow exercise in Stracheyan debunking. By the 1940s, however, Krutch had passed beyond the giddy modernism and literary exhibitionism of *Poe*. His current book would be as cautious as the earlier one had been reckless, as sympathetic as the other had been condescending.

While he had devotedly read Johnson during the thirties, Krutch had been greatly impressed by the example of that deep and hard-won conviction of the great Augustan, coming to respect it far more than the Byronic doubt of his own earlier modernism. As a graduate student, Krutch had preferred the iconoclasm of the Restoration wits to the sober common sense of a moralist like Johnson; rereading Johnson in the thirties, he found in him a new significance. Johnson's conservative leanings in politics and morality corresponded to and reinforced Krutch's own. Johnson had struggled to achieve something of the same social, intellectual, and spiritual stability that had characterized the Knoxville of Krutch's youth, and which Krutch himself craved as he passed through the disillusionment of the twenties and the fanaticism of the thirties. With far more subtle understanding than Krutch's family or his Knoxville neighbors, Johnson had subscribed to attitudes and values by which Krutch's temperament had been shaped and which he had, not wholly successfully, tried to shake off as he strained to become a sophisticated, modern thinker in New York. Johnson's literary achievement, moreover, bestowed a sanction on those beliefs which the culture of turn-of-the-century Knoxville never had given. As he turned to write *Samuel Johnson* in the 1940s, Krutch sought to revivify that exemplary life, to honor that literary achievement, and to celebrate those humanist values he now greatly cherished.

On none of his other works did Krutch lavish such loving and often anxious effort as on the nearly six hundred pages of this book. As a man of meager scholarly achievement whose last significant academic effort had been his dissertation more than two decades earlier, he recognized that he was "definitely not a member of the sizable group of Johnson specialists who had made him the principal interest of their lives"; he feared they would regard him "as a rash intruder."[21] Recognizing his temerity in attempting the book at all, and eager to justify himself in the eyes of his academic colleagues, he spent several years painstakingly reading and digesting the voluminous material on Johnson, including the illuminating discoveries of several recent generations of scholars, whose research offered insights unavailable to Boswell.

Nonetheless, because he knew that Boswell remained the richest (and most widely known) source of information on Johnson, the shadow of Boswell's achievement hung constantly over Krutch's efforts. "Any general biography of Samuel Johnson," he had observed in 1934, "is bound to contain a great deal that is familiar and not much that is new."[22] Faced with such a situation, the younger, iconoclastic Krutch—eager to display his cleverness and unburdened by scruples of academic responsibility—would have seized the challenge of Boswell's preeminence to offer some novel but misleading interpretation of his subject.

In fact, however, Krutch chose the more difficult, if less spectacular, course by seeking modestly to build upon the foundations Boswell had laid. His own book, he wrote in the foreword, was addressed to "the general reader" and would offer "a running account of Johnson's life, character and work as they appear in the light of contemporary knowledge and judgment."[23] In works as various as *The Modern Temper, Five Masters,* and *Was Europe a Success?* he had demonstrated his considerable talent for digesting, reordering, smoothly joining, and summarizing a large and miscellaneous body of material. The biographical part of *Samuel Johnson,* which was of course the largest part, was a superior demonstration of those skills.

Krutch made no pretense of adding to the vast stock of information about Johnson's life that was available to the diligent scholar. In this first major modern biography of Johnson he did, however, bring together from widely scattered sources the recent findings of specialists, adding them to the Boswellian Johnson in order to present his "general reader" with the most comprehensive portrait of his subject which had yet appeared. The long and widely known anecdotes appeared, together with some new ones. Unfettered by any striving after mere novelty, Krutch was happy to rehearse those familiar parts of the Johnson legend which are so durable as to remain fresh even after repeated retelling.

The anecdotal skill which brought students back to Krutch's Columbia classes to hear the same lecture a second time was everywhere evident in the judicious yet lively narrative of his book. With his characteristic concision, gusto, and sense of the dramatic, he related familiar stories which took on a new life with his recital. "The whole story is too good not to be told from the beginning," he said with obvious delight as he began his account of Johnson's famous letter to Chesterfield.[24] That the story had been told many times before troubled Krutch not at all. His effort, as he saw it, was less to find new stories than to tell the old ones surpassingly well.

That letter, in which Johnson announced his independence of the patron, was of particular interest to Krutch. He felt a special kinship with the man who, like himself, had been born and reared in the provinces and had left his home for the city, there to live by his wit and his pen. Like London for Johnson, New York for Krutch had been "the center of learning and poetry, the market to which any man might bring such wares as he had to sell." Johnson's struggle to make a career as a writer was not unlike Krutch's own. One might well say of Krutch's biography what he himself said of Johnson's *Life of Savage*: "The life owes its vigor to the fact that it is tinged with autobiography in the parts which describe the life of the literary hack as well as enlivened everywhere by Johnson's ability to project himself into experiences which he would, in some sense, have liked to share."[25]

For Krutch, Johnson was important not only as England's first professional man of letters, or as the amiable eccentric of the Boswellian and nineteenth-century tradition who was the source of so many memorable epigrams and anecdotes. He was, moreover, an important writer whose thought and literary achievement deserved the serious consideration largely absent from Boswell's *Life*. Krutch's major contribution—and what ensures his book's continued importance as something far more than an immensely skillful pastiche of other people's work—was his extensive and original appraisal of Johnson's thought and literary achievement.

A critic himself, Krutch devoted his most thorough and sympathetic attention to Johnson's critical works. The poetry he dismissed rather too neatly; and the *Rambler*'s greatest distinction, he concluded somewhat perversely, is its responsibility "for the extent to which many now assume that he is, as a prose writer, quite unreadable." But in the criticism, and most especially in the edition of Shakespeare and his *Lives of the Poets*, Krutch discovered the quality that was, for him, so distinctly Johnsonian: "the play of a vigorous and entertaining mind over a wide range of subjects."[26]

To each of these works he devoted a lengthy chapter—perhaps, in fact, a bit too lengthy for any general reader who was unconcerned with Krutch's scholarly disquisition on Johnson's critical principles and their backgrounds in eighteenth-century literary theory. But even here shone Krutch's admiration for the sanity of a critic who, as in editing Shakespeare, successfully reconciled his allegiance to the neoclassical rules with his deeper sense that the reader's experience constitutes the true test of a work's merit. Johnson passed "the final test of the critic"—"willingness and ability to recognize excellence even when he cannot account for it; to be able to put loyalty to greatness before loyalty to his own theories." Such was also Krutch's own endeavor as a reviewer of plays.[27]

As a writer, Krutch had been aspiring to that broad popular appeal which Johnson in his day had enjoyed. The source of Johnson's success offered confirmation of Krutch's growing understanding as to how he might achieve his own: "Johnson could become a popular critic partly because his premises and his methods were so well adapted to the understanding of the intelligent layman." His had not been the labored, highbrow appeal that had characterized so much of Krutch's own earlier writing; rather, it had been that less pretentious, less self-indulgent approach which had marked Krutch's own work since *Five Masters*. By the 1940s Krutch too sought to address "the intelligent layman." For Johnson, "literary interpretation and judgment seemed . . . to be no more than the application to literary questions of that generally applicable common sense in which the eighteenth century placed its faith."[28] For Krutch, common sense now seemed a precious guide not only to criticism but also to life.

The way in which such common sense informed Johnson's life and thought had especially drawn Krutch to Johnson. His book was a biography, not an interpretation; but throughout can be seen the biographer's admiration for a man who, as he announced in the opening sentence, "was a pessimist with an enormous zest for living." For the author of *The Modern Temper*, that fundamental pessimism had been all too real; like Johnson, Krutch had felt that "human life is everywhere a state, in which much is to be endured, and little to be enjoyed." Like Krutch in the 1920s, Johnson in the Enlightenment had been bewildered by the transition from one intellectual and spiritual dispensation to another and had "clung to old-fashioned ways of feeling even more than he did to old-fashioned ways of thinking."[29] But, as Krutch later recalled, one of the most powerful attractions of his subject was "the presence in Johnson of an underlying somberness of temperament, accompanied by a keen delight in those pleasures which existence nevertheless offers us."[30] Common sense had saved Johnson from the despair in which Krutch had wallowed in *The Modern Temper*.

"'Common sense,'" Krutch explained in *Samuel Johnson*, was "the acceptance of certain current assumptions, traditions, and standards of value which are never called into question because so to question any of them might be to necessitate a revision of government, society, and private conduct more thoroughgoing than anyone liked to contemplate."[31] In *The Modern Temper* the dictates of common sense struggled against the apparently contrary evidences of science

147

and nature which indicated that those assumptions, traditions, and standards of value were bankrupt. In the late twenties, eager to present himself as an advanced thinker of "robust but serious mind," Krutch had called everything into question—and had found no satisfactory answers. In the thirties he had witnessed among the Marxists a similar questioning, also lacking common sense, of the fundamental values of European civilization. Their answers proved no more satisfying to him than his own, earlier doubts. Arguments had proceeded from dogmatic conclusions back to convenient premises; human reason had been replaced by an arrogant, narrow logic in which history was disregarded, tradition derided, and unwelcome realities facilely dismissed. Everything was neatly simplified and categorized so that all was explained but nothing was understood. Just as Johnson had urged Boswell, Krutch, in writing *Was Europe a Success?*, had urged his age: "Clear your mind of cant." He was doubtless thinking of his own recent writing when Krutch said that Johnson "genuinely believed that the [political] current was running so strongly in one direction that someone ought to say what could be said against the prevailing tendency."[32]

By the 1930s Krutch had come to share Johnson's assumption "that the risks involved by change are risks taken without real chance of betterment."[33] He had also come—partly through Johnson—to recognize that common sense was precisely the quality lacking both in his own thoroughgoing modernist skepticism and in the revolutionary dogmatism of the Marxists. Now, chronicling Johnson's life and works, Krutch revealed some of the convictions he had gained from nearly fifteen years' thought: that common sense might be not only a check upon the excesses of radical doubt and radical conviction, but also something precious in itself; that common sense might be at least as useful a guide to philosophy and life as the labored denials of the modernists or the equally labored affirmations of the Marxists; that the evidences of feeling and common sense could be, in their ways, no less compelling than those of reason and science. Informed by the great common sense of a man like Johnson, one could be a pessimist and still retain an enormous zest for living.

Read in the context of his earlier work, it is Krutch's quiet celebration of Johnson's common sense which is the most striking aspect of his biography—even though the point, while everywhere apparent, was nowhere insisted upon. He was writing a biography, not an autobiography. He was here as reticent as he had earlier been brashly outspoken, and in his study he offered no confession of the great personal relevance he found in his subject. Edmund Wilson was just to complain, in an otherwise admiring review, that the book "a little bit lacks impact." And he may equally have been correct (if also characteristically anti-academic) in charging this failure to "the habitual blankness of the outlook of academic scholarship. . . . When Mr. Krutch wrote 'The Modern Temper,' " Wilson remarked, "he had a much more definite point of view as a general critic of life."[34] In fact, Krutch's point of view was far clearer and far more affirmative in 1944 than it had been fifteen years before. In broad outline, if not in every detail, it was markedly Johnsonian. His biography was a statement, though never more than implicit, of many of the social, literary, and human values which Krutch himself—largely through Johnson—had once again come to respect.

The devoted attention expended in the preparation of *Samuel Johnson* seemed richly justified by its reception. In the popular press it was extensively and enthusiastically reviewed, and for two weeks it enjoyed a place on the best-seller list of the New York *Times*. Academic reviews were equally flattering, and even the crusty F.R. Leavis conceded that "Mr. Krutch's book . . . is not only inoffensive, it is positively good. . . . An Englishman," he went on, rather differently from Edmund Wilson, "must see in him something very much to the credit of American academic letters."[35] Harvard University apparently thought so as well and in 1945 invited Krutch to become a professor there. Happy though he was to have Harvard's imprimatur on his newly earned academic respectability, he declined. His home in Redding was by then far more important to his life than any English department, however celebrated.

The publication of *Johnson* was doubly significant in Krutch's career. It was his greatest commercial success to date; indeed, it has remained one of his most popular books. For the man of letters, such sales count for quite as much as any number of flattering reviews. After a long drought, both his reputation and his self-confidence as a writer were rapidly renewed. Moreover, in his celebration of Johnson, Krutch clearly implied that he had put behind himself the modernism with which he was still popularly associated. The pessimism of *Rasselas* had been as real to Johnson as that of *The Modern Temper* had been to Krutch. But it was the witness of Johnson's life—increasingly confirmed in Krutch's own—that such pessimism need not be total. At Redding, Krutch had his Happy Valley; and, like Rasselas, at the end of his melancholy intellectual journeying he was discovering at home such not inconsiderable pleasures as life allowed.

Twelve years had separated the publication of *Samuel Johnson* and *Experience and Art*, Krutch's previous major book. Only four years would pass, however, before the appearance of his next important work, *Henry David Thoreau*. Again enjoying the literary recognition which had eluded him during the 1930s, and stimulated by subjects he greatly cared about, Krutch rediscovered his enthusiasm for writing.

It may seem curious that, having just published a sympathetic life of Johnson, Krutch should immediately turn to write an equally warm biography of so different a figure as Thoreau. The paradox, if any, is apparent rather than real. In the years since *The Modern Temper*, Johnson and Thoreau had been the two leading influences on Krutch's thought and life. While Johnson had helped him clear his mind of the cant of a labored modernism, Thoreau at the same time had offered a model of a life—more relevant to Krutch than Johnson's life of Christian piety—in which one might enjoy such pleasures as existence does afford. Like *Johnson* (1944), *Thoreau* (1948) was a belated tribute to a man to whom Krutch had been indebted long before the book appeared.

Krutch had doubtless first encountered Thoreau as early as 1915, in discussion with Mark Van Doren. Although his University of Illinois master's thesis on Thoreau was then in press, Van Doren could hardly have been very enthusiastic in recommending that writer to his new friend. His disdain for Thoreau was nearly complete: his "main product was nothing," he had written, "and his main effort vain." [36] Thus it is not surprising that another fifteen years passed before Krutch himself first read *Walden*, while returning east from his cross-country lecture tour promoting *The Modern Temper*. As he read the book in 1930, Krutch scribbled on the flyleaf of his copy some notes: "Man must be reformed first," he wrote, summarizing Thoreau's and declaring his own suspicion of movements for mass social reform. And: "The true moral of the book and perhaps one which Thoreau would have accepted is not that men should do as he did and society attempt to compose itself of Thoreaus but that every man should lead the kind of life which seems best to him."[37]

During the thirties Krutch would come to share even more passionately Thoreau's distaste for politics and his appreciation of individualism. Moreover, he would come to value an aspect of *Walden* that he did not explicitly remark upon at the time: Thoreau's demonstration that "there can be no very black melancholy to him who lives in the midst of Nature and has his senses still."[38] In *The Modern Temper*, nature had struck "terror to [Krutch's] soul."[39] Seen as Thoreau saw her, and as Krutch under Thoreau's aegis would shortly come to see her in Redding, nature could also bring great joy.

During the 30s, when Krutch wrote occasionally on politics and hardly at all on nature, he cited Thoreau only to help rescue him from the hands of those politically inclined critics who found in his writings the makings of a Marxist analysis of society and in his life a model for the social reformer. "He sought first of all his own salvation," Krutch insisted in 1933.[40] "How can it be," he asked impatiently a year later, "that even a mere forerunner of Communism . . . could have happened to say as he did: 'I came into this world, not chiefly to make this a good place to live in, but to live in it, good or bad.'"[41] Thoreau's goals were, of course, Krutch's own.

But Thoreau had not merely fled from politics and society; more important, he had fled to nature. By the 1940s, when Krutch too was confirmed in his belief that nature offers an alternative to the black melancholy of the modern temper, he was eager to pay public tribute to a man who, like Johnson, had during the previous decade shown him the way beyond that despair. Like *Samuel Johnson*, *Henry David Thoreau* was a labor no less of love than of scholarship.

Shortly after Henry Holt had published *Johnson* in 1944, Krutch's editor there, William Sloane, had set up his own firm. One of Sloane's first projects was the resurrection of the nineteenth-century American Men of Letters series. As editors for the new series Sloane recruited three Columbia professors, Krutch, Van Doren, and Lionel Trilling, along with Margaret Marshall, Krutch's successor as literary editor at the *Nation*. Together they were to enlist distinguished American critics to write about authors whom they had enjoyed but had not written about. When the board met to select the initial titles, Krutch promptly claimed Thoreau for himself.

Though he was happy enough to draw upon the scholarship of others, with Thoreau, as with Johnson, Krutch was little inclined to devote himself to original biographical research. Happily, that task had been performed (for the time, it seemed, definitively) as recently as 1939, when Henry Seidel Canby had published his massive account of Thoreau's life. That, combined with the fact that Thoreau's life was none too eventful (at least when compared to Johnson's), freed Krutch to subordinate biography to criticism and to present—again, for the general reader—an analysis of Thoreau's major ideas and an assessment of his literary achievement.

Even in 1948 Krutch felt it necessary to try, as he had fifteen years earlier, to detach Thoreau from the "specifically political criticism of contemporary society [which] has become so dominant a feature of our intellectual life." Krutch's Thoreau was nearly as apolitical as Krutch himself. "Reform was never with him more than a secondary purpose"; notwithstanding his indignation against slavery or his refusal to pay the poll tax, Thoreau was "at most . . . a very reluctant crusader."[42]

Effectively describing himself as well, Krutch wrote that Thoreau "never supposed that social organization itself was an interesting subject, that politics should or could be one of the important sources of satisfaction, and one of the things a man might 'live for.'" For Krutch, the 1930s had provided dreary evidence of the justness of Thoreau's conviction, that "reform is possible only in so far as each man reforms himself, and that all attempts to save mankind through concerted efforts are vicious and self-destructive."[43]

But Thoreau had offered something beyond a confirmation of Krutch's temperamental apoliticism. He had, moreover, reinforced Krutch's growing conviction that immediate palliatives for the individual should be sought before remotely possible panaceas for society at large. The great value of Thoreau's writing and the example of his life, he wrote, lay in their proposal of "a revolution which each man can make for himself." Even in 1948 Krutch's description of Thoreau rang with something of the rhetoric of the 1930s: "The whole of his mental and emotional life could exist only in so far as he assumed that it was possible for a man to resist 'forces,' to refuse to be a 'product,' or, what is the same thing, a 'victim.'"[44] If the reference is most obviously to man's passive role in the deterministic scheme of dialectical materialism, it also suggests the passivity of Krutch himself in the fatalistic conclusion to *The Modern Temper*. Thoreau's kind of resistance had become Krutch's own. "He went off to Walden," Krutch continued, "to demonstrate that if you do not like the world you find yourself in and do not think you can change it very soon, you can at least move away from it. Thus he brings tidings of great joy and demonstrates their truth by being himself filled with that joy."[45] Less dramatically than Thoreau, Krutch too had moved away — to Redding. And he came to be filled with that joy he failed to find in either modernism or Marxism.

Unsatisfied by the abstractions of scientism, humanism, or more recently Marxism, Krutch in the early 1930s was an unbeliever searching for something in which to believe. "*Walden*," he wrote in his biography, "was, among other things, an attempt to speak of matters simple and practical enough to be meaningful to those whom high abstractions left cold." Krutch was one of those, and Thoreau's book had spoken forcefully to him. "Thoreau," he remarked, "unlike many other mystics and transcendentalists, had accepted the one world of external reality — a world not to be neglected while the search for the other world beyond it was still on." Thoreau's example had led Krutch toward a similar acceptance. His retreat to Walden Pond, Krutch wrote, was a retreat from the abstract to the concrete, "not an escape toward the strange, but a digging into the familiar."[46] At Redding, Krutch had likewise gone beyond his modernist speculations about the abstraction of Nature (whose "purpose, if purpose she can be said to have, is no purpose of [man's] and is not understandable in his terms"[47]) to dig into the more familiar reality of concrete nature and to understand it for the first time.

Thoreau, Krutch said, moved "away from the transcendental

assumption that the meaning of nature can be reached by intuition and toward the fundamentally scientific assumption—namely, that only through observation may one ultimately reach not merely dead facts but those which understanding can make live." If Thoreau's approach was fundamentally scientific, it was not merely so. As for Krutch in *The Modern Temper*, "official science" was for Thoreau "the antithesis both of any genuine familiarity with even the living facts of nature, and of any emotional participation in her mysteries."[48]

In Cornwall during the late 1920s, Krutch's observation of nature had been largely a matter of field guides and handbooks; experimenting with *Mimosa pudica*, he had simply been aping the "official" scientist whose activity was limited to collecting, dissecting, and classifying. But when he first read Thoreau in 1930, Krutch found the example of a different and richer approach to nature. Thoreau's goal in his observation of nature, Krutch wrote, "was what he himself would have been inclined to call, rather vaguely, 'poetic,' and it aimed at familiarity with, rather than knowledge about, living things." For Thoreau, the mere intellectual understanding of nature was hollow if not accompanied by an emotional participation in her processes: "What Thoreau always sought in his intercourse with living things and even with the very hills and fields themselves was that warm and sympathetic sense of oneness, that escape from the self into the All, to which psychologists have given the chilly name 'empathy.'"[49] Thoreau's example had led Krutch to make a similar effort, and during the 1930s he had found in nature something far more precious than his earlier despair, far richer than the literary fame which seemed for the moment to have eluded him, far more satisfying than the fellowship and admiration of advanced thinkers from whom he now felt alienated.

Indeed, for both Thoreau and Krutch, hardly the least of nature's attractions was her offer of a refuge for men who were fundamentally asocial, if not quite misanthropic; who briefly embraced, then became disillusioned with, and finally rejected the intellectual coteries of their day; and who found more pleasure in the company of animals furred and feathered than in those who were human. What he wrote in 1948 of Thoreau was by then true of Krutch as well: "He was sure that he was more nearly of the frogs' fellowship than he was of any fellowship gathered in towns; more a part of their ancient world than of that newer one which had created needs to which it was now enslaved." For Krutch as well as Thoreau, "It was the solitary rather than the social aspects of life which seemed to him the more important, the nonhuman rather than the human part of the universe the more significant." The author of *The Modern Temper* had finally concluded, like Thoreau, that "the proper study of mankind . . . is not man but nature."[50]

During the thirties and most of the forties, it had been enough for Krutch to follow Thoreau in that study. Thoreau's life and thought had been far more important to him than the literary achievement of Thoreau's writing. But as he prepared his critical biography, Krutch considered Thoreau's distinction as a writer; and as he did so—while also hoping for the renewal of his own literary career—he made an important discovery.

The final chapter of his biography was devoted to a detailed analysis of various aspects of Thoreau's literary art—in fact, his most extensive exercise in purely stylistic analysis. Great as *Walden* is, he said, one must go to Thoreau's *Journal* "for any adequate idea of the bulk or importance of a kind of writing which will contribute more to Thoreau's fame than it yet has." That kind was, of course, the nature writing: "a vast record of his intercourse with trees and flowers, with animals, wild and domestic, and with inanimate nature as well."[51] Studying carefully the fourteen volumes of that *Journal*, Krutch recognized that Thoreau's achievement, unique among American writers, had been to understand that nature, faithfully rendered, requires no moralizing interpretation, and then to have set himself to recording simply but vividly his own empathic observation of the natural world.

Thoreau attempted, Krutch said, "to keep attention fixed upon the object itself, to return again and again to its own various aspects rather than merely to use the object as something from which the mind can take off. . . . Experience itself rather than any explanation or interpretation of it is what he is trying to communicate." For Thoreau, the distinctive quality of that experience was "delight." "The distinguishing character of that delight," Krutch wrote, "arises out of the fact that it is something that he is *sharing*, both with the beasts themselves and with the universe as a whole."[52]

For some time, Krutch in Redding had also known that delight and sense of sharing. But his Thoreauvian explorations of nature had remained distinct from his life of letters—his drama reviews, his political essays, his books on art, his teaching, and most recently his biography of the quintessentially urban Dr. Johnson. Reading more widely and deeply in Thoreau (and especially in the *Journal*) than he ever had before, and reflecting on the character of Thoreau's achievement as a writer, Krutch came to recognize the literary as well as the spiritual inspiration to be found in nature. Writing about Thoreau, Krutch sensed that his own interest in nature might at last find expression in his literary career. He was not long in acting on his intuition.

7.

A NEW BEGINNING

Like many an undergraduate, Krutch looked forward impatiently to each of the generous vacations in Columbia's academic year. He relished his classes far less than most of his students did, and he was increasingly eager to spend his days in Redding, uninterrupted by the tiresome journey to and from New York. The 1947 Christmas holiday promised to be especially luxurious. Having just sent back the galley proofs of *Thoreau*, he had borrowed from the Columbia library several volumes of nature writing in order to extend his acquaintance with a literary genre whose importance he had come to appreciate while working on that manuscript.

He was also turning over in his mind further projects for himself. The new momentum in his literary career was not to be lost, and he was eager that *Thoreau* be followed soon by another book. His desultory reading presently took on purpose; shortly before Christmas he decided that his next book should be an anthology of American nature writing. It might, he thought, enjoy a certain popular appeal. Moreover, he imagined that systematic reading of other peoples' nature essays might hasten the day — not too distant, he hoped — when he would feel ready to write his own. In fact, the inspiration came far sooner than he had anticipated. Late that December, while reading a nature essay which particularly pleased him, he suddenly felt the impulse to try his hand at something similar. A draft of "The Day of the Peepers" was completed by New Year's Eve.

His theme was springtime, the most conventional of the nature writer's themes—and one all the more refreshing in the dead of a Connecticut winter. His subject was the tiny tree toad *Hyla crucifer*, whose spring song is one of earth's oldest. And his form was for him a new one, the familiar essay. "*Hyla crucifer* is what the biologists call him," he began, "but to most of us he is simply the Spring Peeper." Here there was none of the breathless intensity of his *Modern Temper* essays, or the pointed polemicism of *Was Europe a Success?* Instead, he sought the cordial familiarity which would characterize his nature writing for more than a decade. From the start he spoke simply, directly, in the first person, and from a perspective distinct from that of the scientist.

It was curious, he observed, that the beginning of spring should conventionally be marked by Easter, rather than by the peeper's songful proclamation that "life is resurgent . . . the earth is alive again." Man's preference for Easter Day—a date determined by calculations understood by only a handful of theologians—rather than the Day of the Peepers was for Krutch only another example of man's longstanding "tendency to prefer abstractions to phenomena." As man has developed, he said, "more and more he thinks in terms of abstractions, generalizations, and laws; less and less participates in the experience of living in a world of sights, sounds, and natural urges."

Thoreau's wisdom—tested in Krutch's own life—had been the preferability of concrete experience to abstract thought. From the latter, as Krutch had painfully seen, came only such bitter fruits as the despair of modernism and the dogmatic excesses of Marxism. In his essay he called upon others to do as he had lately done: to renew a feeling of active membership in the natural world.

He realized that the peeper, like all reptiles and amphibians, "has an aspect which is inscrutable and antediluvian. His thought, like his joy, must be inconceivably different from ours." But for Krutch the fact was "comforting rather than the reverse." It suggested how vast is the "category of living things which is so sharply cut off from everything that does not live at all." Two decades earlier, Krutch had been distressed by his sense of an irreconcilable conflict between "a stable, essentially animal existence and the . . . life of the society which starts out in pursuit of purely human values." But now for him the mere appreciation of life and the knowledge that man shared that

158

adventure with so many other creatures offered sustenance for a once weary spirit.

He concluded this first nature essay in what would henceforth be the distinctive tone of much of his writing in the genre, at once personal and hortatory: "Surely one day a year might be set aside on which to celebrate our ancient loyalties and to remember our ancient origins. And I know of none more suitable for that purpose than the Day of the Peepers. 'Spring is come!,' I say when I hear them and: 'The most ancient of Christs has risen!' But I also add something which, for me at least, is even more important. 'Don't forget,' I whisper to the peepers; 'we are all in this together.'"[1]

Krutch was not generally given to exhilaration upon completing an essay; after so many years writing so many words, composition had long since lost its novelty. But on finishing "The Day of the Peepers" he again experienced something of the thrill he had enjoyed when writing his earliest pieces. The delight remained partly literary; after many years, his devotion to nature had at last found direct expression in his art, and he was prepared to believe he had just written the introduction to an important new chapter of his literary career. But his satisfaction was also philosophical. More explicitly than had been possible in his reviews or even his biographies, he had articulated the principles of a new faith toward which he had long been quietly moving. " 'We are all in this together,'" he had whispered to the peepers. As he recalled some years later, the apostrophe was particularly significant. "It stated for the first time a conviction and an attitude which had come to mean more to me than I realized." It "summed up," he said, " a kind of pantheism which was gradually coming to be an essential part of the faith" through which he overcame the doubt and pessimism of *The Modern Temper.*[2]

After sending the essay to the *Atlantic Monthly*, which had published his earlier pieces on the modern temper, Krutch was disappointed to receive a prompt rejection. A subeditor there—infected perhaps by the modernist attitudes Krutch had done so much to popularize—dismissed "The Day of the Peepers" as "no more than mumblings in Krutch's beard. They are reasonably entertaining mumblings," he wrote in an internal memorandum, "and their style is attractive, but let's not kid ourselves that anything worth saying is involved here."[3] Other journals to which Krutch circulated his essay were no more enthusiastic. But William Sloane, who had edited his two recent biographies, encouraged Krutch to continue his nature writing. During the spring vacation he began a second essay, this one on the *Meloe*, a blister beetle whose life history seemed to illustrate the contingency of existence in the natural universe.

Though the resumption of classes forced him to put aside this second essay, throughout the spring he considered topics for further nature pieces and assembled material for the anthology of nature writing Sloane was to publish. When the 1948 summer vacation began, he and Marcelle took a month-long motoring holiday in the Southwest. In mid-July Krutch was back in Redding, completing "A Question for Meloe" and ten further essays which, along with "The Day of the Peepers," would make up *The Twelve Seasons: A Perpetual Calendar for the Country*. By September, less than nine months after impulsively composing the volume's initial essay, he had delivered to William Sloane the manuscript of his first nature book.

The speed with which he wrote *The Twelve Seasons* is revealing. The remarkable explosion of literary energy he enjoyed that summer of 1948 reflects the renewed confidence as a writer that Krutch had come to feel while preparing *Johnson* and *Thoreau*. After marking time for more than a decade while writing on politics and drama, he had again discovered in preparing his biographies the pleasures of composition and his capacity successfully to undertake major projects. The rapidity with which he completed these essays also suggests that he was not working up a new subject; rather, he was drawing upon a great fund of observation and thought accumulated over a number of years. Perhaps most significant, however, was his sense that he was not so much writing the essays as allowing them to write themselves. "It's still pouring out," he remarked to Marcelle, as one chapter followed another that summer. Never before had writing seemed so easy.

More than any of his previous work — more even than the biographies, which, at least in part, had been undertaken to fulfill his professorial responsibilities — Krutch had written this first dozen nature essays simply because he wanted to. He hoped, of course, that publication would follow. But he was neither straining to fashion some distinctive reputation for himself nor (as in *The Modern Temper*) at-tempting to display the stunning brilliance of his prose and the origi-nality of his thought. He had not taxed himself as a writer, and he would not tax his reader; easy writing would make for equally easy reading. If these essays were to enjoy popular appeal, it would be an appeal far different from his early work, which was as labored as this was casual, as urgent as this was relaxed, and as impressive as this was simply charming.

Having long been an essayist, Krutch was now writing familiar essays for the first time, and he discovered that the form was genuinely his. The emphasis throughout *The Twelve Seasons* was on familiarity, and he addressed his reader with the simplicity and candor with which one might address a friend in conversation. Indeed, like pleas-ant conversation, the essays are loose and associative as they ramble genially from one topic to another. Occasionally the amateur natural-ist, eager to display his accumulated learning, lapses into amiable ped-antry to share some curious fact or other; occasionally the professorial Krutch obtrudes, as in the many literary and philosophical allusions gratuitously scattered throughout the book. But generally he en-deavored to do no more than describe some of the things he had ob-served in nature, and to explain what those observations had meant to him.

The very subjects of the essays are as unextraordinary as their form: the hibernation of the caterpillar; changes in the weather; a cat's playful rolling on a snake; the feeding of birds and squirrels; the ap-pearance of wildflowers; the habits of the katydid and the 'possum; the lushness of summer's verdure and the bleakness of winter's snow cover; and the peeper's spring song. Krutch took obvious pleasure merely in describing the commonplace phenomena he had noted during the previous fifteen years around his Redding home, and *The Twelve Sea-sons* was fundamentally a celebration of that natural universe.

But the further point of his book — never insisted upon, but ev-erywhere apparent — was that those commonplace natural phenom-ena, when thoughtfully and closely observed, can be rich in human meaning as well. "Anxiety and distress, interrupted occasionally by pleasure, is the normal course of man's existence," he remarked. In those commonplace occurrences he had observed at Redding and re-created in his essays, he had discovered that "Joy, interrupted now and again by pain and terminated ultimately by death, seems the normal course of life in Nature."[4]

Rather than arguing abstractly against the despair of modernism beyond which he had passed, Krutch concretely illustrated an alternative to that despair in the contentment he had found in nature. "The privilege of being permitted to be continuously aware that I am indeed alive" was for him the greatest and most inclusive advantage of the life he had been fashioning for himself among the commonplace realities of nature.[5] He would try to extend that privilege to others by presenting the example of his own experience in the new literary life he began with *The Twelve Seasons*.

In the fall Krutch returned to the preparation of his anthology of American nature essays, no longer considering it merely a useful exercise to facilitate his own similar writing. In his choice of selections, and above all in his own lengthy and learned introductory essay, he tried to define "a genre which has, perhaps, not been so clearly recognized as it might be."[6] Judging on strictly literary merit, one might question whether all of the essays deserve to appear under the title *Great American Nature Writing*. But as with Krutch's own nature writing, the intended audience for his anthology was the general reader of less austere standards. The book was not to be read and puzzled over, but to be browsed in and enjoyed. Krutch was content to hope that his volume might provide pleasantly light reading for the urban reader, and that it might introduce that reader to a kind of writing in which Krutch himself hoped to work further.

His commitment to the genre was reinforced in spring 1949, when *The Twelve Seasons* appeared, to generous reviews and gratifying sales. With his first effort at such writing, Krutch even enjoyed another brief appearance on the New York *Times* best-seller list. Having suddenly demonstrated the popular appeal of his nature writing, he found that editors who had rejected his essays a year ago were now eager to publish them. Further pieces began to appear in periodicals ranging from the *American Scholar* and *Virginia Quarterly Review* to *Mademoiselle* and *House Beautiful*. The very range bespeaks the breadth of appeal his essays enjoyed. These further reflections on the natural world of rural Connecticut were collected in 1953 as *The Best of Two Worlds*.

Like those in *The Twelve Seasons*, these later essays are rooted in the commonplace experiences any alert person might enjoy while living in the midst of nature. Again Krutch celebrated the familiar, rather than the exotic: spiders, weeds, snowstorms, and dozens of his animal friends, wild and domestic. The book radiates the quiet contentment he felt in nature. With neither belligerence nor shame, he remarked: "I always feel more serene after a conversation with a few friendly animals than I do after an evening with even the most brilliant of my human acquaintances."[7] That aside was characteristic of the cordial geniality which informed his nature writing. He rambled unhurriedly and unselfconsciously from one topic to another, from describing something he had seen, to sharing what he had learned, to recording what he had thought. In this second group of New England essays, his descriptions of natural phenomena were even more vivid than in the first. Capturing in words the sights he delighted in, he seemed often content merely to re-create in prose that greater creation on whose variety he feasted.

But he was also seeking "contemplative participation" in that natural universe, and in these further essays he became even more insistently and explicitly philosophical. "All of those nature writers who stem ultimately from Thoreau are concerned not only with the aesthetic and hedonistic aspects of the love of nature, but also with what can only be called its moral aspect," he remarked. "Nature writing . . . raises the question of the effect which forgetting that he is alive may have on man and his society." In his meditative asides, the wisdom of the moralist grew unobtrusively from the experiences of the naturalist: "What seems to me so terribly, perhaps fatally, wrong with the present stage in the evolution of the human spirit is not its tendency to go beyond a mere 'life in nature,' but its tendency to break completely the connection which it cannot break without cutting off its roots; without forgetting with desperate consequences that the human arises out of the natural and must always remain to some extent conditioned by it."[8]

Having been such a promising but unhappy student of modernism at the beginning of his career, Krutch in Redding had enrolled himself as a pupil in nature's school. After nearly twenty years there, Krutch could say of the little universe around his Redding house that he knew "it better than I have ever known any other place on earth." His essays testified to that knowledge, as well as to his feeling that "It is here and here only that I ever really feel 'at home.'"[9] But even as he was writing his accounts of life amid the natural phenomena of New England, he realized that elsewhere lay a world of nature far different from that so comfortably familiar in Redding—a world whose acquaintance he might profitably make. With the prospect of another sabbatical year from Columbia, he decided to put himself to school once again, this time in the desert of the American Southwest.

The choice was hardly surprising. Krutch had first been smitten by the desert more than a decade before, and he had returned there several times since. Marcelle, who had first lured Krutch from Greenwich Village to Cornwall in 1925, had also convinced him to spend part of his first summer vacation from Columbia in the west. Feeling that there was world enough for him in Redding, he was reluctant to go. But in late June 1938, as they drove south from Colorado toward the deserts of New Mexico, Krutch found "a new, undreamed of world."[10] As he recalled later, he felt "a sudden lifting of the heart" in discovering "the combination of brilliant sun and high, thin, dry air with a seemingly limitless expanse of sky and earth."[11]

For three successive years following, until the war interrupted their travels, they returned each summer, crisscrossing New Mexico, Arizona, southern Colorado and Utah, venturing as far south as the Mexican border and as far west as California's Mojave Desert. His delight in the more obvious spectacles of the area, the great vistas and the dramatic buttes and canyons, was soon complemented by his discovery of plants and animals nowhere to be found in New England. Some of those plants the Krutches took back to Redding, to cultivate in their home. As they nurtured their cactuses throughout the war, they impatiently awaited the opportunity to return to the desert. By 1948 they had resumed their visits and discovered Tucson, where two years later they would spend their sabbatical.

For the Krutches, as for many others, the most immediate attraction of the Southwest was its climate. Approaching sixty, Krutch
was finding the New England winters less compatible with his never
robust health; he hoped in the desert to find freedom from the
chronic colds and 'flus of the East. Moreover, he looked forward to
extending in a new environment the nature study he had been pursuing and writing about in Redding. During his earlier visits he had
been fascinated by the plants and animals of the desert; but his had
been the tourist's fascination with the exotic. He hoped that, as he
began studying what he had been content earlier merely to observe,
the novelty of the strange and mysterious would yield to the more
powerful charm of the known and familiar. Above all, he hoped he
might find in the desert the same literary inspiration he had found so
abundantly in rural Connecticut.

After house-sitting for the summer in a spacious home ten miles
north of Tucson, in the middle of the desert, the Krutches were invited to spend the remainder of their year in one of two guest houses
behind the home of Mrs. Helen d'Autremont, the widow of a former
state senator and herself a prominent Tucson civic leader and philan-
thropist. The other cottage was occupied by the composer Elliott
Carter and his wife, and the Krutches enjoyed their company, as well
as that of other Tucsonians they met through Mrs. d'Autremont.
But, as in Redding, the companionship Krutch valued most, apart
from Marcelle's, was that of nature. He reveled in the society of the
plants and animals surrounding his new desert home.

Each day seemed an adventure. In the morning as he awakened
and heard some unfamiliar birdsong, he was happy for the reminder
that he was in a new land. In the distance, visible from the window of
his cottage, the Catalina Mountains loomed dramatically. All around
were the characteristic flora of the Lower Sonoran Desert: prickly
pear, creosote, ocotillo, paloverde, mesquite, and the giant saguaro
cactus, with its awesome and twisting columns. New animal friends
were readily found: lizards, scorpions, horned toads, coyotes, taran-
tulas, jack rabbits, and roadrunners. Though a stranger in Tucson,
Krutch hardly lacked company.

Invigorated by the brilliant flood of sun pouring through the
dry southwestern air, he set off almost daily on foot or by car to mar-

vel at the ways in which so much plant and animal life sustained itself in the forbidding desert environment. The adventure of life, he discovered, was even more varied, even more marvelous than he had imagined. He began keeping a bird list and was proud when it grew to well over a hundred different species, many of them previously unfamiliar. Even the inanimate stars, so vivid in the clear, wide skies, proved fascinating; each evening, just after sunset, he and Marcelle went out to watch them as they one by one appeared.

Krutch, however, was not satisfied by the mere spectacle of nature. Though his were perhaps unconventional interests for a professor of English, he was in fact devoting his sabbatical to research and a kind of scholarship. He puzzled over the phenomena he observed: how the Sonoran spadefoot toad could live in a world largely without water; how tadpoles matured into toads in the brief time that puddles lasted there; how *Dipodomys*, the desert mouse that never drinks, makes water for himself from the starchy carbohydrates he eats; and why bats, when leaving a cave at dusk, invariably fly in a counterclockwise spiral. Periodically he consulted books and journals in the nearby University of Arizona library. If his curiosity remained unsatisfied, he put his questions to biologists there or wrote to other specialists to whom he was referred. To his study of the desert he brought the same scholarly thoroughness he had recently brought to his biographies of Johnson and Thoreau.

The ultimate goal of his sabbatical in Tucson was, however, neither recreational nor educational. It was, of course, literary. Encouraged by the success of *The Twelve Seasons*, he had agreed to do another nature book for William Sloane. In all of his desert explorations and researches he was looking, as he wrote Mark Van Doren, for "a usable emotional attitude." He was not long in finding it. Shortly after he arrived, he was writing the first of the sixteen essays which were published as *The Desert Year* (1952). Like the essays he had written in Redding, these flowed with remarkable ease; and he wrote Van Doren, "I find more satisfaction in writing this sort of thing than in almost any sort of writing I have tried."[12]

Addressing, one imagines, Eastern colleagues and friends who found his passion for the desert curious, Krutch's first essay explained "Why I Came." The appeal of the desert, he acknowledged, was "not

166

the appeal of things universally attractive. . . . Its beauty is no easy one. It suggests patience and struggle and endurance. It is courageous and happy, not easy and luxurious. In the brightest of its sandstone canyons, even in the brightest colors of its brief spring flowers, there is something austere." That austerity, like Johnson's pessimism, corresponded to something in Krutch's own spirit. But the desert, like Johnson, had an enormous zest for living. "This seemingly difficult land," he wrote, "nevertheless flourishes vigorously and lives joyously." Everywhere he found "some kind of gladness," and *The Desert Year* is, in part, a record of the gladness it inspired in him.[13]

The quantitatively greater part of the book is devoted to a description not of what Krutch felt, but of what he did and saw. In discussing such topics as the virtue of the adaptability desert life displays, the meaning of owning land, the ways in which deserts (like mountaintops) are conducive to meditation, the pleasures of solitude, or the impulse which led him to rescue a bat from a swimming pool, Krutch occasionally indulged in philosophical asides. But in his first nature writing from the desert he was less reflective and more narrowly descriptive than he would later be.

For Krutch, and doubtless for most of his intended readers, the commonplace phenomena of the desert were rather less commonplace than those of New England, so much of his book is devoted to a narrative of what it was like to live in and discover that strange and unaccustomed world. Like Adam, Krutch goes about naming the plants and animals; like a teacher, he patiently explains the curiosities he has observed and come to understand; like a travel writer, he extols the charms of the area — giving others the vicarious experiences of his desert year, and suggesting that they might well enjoy one of their own. In short, he composed a volume which, if not profound, is consistently engaging. It was not so much profundity which Krutch was now seeking as the conversational engagement of a man with his fellows.

By the time he returned to Columbia in September 1951, he had "stayed in a strange place long enough to observe the process by which the strange is transformed into the familiar."[14] But by then Krutch had come to desire not merely familiarity with the place, but intimacy. As he left Tucson, he knew he would soon return.

᠅ Shortly before their return to New York, Mrs. d'Autremont had offered the Krutches five acres near her home on which to build a house for themselves. That offer, combined with happy memories of their desert year and the suggestion that Krutch's recent freedom from illness might be attributable to the Arizona climate, sealed their resolve that the coming year would be their last in the East.

After more than twenty-five years of drama reviewing, regular, obligatory attendance at the theater was wearisome, rather than exciting. Krutch would have no regrets about placing a continent between himself and Broadway. Nor was he so attached to teaching that he would greatly miss it. Even before beginning his sabbatical, he had considered early retirement from Columbia. He had accepted his position there fourteen years earlier, when his literary career had apparently reached a dead end. Now, with the successes of his biographies and his more recent nature writing, that career seemed at last to have been resuscitated. But the renewal of his literary ambitions coincided with an increase in his academic responsibilities. With the great influx of students (especially graduate students) after the war, his classes were larger than ever, and his desk was piled high with dissertations, supervised by his colleagues, which he was expected to read. Because the leisure he had valued in the academic life had abruptly disappeared, he concluded, none too regretfully, that to continue his writing he must abandon his teaching.

As he gave notice to the *Nation* and to Columbia, Krutch thought of himself less as a man prematurely retiring at fifty-seven than as a man belatedly resuming the full-time literary career he had suspended in 1937. Ever since the Depression, financial considerations had not been far from Krutch's mind; he knew how elusive the rewards of a writer's life could be. But he was again optimistic about his career, and he hoped that his writing in Tucson would bring in at least as much income as had his teaching and reviewing. Even as he left New York in June 1952, he had two major projects in mind: a book reconsidering, twenty-five years later, the conclusions of *The Modern Temper*, and a series of lectures on modern drama to be delivered that fall at Cornell. Because he was hopeful, rather than confident, of his prospects, instead of making the irrevocable commitment of retirement, he requested and received merely another year's leave from Columbia and the *Nation*. He was reassured to know that he would be able to return if, by the next fall, his hopes seemed unlikely of fulfillment. The arrangement had the further advantage of allowing him to avoid the retirement dinners and farewell parties he was far from eager to attend.

Moving is, of course, a time for dispossession. The Krutches were saddened to sell the Redding home where, for twenty years, they had together enjoyed the happiness that had sustained them even when Krutch's career brought little. With rather less regret Krutch also sold the library he had accumulated during years of reviewing and teaching, retaining for shipment to Tucson mostly books concerning the eighteenth century and, of course, nature.

For the Krutches, however, the process of dispossession that spring of 1952 was more complete than they had intended. As Marcelle burned some trash behind the house, she accidentally set ablaze a disused chicken coop in which they had stored cartons of personal papers, manuscripts, photographs, and correspondence since renting the house in 1950. Though the fire was confined to the chicken coop, all its contents were lost. The Krutches, however, were looking ahead to their new life, rather than behind to the old.

In May, Krutch wrote—with weariness and relief—his last drama review for the *Nation*, describing a work "not thoughtful enough to be a play of social significance, not simple enough to be a first-class melodrama."[15] Thus he concluded his quarter-century of reviewing not with a grand summing-up or nostalgic farewell, but merely with another matter-of-fact review of yet another uninspiring play. His departure from Columbia was equally unceremonious. Still insisting that he might return a year later, he gave his final lectures, marked his last blue books, and was gone.

Shortly after his arrival in Tucson, however, he received news which reassured him that he would not need to return. Some months earlier he had applied to the Bollingen Foundation for a three-year grant to assist him "in connection with the writing of an extended philosophical essay surveying the present attitudes of western man toward his nature, powers and destiny"—in fact, his review of the modern temper.[16] With word that the grant had been awarded, and with the appearance of enthusiastic reviews of his second nature book, *The Desert Year*, he was relieved to be able to tell Columbia and the *Nation* that he would not be returning.

⁓ The intellectual distance which separated the Krutch of the early fifties from the young modernist of the late twenties would have been apparent to the reader who had followed him attentively from *The Modern Temper* through his books on art, his essays on Communism, his biographies, and most recently his writing on nature. But the evidence of Krutch's odyssey was largely implicit in those works; explicit formulations of his new position were generally buried in a sentence or two here, a paragraph there. Since his eloquent exposition of the modern temper, a temper he had presented as his own, he had yet to disavow the modernism with which many still associated him.

He arrived in Tucson in the summer of 1952, precisely twenty-five years after his first "Modern Temper" essay appeared. As he settled into his new life, it seemed appropriate formally to announce the renunciation of his earlier skepticism and to express his renewed appreciation for human capacities and values he now felt he had been too ready to dismiss. While supervising the clearing of desert brush for the construction of his new home, he was also working on two books which represent a kind of intellectual ground-clearing. *"Modernism" in Modern Drama* and *The Measure of Man* look both back and ahead: back, in reconsidering the modernism he had done so much to popularize and now had come to reject; ahead, in stating some of the convictions he would be arguing in the social criticism which, with his nature writing, would constitute most of his future literary effort.

Several hundred students and teachers crowded into the first of Krutch's lectures at Cornell in October 1952, doubtless with clear expectations of what the veteran drama critic, Columbia English professor, and author of *The Modern Temper* might have to say about "'Modernism' in Modern Drama." They were promptly disabused of their expectations. He would not, Krutch announced, concern himself with "the greatness or the defects of the modern drama considered as a contribution to world literature." Instead, he would trace in the plays he discussed "the development of ideas that have affected and continue to affect most of us very profoundly."[17] His sympathy for those ideas was far less than many may have expected.

In the foreword to the published lectures, Krutch explained that he had written "as a moralist, not as a critic." Behind his remarks lay something of the spirit of Johnson's criticism, which Krutch had remarked approvingly mingled "moral, social or even merely prudential considerations with aesthetic ones."[18] For Krutch now, criticism of literature was part of the more general criticism of life to which he would presently be turning. As he explained: "My purpose is frankly polemic. I had and I have an axe to grind. I seek to persuade my readers that much of what others have presented to them as the convictions necessary to anyone who wished to believe himself 'modern' is actually incompatible with any good life as the good life has generally been conceived of during many centuries before the nineteenth."[19] The "others" is perhaps slightly disingenuous; Krutch had himself been a persuasive spokesman for the very attitude he was now attacking. *"Modernism" in Modern Drama* marked the beginning of his public recantation.

"The modern drama," Krutch asserted, "is . . . open to the same charge that may be made against modern literature as a whole. Its tendency has been to undermine the foundations of post-Renaissance civilization." Among the premises of that civilization, he said, were the beliefs that man is a creature capable of dignity; that life in this world (not some future world) is worth living; and that life may be most fruitfully led by the light of human reason. To the self-consciously "modern" thinker, however, such traditional beliefs were self-evidently bankrupt. Past and present were discontinuous. As Krutch knew from his own experience, "to be 'modern'" was to see oneself as "in many important ways different from any one who ever lived before."[20]

The tendency of modern drama, he said, "has been in the direction of realism, of sociological concern, of dissonant sonorities, of an obsession with irreconcilable conflicts, and, therefore, in the direction of despair." Beginning with the plays of Ibsen, he surveyed the symptoms of the "subtle disease" of modernism.[21] Denying the absolutes of wisdom or morality, Ibsen, Krutch said, satisfied himself with an "all-inclusive relativity" which "cuts the ground out from

under one's feet [and] digs a chasm into which it is possible to fall."
With Strindberg, however, the possibility becomes reality. Man is
seen as fundamentally irrational, a helpless victim of conflicting desires, and life is "a hell of conflict and frustration."[22] With Chekhov,
the very form of the drama reflects the dreariness of the human life it
portrays, "a flat, melancholy, and featureless plain." In Pirandello,
Krutch found the most inclusive denial of all: the denial of that most
basic human attribute, a consistent character and personality. Even
Shaw, so apparently optimistic and the object of Krutch's early adula-
tion, seemed to Krutch to share the modern despair; his utopian vision (in *Back to Methuselah*) of a radically changed human nature and
society remained for Krutch "both unrecognizable by, and rather du-
biously attractive to, those of us who are still dominated by old-
fashioned human nature."[23]

For Krutch, the ideas of the leading modern playwrights led,
like modernism generally, "not to a bright future, but to something
like intellectual and moral paralysis." "Soberly to acquiesce in any one
of these negations is to surrender a premise upon which most men at
most times have relied," he said. "To acquiesce in all of them is to enter a new and bewildering world which has lost almost completely its
familiar shape."[24] In *The Modern Temper* Krutch had thus acquiesced,
almost gladly. Once modernism's sympathetic expositor, he was now,
as a moralist, its implacable foe.

The modern drama was in fact less the subject of than the text
for his lectures. Those Messenger Lectures on the Evolution of Civilization had been established at Cornell "for the special purpose of raising the moral standards of our political, business and social life." The
young writer who twenty-five years ago had been so eager "to be
'modern'" and to associate himself with the advanced thought of the
day would hardly have found such a charge congenial. Now, however, the endowment's purpose corresponded closely to his own. He
was unwilling to see man as the modernists did, as a passive, despairing victim of uncontrollable forces. He now doubted the very doubt
in which he had earlier gloried. "Old-fashioned human nature" still
dominated him; notwithstanding the negations of modernism, he
believed that man was responsible for his actions, that he had dignity,
and that, guided by reason and common sense, he could fashion for

himself a life worth living. When he returned to Tucson from Ithaca, he began work on a book which would elaborate on those beliefs.

❧ During his sabbatical in Tucson, Krutch had written that "no man in the middle of a desert or on top of a mountain ever fell victim to the delusion that he himself was nothing but the product of social forces. . . . No such man . . . ever thought anything except that consciousness was the grandest of all facts and that no good life for either the individual or the group was possible on any other assumption."[25] In his Cornell lectures he had pointed to Freud, Marx, and Darwin as three determinists whose writings had popularized that delusion, and had thus undermined man's self-confidence by apparently stripping him of the power to control his own destiny. Afterward, back in the middle of the desert, he examined some assumptions of the determinist ideas which lay behind the spiritual paralysis of modernism, offering in its place his own more affirmative estimate of *The Measure of Man.*

The book grew from a suggestion by Hiram Haydn, then an editor at Bobbs-Merrill, that Krutch consider the change in the contemporary intellectual climate since the publication of *The Modern Temper.* It was still, Krutch found, "an Age of Anxiety" in which man was torn by "the contradictions inevitably incident to a life in two irreconcilable worlds — the world of intimate experience and that world of abstract convictions in which the validity of intimate experience is categorically denied."[26] The former was of course the humanist's world of poetry, mythology, and religion, whose passing Krutch had so eloquently lamented in *The Modern Temper;* the latter was the world of science, whose advent he had gloomily bemoaned.

But if Krutch still recognized the tension between value and fact, he was no longer willing to grant, as he had earlier, that "the universe with which science deals is the real universe."[27] In particular, he was unwilling to concede that the evidences of the social sciences, whose findings most closely touch man's understanding of himself, were the only ones worthy of credit. Mustering some of the same polemical vigor that he had just used in attacking the modernism of modern drama, he addressed himself to the determinism of contemporary social thought, proposing that the despair he had earlier assumed to be inevitable to any thoughtful man was in fact a consequence of man's not having been thoughtful enough.

It would not be unreasonable, he said, to imagine "that the Grand Strategy of nineteenth-century thought had as its aim the destruction of man's former belief in his own autonomy." As popularly understood, Darwinism explained man's evolution by "natural selection, operating with mechanical inevitability." Marxism insisted that man was merely a product of society "which is, in its turn, inevitably produced by the dialectic processes of matter." Freudianism reduced "what we call our unique self" to "the result of the way in which the fixed 'drives' of human nature have been modified by the things which have happened to us."[28] Surveying a variety of popular sources —including public statements of social scientists, *New Yorker* cartoons, and *Walden Two*, the novel by the Harvard behaviorist B.F. Skinner—he illustrated the extent to which those deterministic assumptions were current in contemporary thought.

Although Krutch recognized that man was partly a product of forces beyond his control, he resisted a notion which he felt enjoyed increasingly widespread and uncritical acceptance: that if man is partly a product of such forces, he is nothing but a creature whose life is absolutely determined, predictable, and controllable.

The social sciences, he insisted, took at best a partial measure of man. "The methods employed for the study of man," he said, "have been for the most part those originally devised for the study of machines or the study of rats, and are capable, therefore, of detecting and measuring only those characteristics which the three have in common." Human consciousness may not lend itself to quantification in the laboratory or examination by questionnaire, but the commonsense evidence of experience shows it to be "the one thing which incontrovertably *is*," Krutch insisted. "To refuse to concern ourselves with it is to make the most monstrous error that could possibly be made."[29]

Striving to be scientific, the social sciences concentrate on the predictability of masses and largely ignore the randomness of individuals. The statistics with which social scientists are preoccupied may describe fairly the behavior of the group, but implicitly they deny the freedom of the individual. Even the physicist, Krutch pointed out, had rejected the concept of strict determinism, had recognized that

174

the unpredictable and the indeterminate are part of physical reality, and had acknowledged "that statistical results are *merely* statistical, and that no fully determining laws are operating."[30] The mind of man is no less mysterious than the physical universe, but many sociologists seem to deny to man the "free will" physicists had granted the atom.

Studiously blind to judgments of value and confident in the adequacy of their statistics, the social sciences gave support to a moral relativism which assumes that "right" behavior is "normal" behavior, when "normal" has come to mean simply "average." "Many 'advanced thinkers,'" he went on, clearly excluding himself, assume "that the concept represented in the word 'ought' is radically meaningless."[31] For Krutch, however, man's ability freely to choose one thing over another and man's need to create and act upon values were two of his distinctly human characteristics.

The social scientists implicitly and often explicitly suggested that man is a machine, determined in his behavior and lacking the consciousness by the exercise of which he might make free choices. That suggestion was both a symptom and a contributory cause of modernism's more general denial of human dignity, and it led Krutch to ask, "What are the *minimal* powers and characteristics one would have to possess to be worthy of the designation Man?" He continued, "Grant us only that what we call 'reasoning' is not always rationalization; that consciousness can sometimes be more than merely an epiphenomenon accompanying behavior; that 'value judgments,' even if never more than 'tastes' or 'preferences,' are nevertheless not absolutely and 'nothing but' what we have been conditioned to accept — grant us this and those minimal concessions will free us from the dilemma in which the refusal to make them has placed us." Such beliefs in the reality of what he spoke of as "Minimal Man" were, Krutch insisted, "levers with which, once more, we can move our world."[32]

Twenty-five years earlier, in *The Modern Temper*, Krutch had announced the advent of "not a changed world but a new one" — a world where science had so thoroughly undermined the premises of humanistic thought that "the values which [man] thought established have been swept away along with the rules by which he thought they might be attained."[33] Now, however, he insisted that "Belief in the reality of values and in man's ability to recognize or to establish them is the *sine qua non* for any world which is to remain what has previously been thought of as human."[34] He was convinced that such belief was again possible, if man would critically examine the doctrines of a paralyzing determinism and use the levers of a recognition of man's minimal capacities to move his world of thought.

For Krutch, the only alternative to the passive acceptance of modern despair was the deliberate resumption of "that Moral Discourse which has gone on in Western Civilization uninterruptedly for at least three thousand years." He was not suggesting "that we must return to theology, to simple Christian belief, or to anything else"; nor was he suggesting that renewed belief in the reality of consciousness, values, and free will were in themselves sufficient. He recognized that "intelligence and knowledge" were also necessary, "and knowledge includes much of what we know about science and technology." But respect for that knowledge did not preclude a similar respect for the value-making function of man about which science had little constructive to say. The Moral Discourse was, in its way, as real as science; it alone could "prevent our understanding of the meaning of human life from degenerating into the 'nothing but' to which all of the sciences, because of the simplicity of their conceptions and the crudity of their instruments, tend to reduce it."[35]

His purpose in *The Measure of Man*, Krutch said, had been "to raise doubts and reveal paradoxes"[36]; however, the object of that skeptical inquiry was not now (as in *The Modern Temper*) the meaning of life itself, but those scientific notions which had undermined that meaning. The later book is in many ways the obverse of the earlier. While the one had set out to portray and confirm the doubts of "advanced thinkers" with whom Krutch was then eager to associate himself, the other endeavored to repudiate the bases of that doubt and to reinforce the self-confidence of those people who, like Krutch himself, were "still dominated by old-fashioned human nature."

In a contribution during the early 1950s to the nationally broadcast CBS series, "This I Believe," Krutch recalled his early writing.

> I thought I was an intellectual because of the number of things I did not believe. Only very slowly did I come to realize that what was really characteristic of myself and my age was not that we did not believe

anything but that we believed very firmly in a number of things which are not really so. We believed, for example, in the exclusive importance of the material, the measurable, and the controllable. We had no doubts about 'what science proves' and we took it for granted that whatever science did not prove was certainly false. . . . The trouble was not that we were skeptical but that we were not skeptical enough.[37]

In *The Measure of Man* he offered his mature reconsideration of that earlier skepticism.

In characterizing the premises of social scientific thought and in describing the current intellectual climate, Krutch may well have exaggerated the strength of deterministic and mechanistic theories of man and life. But he was writing less as an intellectual historian than as a concerned amateur student of contemporary life and thought. His inquiry partook of the spirit of the age of Johnson, when, as he had written a decade earlier, "the assumption is that truth can most often be arrived at not, as the Middle Ages believed, by metaphysical argument and not, as we profess to hold, by scientific method, but by the application of 'common sense.' " In *The Measure of Man* Krutch had applied such common sense to some of those debilitating modernist attitudes he had earlier accepted.

Clearing the ground of the doctrine of "forces," he had tried to show that the human being can, at least to some extent, enjoy freedom, rationality, autonomy, and a sense of purpose. The book was a brief for the reality of man's spirituality, and for the possibility of that individualism of which its author had written as an undergraduate: "Real success or failure comes only from within and society cannot impress it from without. Only the individualist succeeds for only self-realization is success." During the twenty-five years since writing *The Modern Temper*, Krutch had been resisting the forces of intellectual fashion and social conformity and had achieved that "real success" in his life.

The Measure of Man was, of course, another contribution to that debate between science and the humanities which had erupted in the nineteenth century, the same era to which Krutch traced the beginnings of modern determinist thought. In barest outline, much that he said about human nature had been said before—and often more fully and dogmatically. It is fair to remark that his notion of Minimal Man was very minimal indeed; the Moral Discourse whose renewal he urged was characterized more by its form (the enterprise of seeking values) than by its substance (the assertion of specific values which could be recognized as, in some absolute sense, true.) Rather than rushing to embrace theology or mysticism, Krutch stood squarely on humanist grounds. If he lacked the certainty of conviction which would allow him dogmatically to assert a system of values as compelling as the value-free relativism he endeavored to refute, he had at least taken his argument as far as he honestly could.

The very modesty of its assertion was in fact one of the attractions of the book. His was a gallant attempt to defend truths so simple and fundamental as to be easily overlooked. He had taken abstract ideas and had translated them, through his clear argument and his concise and forceful prose, into terms comprehensible to those intelligent laymen like himself for whom he was now writing. True, celebration of common sense is a distinctly less promising subject for stunning literary success than the celebration of despair which had brought Krutch his early fame; but in the early 1950s, a Depression and a World War after *The Modern Temper*, his more modest effort corresponded to the mood of the nation.

When it was published in spring 1954, *The Measure of Man* received extensive and enthusiastic reviews. Granville Hicks, who had earlier described *The Modern Temper* as "one of the crucial documents" of the 1920s, now praised Krutch's "carefully reasoned, carefully qualified statement of a kind of humanism that I find admirable."[39] The great success of Krutch's first extended exercise in social criticism encouraged him to write further in the same vein. His commitment to this new literary vocation was confirmed later that year, when the jurors for the 1954 National Book Award described *The Measure of Man* as "a courageous statement of the humanist position, and an inquiry into fundamentals at a moment when the world is distracted by superficialities," awarding it the prize for nonfiction. A New York *Times* editorial lavishly praised the book and described the award as "particularly gratifying."[40]

In January 1955, Krutch traveled from Tucson to New York to

collect his gold medal. (William Faulkner and Wallace Stevens received the awards for fiction and poetry.) The visit, however, was brief and unsentimental. He was eager to return to the desert, to that communion with nature which in large measure had brought him beyond modernism to the modest but sufficient faith he now enjoyed. And he looked forward to the completion of *The Great Chain of Life*, the book which most clearly demonstrated how his understanding of nature had led him to his new understanding of the measure of man.

8.

🎵 THE HAPPIEST YEARS

"At some time in his experience," Krutch wrote around the time he decided to leave the East, "every man should rub shoulders with his fellows; experience the excitement of a metropolis' nervous activity; live close to the great, the distinguished, the famous, and the merely notorious—if for no other reason than because only so can he learn properly to discount them." During more than thirty-five years in and around New York, Krutch had experienced that excitement and had rubbed shoulders with the intellectuals whose admiration he had once coveted. By the end he, too, had discounted them.

"Urbanity," he continued, "seems to be literally that: something impossible to acquire except in cities." In his early writing—his dispatches from Dayton, his biography of Poe, and the "distinctly high-brow" *Modern Temper*—he had proudly announced his own urbanity. "But," he added in the early 1950s, "one need not, and one should not, I think, spend a lifetime in getting it, for in that respect, as in many others, the city pays a diminishing return."[1] Though he valued the city's literary and academic opportunities, he had recognized during the thirties and forties that life in New York was paying him that return. Moreover, he had come to feel that the intellectual urbanity he had sought was hardly an absolute good.

Even while displaying his new sophistication, Krutch had shown, in his early writing, vestiges of a temperament shaped in Knoxville. His sympathy for the experiments of modern art was never complete. Even as he expounded the principles of modernism, he remained nostalgic for the old truths it denied. Later, when the Marxists celebrated the prospects of a radically changed future, he preferred the comforts of a known past. Though he had lived in the Village, he had never been of it, remaining intractably the child of his East Tennessee hometown.

In May 1952, Krutch drove from New York to Tucson by way of Knoxville. In fact, he stopped there to visit his brother Charles. But the return to Knoxville was appropriate. After his emigration to New York and his condescension in the *Nation* to his native state, after his studied modernism and his flirtation with the intellectual avant-garde, after his disillusion with many of the people and ideas gathered in the metropolis, he was at last coming home to resume — in Arizona, if not in Tennessee — the kind of life he had been so eager to escape nearly forty years before.

At nearly sixty, Krutch looked forward to making a new life in Tucson. He sought there not only the desert's proximity and a warm, dry, and healthful climate. He looked as well for a climate of life and thought which would be more congenial than New York's and which in many ways resembled Knoxville's. Though twice the size of Krutch's boyhood Knoxville, Tucson in 1952 was still essentially a small town whose largely middle-class residents lived comfortably by those bourgeois values of Krutch's own family. Like Knoxville, it was the seat of the state university. But, compared with New York and many lesser cities, it was an artistic and intellectual backwater. The restaurants, lectures, theaters, the concentration of distinguished writers and thinkers — all the activity of the metropolis was almost wholly absent. Sated by his years in New York, Krutch felt no sense of deprivation; indeed, he was happy to exchange the cultural amenities of the big city for the simpler human pleasures he had failed to find there. Many aspects of the kind of life he had known in Knoxville seemed once again attractive, and he was returning to it not merely with a new tolerance, but even with a new appreciation.

During his sabbatical year in Tucson, Krutch had discovered not only the desert but also the virtue of those simple pleasures of life in a small middle-class town which were, in their way, as bracing as the Arizona sun. If he found few people there as brilliant, learned, or famous as his literary and academic colleagues in New York, neither did he find the pretensions, the pettiness, or the intellectual arrogance from which he had fled to a nearly reclusive life in Redding. In Tucson he felt less apologetic in preferring the works of nature to those of man, less uneasy about his impatience with the tortured artistic obscurity that others saw as beauty, and less peculiar in believing that moral questions and old-fashioned values were still important. Conventional tastes and ideas were here not rejected simply for their currency; the popular was not automatically dismissed as the inferior. If the average Tucsonian was not in the vanguard of contemporary thought, neither was he infected by the paralyzing skepticism — or its contrary, the self-assured dogmatism — that Krutch had found so common in New York. If they were not deeply and systematically reflective, they nonetheless respected that common sense Krutch himself had come to value.

By contrast with the intense professionalism of New York, the amateur spirit which informed so much of the intellectual and cultural life of Tucson was also refreshing. His professional life having brought him little satisfaction, Krutch in Redding had been sustained by his private life as an amateur naturalist. He had brought no certified expertise to his early nature writing, not would he to his later social criticism. But in Tucson the sincere effort of the amateur was honored along with the distinguished achievement of the expert, and his writing there bespeaks Krutch's comfort in his new environment. The style as well as much of the substance of Krutch's later essays and books resembles that amiable small-town discourse where people plainly and candidly share their ideas with one another, where apparently trivial events and incidental information become the subject of pleasant, often illuminating, conversations.

His writing had ceased to strive for effects. In his life he had also ceased straining, and at last he was living authentically. No elaborate psychosomatic theory is required to see a connection between emotional distress and physical illness. The uneasiness Krutch felt with his New York career had its counterpart in a chronic malaise. It was hardly coincidental — and a result of something more than the Arizona climate — that Krutch in Tucson enjoyed more consistently good health than he had since his youth in Knoxville.

When he was starting out as a writer in 1920, Krutch had installed on the desk in his Greenwich Village apartment a bronze bust of Voltaire. In Tucson, nature, rather than art, was his inspiration. His desk in the house which he designed for himself faced out upon a desert scene whose austere beauty and courageous affirmation of life subtly informed many of the essays and books he wrote there. From the window of his study he looked out across several miles of desert vegetation toward the rugged, occasionally snow-capped Catalina Mountains. The living room, with its long, high wall of windows, framed the same impressive scene. From the living room a door opened onto a small terrace, the terrace led to a modest garden of desert plants, and the garden melted into the untouched desert beyond. He had designed his modest, functional surburban bungalow to blend into, rather than be separated from, its surroundings, and to help him achieve intimacy with nature.

From the time he moved into his new home in November 1952, Krutch settled into the routine he followed contentedly throughout his years there. Arising early, he spent an hour or so watering the shrubs and trees he had planted around his house, or greeting the birds and desert animals he lured to his terrace with sugar water and other attractions. Then he closeted himself in his cluttered study for several hours at the typewriter. By lunchtime he would emerge with the fruits of his morning's labors and read to Marcelle what he had written. Afternoons he spent reading under a paloverde tree behind the house, going the few miles to the University of Arizona library to consult a book or journal (often on a scientific topic), or, most frequently, exploring the nearby desert. After dinner, and perhaps a bit more reading in preparation for the next day's writing, he was ready for bed by ten. His was a daylight world, and he was eager to be up early again to enjoy the desert, the mountains, and his nonhuman visitors as they revealed themselves anew.

To the end, the desert and its flora and fauna held a greater fascination for Krutch than any other place, work of art, or person (save only Marcelle) ever had. Novelty gave way to familiarity; familiarity, to devotion. The desert became the temple where the former agnostic, now a pantheist, went to worship. Like a conscientious theologian, he studied his god, keeping lists of its various manifestations in birds, plants, and animals. He recorded in his journal whatever phenomena, ordinary and unusual, he had witnessed; he consulted learned scientific treatises; and he discussed vexed topics with specialists.

He made pilgrimages as well—but these were not distant, for shrines were everywhere. Just a few yards from his home were plants and animals to which he was devoted, and several miles of driving would take him to various other parts of the desert where still more wonders could be found. In less than an hour's drive he could be ascending Mount Lemmon; passing from the characteristic vegetation and animal life of the desert to that of Canada, he also had at hand a natural world different from, but hardly less splendid than, that on the desert floor.

Enjoying sunshine nearly every day, and invigorated by the dry heat of the desert, he became again at sixty an avid walker. With his large straw hat, his baggy trousers, and a shirttail flapping behind him, he traveled countless miles of untrod desert land, always careful not to step upon some small plant struggling to make a life for itself there. Often accompanied by Marcelle and occasionally by friends, he paused frequently to identify and discuss the curiosities he encountered. He was generous with his considerable knowledge of the desert, but sparing of pantheistic effusions. His meditations on the significance of what he saw were reserved for solitary contemplation, and for his nature writing.

Rambling through the desert, Krutch enjoyed not only a quiet spiritual nourishment but also recreation after a busy morning of writing. For him, the desert was an ample theater and concert hall; after a few hours out of doors, he felt little need of further entertainment. Only reluctantly did he eventually admit a television to his home—and even then it was the weather forecast, with prospects for the next day's explorations, that he followed most intently.

Shortly after arriving there, Krutch described Tucson as "the pleasantest place in the whole [Southwest] for those who want isolation when they want it and yet want to have company within reach."[2] Set back fifty yards from the quiet rural road which, several miles on, led to more densely populated areas, Krutch's desert house was a symbol of the isolation he sought in Tucson. But he found increasingly that he also wanted the company which was within reach; and among a small circle of friends he enjoyed a social life more effortless and more personally rewarding than any he had known before. He preferred the suburban informality of a backyard barbecue or a picnic in nearby Sabino Canyon to the stiff dining-room entertainment he had eschewed in the East. When friends dropped by unannounced, he never begrudged the interruption; almost all of them shared his interest in nature and his passion for the desert. Though they were entertained by the stories he enjoyed telling about his years in New York and impressed by the wealth of allusion he brought to conversation, they were indifferent to the literary and academic politics Krutch had found so tedious. With the exception of a few scientists from the University whose company he also enjoyed, his friends were amateurs in those areas in which he himself was most interested: nature, and current events and social trends. He was eager to hear about their experiences and ideas; they, in turn, valued his.

Above all, most of his friends shared Krutch's active interest in the Arizona-Sonora Desert Museum, which opened around the time he arrived there. Jealous of his independence and loath to join groups of any kind, Krutch had always been a writer and a thinker, rather than a doer. The museum, however, engaged his imagination as no other civic project ever had, and he was intimately involved with its affairs throughout his years in Tucson. Located fourteen miles west of the city, the museum was established to encourage appreciation of the plants and animals native to the Sonora Desert in which Tucson lay. The museum's purpose closely resembled that of Krutch's own nature writing. Moreover, its conception as a "*living* natural history museum" corresponded to his own long-standing feeling that nature should be seen alive and naturally—not, as in most museums, dead and along marble corridors. Wherever possible, cages were replaced with large, open areas surrounded by moats, so the prairie dogs, bobcats, mountain lions, bears, deer, and desert bighorn sheep lived and were seen in conditions similar to their native habitats. Cacti were likewise to be found along the nature trails which wound through several acres of desert vegetation.

The museum opened with high ambitions but meager endowment; for a time its very survival was in doubt. At the first meeting of a reconstituted board of directors in 1953, Krutch was elected secretary-treasurer, and he remained a zealous participant in its work. Nearly every week he drove the forty-mile round trip to the museum, and visitors to the Krutches in Tucson were invariably taken there as well. It was for him an expression of his interest in nature more concrete than any number of essays. Having adopted the museum's cause in its infancy and having nurtured its growth, he was proud finally to see it internationally recognized as one of the finest institutions of its kind.

After a few years in Tucson, Krutch wrote a friend that "these have been the happiest years of my life so far."[3] They were also to be the most productive. In his first year alone, he had written between 125,000 and 150,000 words—"a possibly shocking number," he admitted.[4] And for most of the following years he maintained that pace.

His uncertainty as to whether he would be able to support himself wholly by his literary earnings proved unfounded. He continued to provide the *Nation* with book reviews and essays. In *Theatre Arts* he published a series of articles on various topics concerning drama. He contributed frequently to the book review supplements of the New York *Herald Tribune* and the New York *Times*, and to the *Times* Sunday magazine. He agreed to do a quarterly column for the *American Scholar* and was on retainer to contribute periodically to the *Saturday Review*. During the 1950s his essays were also appearing in such diverse publications as *The Freeman, Harper's, House and Garden,* the *New Leader*, and the *Saturday Evening Post.*

He found, too, that he was again in demand as a lecturer. As at the beginning of his career, he seized the opportunity to supplement his literary income and help create a still larger market for his books. During the 1950s he often traveled several times a year to address conferences on the teaching of English, to speak to Phi Beta Kappa alumni, to lecture on one or another literary topic, or, as he wrote Mark Van Doren from one of his many college and university engagements, to participate in "a round-table discussion on things in general."[5]

The great productivity he enjoyed in Tucson was partly a function of the good health he at last enjoyed; partly, too, he was free from such enervating distractions as teaching and reviewing. But above all, his productivity resulted from his having redefined his literary ambitions. He no longer strained to affect the smart intellectual urbanity of his earliest writing, or to address the "distinctly highbrow" readers to whom *The Modern Temper* had been addressed. He was now writing, frankly and simply, about nature and contemporary society, matters that he cared about greatly. His audience was now "the general reader," the intelligent layman—indeed, the kind of person with whom he felt so comfortable in Tucson.

With the success of his biographies and his early nature writing, Krutch's self-confidence as a writer had been renewed. In 1954, shortly after he arrived in Tucson, he was fairly showered with honors. The achievements of the first three decades of his career were recognized when Columbia awarded him a Doctor of Letters degree, and the American Academy of Arts and Letters elected him to membership (along with W.H. Auden, Aaron Copeland, and Allan Nevins). But for Krutch, two other literary awards he received that year were perhaps more significant auguries of his future success. For *The Measure of Man* he had been selected to receive the National Book Award; and for *The Desert Year* he was presented with the annual John Burroughs Medal of the American Museum of Natural History. Social criticism and desert writing were the two kinds of writing he was to pursue. The official recognition accorded his first such efforts in Tucson anticipated the enthusiastic popular reception similar books and essays would shortly receive.

Of all the many literary genres in which he worked, his nature writing brought Krutch his widest and most devoted readership. The 200,000 copies of his nature books published since *The Twelve Seasons* appeared in 1949 constitute the greatest single part of his sales. If, years hence, only *The Modern Temper, Johnson,* and perhaps *Thoreau* should enjoy broad recognition within the academy, it is likely that a much larger public, probably unaware of his other achievements, will still be appreciating his account of his social life in nature. The situation is understandable, both because the nature essay has never enjoyed the prestige of other literary genres and because Krutch's essays were patently written to be read, rather than studied.

In fact, they were written simply because he wanted to write them. Rather than reflecting any professional ambition to distinguish himself as a writer, they demonstrate his personal desire to organize and articulate his experience in the world not made by man. While most of his other work was written at the behest of an editor and to the dictates of the literary marketplace, his nature writing was undertaken with no immediate prospect of publication.

Compared, for example, with his essays on the modern temper, Krutch's nature essays are charming rather than impressive, discursive rather than highly wrought, and familiar rather than rhetorical. Though they offer (almost incidentally) any number of truths, they presume to present less a Final Truth about man and his condition than a narrative of what one man saw, heard, learned, thought, and felt in the natural world. Krutch had earlier been eager to portray himself as a man exceptional among men; now, in his nature writing, he sought to demonstrate that all men could enjoy experiences like his if they have eyes to see, ears to hear, perhaps a few books to consult, and a mind to contemplate. The essays offer not only an opportunity to participate vicariously in Krutch's experience, sharing the knowledge, refreshment, and inspiration he derived, but also a quiet challenge for the reader to go forth and do likewise.

Though reviewers and publishers described him as a "naturalist," Krutch was content simply to say, "I probably know more about plants than any other drama critic and more about the theater than any botanist."[6] That amateur spirit informs all of his nature writing and constitutes much of its charm. For the amateur, he remarked, "there are few places not covered with concrete or not trod into dust where he does not find something to look at. . . . He feels no pressing responsibility to 'add something to the sum of human knowledge.' He is quite satisfied to add something to *his* knowledge. . . . Any flower he has never seen before is a new species so far as he is concerned."[7]

His nature writing in New England was largely concerned with common phenomena, familiar even to those urban readers who doubtless comprised most of his audience. Through his vivid description, however, those common phenomena come to seem almost novel; refracted through Krutch's contemplative mind, they take on a significance they never had before. All of his essays were designed to heighten an awareness dulled by man's familiarity with the commonplace, and to show that even (indeed, especially) the commonplace was fraught with meaning.

His desert writing, however, offers something more: an introduction to a world of plants and animals largely unknown outside the Southwest. This strange and initially alien world becomes, on the pages of Krutch's books, familiar and reassuring. Effortlessly weaving into his narrative the information he has accumulated and unpretentiously sharing the insights he had gained, he provides not only an account of some of nature's less well-known curiosities, but also an understanding of their role in her larger scheme and the relevance of that scheme to man himself.

"The Colloid and the Crystal," the most frequently anthologized of all Krutch's nature essays, is representative.[8] Written in Redding, it recounts his experiences and reflections one January morning. Coming downstairs to breakfast, he saw that it had snowed while he had slept. "On the snow-capped summit of my bird-feeder a chickadee pecked at the new-fallen snow," and "a downy woodpecker was hammering at a lump of suet and at the coconut full of peanut butter." He further noticed the overnight frosting of his windowpanes, which "were etched with graceful, fernlike sprays of ice which looked rather like the impressions left in rocks by some of the antediluvian plants." Recalling the brief temptation to scratch his initials into the icy surface, he observed, "The impulse to mar and to destroy is as ancient and almost as nearly universal as the impulse to create."

These leisurely opening paragraphs contain many of the elements characteristic of Krutch's nature writing: the setting of the event in his daily domestic routine; the candor in acknowledging that he shares, however briefly, the baser impulses of all men; the almost incidental reflection on that momentary temptation; the affectionate precision of description; and the use of simile to enhance the total effectiveness of his scene.

The domestic setting of "The Colloid and the Crystal" was of course familiar; but Krutch had observed on that January morning the addition of a novel element. A "Christmas cactus" he had acquired on a summer trip to the Southwest had just bloomed on his windowsill. While the description of the cactus is even more vivid than that of the frostflower, the striking portrait is interrupted by Krutch's reflections: "Its lush blossoms, fuchsia-shaped but pure red rather than magenta, hung at the drooping ends of strange, thick stems and outlined themselves in blood against the glistening background of the frosty pane—jungle flower against frostflower; the warm beauty that breathes and lives and dies competing with the cold beauty that burgeons, not because it wants to, but merely because it is obeying the laws of physics which require that crystals shall take the shape they always have taken since the world began." The effect of the red flower against the white tracery on the window prompted Krutch to consider the absolute distinction between the living and the dead, the colloid and the crystal.

As usual, he provided technical information the layman might require. "Protoplasm is a colloid and the colloids are fundamentally different from the crystalline substances," he explained. "Instead of crystallizing they jell, and life in its simplest known form is a shapeless blob of rebellious jelly rather than a crystal eternally obeying the most ancient law." But it was the significance rather than the fact of the distinction with which Krutch was most concerned. The difference between the frostflower and the cactus is the difference between a "thing" and a "creature." The recognition of that difference leads man to understand that he is himself "both a 'thing' which obeys the laws of chemistry and physics and a 'creature' who to some extent defies them."

Recognizing the capacities of the Christmas cactus, one recognizes as well some of the human capacities Krutch later insisted upon in *The Measure of Man*: "It blooms at about Christmastime because it has got into the habit of doing so, because, one is tempted to say, it wants to. . . . His flowers assume their accustomed shape and take on their accustomed color. But not as the frostflowers follow their predestined pattern. . . . He has resisted and rebelled; he has attempted novelties, passed through many phases. Like all living things he has had a will of his own. He has made laws, not merely obeyed them." For Krutch, the recognition of the capacity of the Christmas cactus to resist and rebel was a stay against the invitations of determinist thinkers "to submerge myself into a crystalline society and to stop planning in order that I may be planned for."

"Wordsworth's God," Krutch concluded, "had his dwelling in the light of setting suns. But the God who dwells there seems to me most probably the God of the atom, the star, and the crystal. Mine, if I have one, reveals Himself in another class of phenomena. He makes the grass green and the blood red." It was the God of living nature, illuminated by science and patiently observed by man, rather than the God of romantic ecstasies. The reassurance that came to Krutch that January morning in Redding—and that he would enjoy in the desert as well—was equal in scale to Wordsworth's. The romantic need to believe, so obvious in *The Modern Temper*, was satisfied in his intercourse with nature.

Nearly all of Krutch's nature essays share, in varying measure, the elements distinctive of "The Colloid and the Crystal": a matter-of-fact narrative of how he discovered, often quite by chance, some curious natural phenomenon, or how he rediscovered some familiar one by seeing it anew; a scientific explanation, as extensive as necessary, of what he had observed; and his reflections upon the human significance of his experience. In some of his essays, especially those concerning the desert, the second element predominates, as he describes plants and animals he has only recently come to understand and with which he assumes many of his readers will be unfamiliar. Occasionally, therefore, his desert writing comes to resemble popular science more than belles lettres. But that apparent fault becomes a virtue; length lulls disbelief, and the unlikely phenomena he so fully describes come nearly to seem inevitable and familiar.

Doubtless much of the appeal of his books and essays about the desert lay in his vivid description of the face of nature there. Furthermore, Krutch lucidly explained *why* nature appears and behaves as she does, and few laymen could read Krutch's nature writing without learning a great deal. But what makes most of his essays something more than informed travel writing about an exotic land—and, indeed, what gives them permanent literary value—is the reflective element, the meditative intelligence, which is present in nearly all of them.

Part of the impulse behind Krutch's nature study was of course a simple, nearly childlike curiosity. He tried to recapture something of the experience of Adam, who "had the privilege of first looking at the world through eyes capable of wonder."[9] But he also sought (and, in the most memorable part of his essays, captured) that more deeply spiritual, fundamentally romantic appreciation of nature and of man's place in it that modernism seemed to preclude. He had passed beyond modernism by discovering what he had previously denied: that nature has a purpose, and that it is understandable in man's terms. For him, as for the romantics, it was "the great reservoir of energy, of confidence, of endless hope, and of that joy not wholly subdued by the pale cast of thought."[10]

If Krutch's goal was fundamentally romantic, his approach was not the traditionally romantic one. If he had escaped the suffocating doubt of modernism, he remained modern nonetheless in feeling that the facts of the scientist, rather than the intuitions of the poet, were the proper bases for the appreciation of nature. "It is not ignorance but knowledge which is the mother of wonder," he said, and he was unwilling to "exchange the puzzle and the excitement of the Nature which science has helped us see for the eighteenth century's mere illusory idyll."[11] He resisted "that cult of the sublime" in much nineteenth-century romantic nature poetry. Encouraging "a mere vague ecstasy" and projecting upon nature "their own fancies," those poets were, he felt, hardly less self-absorbed than many other men wholly blind to the natural world.[12] Wordsworth's "Only in ourselves does nature live" was for Krutch "less true than its opposite: 'Only in nature do *we* have a being.' "[13] He was not by temperament a mystic, and he preferred "to live under the dome of many-colored glass and to rest content with the general conviction that the white radiance of eternity has something to do with it." He sought "less to meet God face to face than really to take in a beetle, a frog, or a mountain when I meet one."[14] "The human mind," he insisted, "can appreciate the One only by seeing it first as the Many."[15] His own experience indicated that "Acute awareness of a natural phenomenon, especially of a phenomenon of the living world, is the thing most likely to open the door to that joy we cannot analyze."[16]

If, as he romantically believed, contemplation of the ultimate meaning of life was the final end of man, the scientist's meticulous attention to penultimate specifics carried man some considerable way toward that goal. At once understood scientifically and appreciated romantically, nature could be both "a challenge to thought and a challenge to emotion."[17] Long before he ever thought of writing nature essays, Krutch had found in scientific books refreshment from a career in which his teaching, reviewing, and writing were largely literary. In Cornwall and Redding he had drawn upon his undergraduate training and his recent reading to conduct simple experiments with plants and animals. Many of his essays reflect that reading (as when he lapses amiably into technical polysyllabics) as well as the pleasure he took in experimentation. But Krutch's pretensions as a scientist were only those of the *amateur*, the lover. He neither sought for himself nor imposed on his reader more knowledge than was necessary to understand and better love the plants and animals he found around him.

Krutch was clearly indebted to Thoreau for his appreciation of the ways in which the facts of science can enhance one's feeling for nature. He also shared Thoreau's impatience for what Krutch called "official science." In the first sentence of his first nature essay — "*Hyla crucifer* is what the biologists call him, but to most of us he is simply the Spring Peeper"[18] — he had announced that his perspective was different from that of the narrowly focused scientist. Biologists, he wrote elsewhere, spend too much time in laboratories and "too little observing creatures who are not specimens but free citizens of their own world. The odor which clings to these scientists is too seldom that of the open air, too often that biologist's odor of sanctity, formaldehyde."[19] Literally murdering in order to dissect, the scientist is, of necessity, not drawn into that emotional relationship with animals and plants which enhances reverence for life; for Krutch, the scientist was likely to be "more rather than less callous than the ordinary man."[20]

As he was working on *The Twelve Seasons*, Krutch wrote a review in which he described the tradition of nature writing, beginning in America with Thoreau, which he most admired. It was, he said, "Writing which takes as its subject some aspect of life other than human but which is distinguished from science by the fact that an emotional attitude is sought for rather than avoided, and distinguished from pure mysticism or mere rhapsody by the fact that it takes as its starting-point some scientific observation or knowledge rather than simple intuition."[21] Rejecting the extremes of both uninformed romanticism and unfeeling scientism, Krutch throughout his nature writing tried to show how his moments of privileged insight were earned through the patient and disciplined observation which validated them. He sought to present not a philosophy of nature, but a narrative of his own experience there. Like that experience, the largest part of his essays centers on what he saw and learned. But from the passages which recount his emotions during those moments of observation and insight, one can understand why he recognized, after completing his first essay, that his apostrophe to the peeper—"We are all in this together"—summarized a faith which had taken him decisively beyond the doubt of modernism.

To turn directly from *The Modern Temper*, with its haughty assurance of man's unique and privileged status, to the respectful geniality of these nature writings is to be struck by the intimacy Krutch had achieved with those other forms of life, and by his continuous indulgence in that fallacy which scholars curiously describe as pathetic. In Krutch's world, birds and butterflies "learn"; the cactus "discovers"; animals "dare"; the paloverde is prudent, foresightful and thrifty; the ocotillo has "virtues" worthy of man's respect; trees speak; frogs "think"; and the entire landscape hums with sentient life. For Krutch, "the risk of attributing too much" to plants and animals seemed now "no greater than the risk of attributing too little."[22] To his mind, the pathetic fallacy was less fallacious than its opposite: the notion that human and nonhuman nature are radically distinct. "Are we so separate from nature that our states are actually discontinuous with it?" he asked. "Is there nothing outside ourselves which is somehow glad or sad? Is it really a fallacy when we attribute to nature feelings analogous to our own?"[23] The courage of desert plants and animals and the joy of birds were real to Krutch, not merely figures of speech.

However deeply and romantically he felt about nature, however hungry he was for the reassurance it provided him, his "robust but serious" modern mind and his knowledge of science generally saved him from the sentimental excesses so common in belletristic nature writing. To find nature as a whole endlessly fascinating and humanly significant did not imply that every creature was equally so. The birds on which he doted with his sugar water "stimulate our imaginations"; but with their simple and repetitive behavior patterns "they are not so much fellow creatures as aesthetic objects."[24] With insects, which lacked individuality and were incapable of reciprocating his interest in them, Krutch also felt "some fundamental lack of sympathy." Even the spring peeper he celebrated in his first essay had an aspect "inscrutable and antediluvian."[25] But such creatures, in their ways, contributed to the sum of life and served as reminders of its infinite variety.

Krutch was also reminded that life often was difficult, that survival was rarely easy and never assured. He did not imagine that "Nature Always Knows Best"; for him it was enough to recognize that in ordering her intricate universe "she has usually hit upon an arrangement which will work, even though often quite inefficiently."[26] To see nature simply as a benevolent mother was to him no more acceptable than to see her as red in tooth and claw: "She is both, or neither, or something that includes and transcends the two." He recognized that nature "is cruel to the rabbit put into the mouth of a fox but kind to the fox's cubs to whom she has given a dinner."[27]

The harshness of nature and the struggle for survival of plants and animals was obvious in the arid Southwest. But even in New England, where life appeared easier, creatures were in constant competition with each other: "Every tree, every bird, every blade of grass is fiercely individualistic. It springs to life, not in order to make its contribution to a pageant, but in order not to be left behind in the struggle for water, and sun, and the few cubic centimeters of soil which this year it will contest not only with the roots of the neighboring plantlet . . . but also with the new seeds dropped perhaps as autumn drew to a close."[28] Along with nature's happier manifestations, Krutch's vision included the disemboweled carcass of a fawn whose belly a hungry coyote had ripped open, the hawk hovering before it strikes, and the buzzard circling as it hunts for the remnants of another predator's kill. His romanticism was checked by his realism; to love nature was to understand and accept her as a whole.

For Krutch, the knowledge that winter's blanket of snow must be stained by the blood of one of nature's sacrifices was far less significant than his recognition of the joy which nature so abundantly manifested. His own experience and his analysis of the modern temper had shown him that "Anxiety and distress, interrupted occasionally by pleasure, is the normal course of man's existence." On the other hand, in Redding, and then in the desert, he had learned that "Joy, interrupted now and again by pain and terminated ultimately by death, seems the normal course of life in nature."[29] Joy was "the one thing of which indisputably the healthy animal, and even the healthy plant, gives us an example."[30] Free of the hypertrophy of intellect and paralyzing skepticism of man, animals offered him a constant reminder of "the fact that joy is real and instinctive." Creatures other than man "know at least one thing which we seem progressively to be forgetting and they have one capacity which we seem to be allowing to atrophy. To them," he said, "joy seems more important and more accessible than it is to us."[31]

Krutch had sought to learn about nature like a scientist, and, more important, to learn from her as a romantic. "Whatever we discover about her," he remarked, "we are discovering also about ourselves."[32] After having rehearsed and partaken of the anxiety and despair of modernism, he was refreshed to find almost everywhere in nature "the example . . . of confidence, of serenity, and, above all, of joy."[33] Man needs a context for his life larger than himself," Krutch said; "he needs it so desperately that all modern despairs go back to the fact that he has rejected the only context which the loss of his traditional gods has left accessible."[34]

It was not, however, a romantic primitivism to which Krutch retreated. Although nonhuman nature offered a context for man's life, he realized that man enjoyed capacities and achievements to be found nowhere else in nature. "Without cities we cannot be civilized," he wrote from Tucson. He knew that in many ways man's art and intelligence had illuminated and improved upon nature. But if man was not to be satisfied merely by nature, he also felt that "neither are we happy without her. Without nature," he said, "we are compelled to renounce an important part of our heritage."[35] For Krutch, the recognition of man's heritage as a child of nature was as comforting as the traditional belief that man was a child of God.

The modern "tendency to get away from nature is an expression of a fundamental perversity which is leading man to prefer a sense of isolation, to stress rather than to minimize his uniqueness and his aloneness." His dismissal in *The Modern Temper* of nature's human significance, his insistence upon man's uniqueness, and his lament over man's loneliness in an alien universe were manifestations of what he now recognized as that perverse tendency. "Personally," he confessed several decades later, "I feel both happier and more secure when I am reminded that I have the backing of something older and perhaps more permanent than I am."[36] Through the nature essays, in which he described the revelation in plants and animals of that "something," he hoped to share that happiness and security with others.

"'Communion with nature' is not merely an empty phrase," Krutch believed. "It is the best corrective for that hubris from which the race of men increasingly suffers."[37] It was also a corrective to the despair of the modern temper. But if an understanding of nature was humbling, it no longer seemed humiliating. Rather, "From Nature we learn what we are a part of and how we may participate in the whole; we gain a perspective on ourselves which serves, not to set us aside from, but to put us in relation with, a complex scheme."[38] Unlike the isolating despair of modernism, such communion fosters a sense of man's fellowship with a larger, more various living community, puts him back in touch with his deepest roots, and resuscitates that most durable, most fundamental of faiths: the faith in life itself.

Because he then enjoyed that faith, shortly after he moved to Tucson Krutch was able to take his new *Measure of Man* and argue that man had capacities not recognized in *The Modern Temper*. With a will which was free to choose, man was no longer to be seen (as in determinist philosophies) as a machine passively acted upon by forces beyond his control. Such mistaken notions about man were partly founded, Krutch believed, upon a misunderstanding of animals. In *The Great Chain of Life*, the book to which he turned after completing *The Measure of Man* and the one in which his thoughts about nature and life were most fully gathered, Krutch demonstrated how his new faith in man grew from his new understanding of nature.

Several years earlier Krutch had written, "Man has never denied anything of the animals without coming, shortly thereafter, to deny it of himself also."[39] Behind modernism's denial of man's consciousness, purposefulness, and will lay similar denials of those capacities in animals. In *The Measure of Man* he had argued that man was not the machine pictured by behaviorist social scientists. Now—addressing himself to popular ideas of Cartesian mechanism, Darwinian determinism, and the "mechanomorphism" of much contemporary biological science—Krutch argued that animals are not machines, either. More than a quarter-century of patient, informed observation of nature had shown Krutch that "not everything about the beast is beastly." To comprehend "what being 'like an animal' means" was to begin to understand what it is to be a man.[40]

The *Great Chain of Life* was the most ambitious, most philosophical, and most closely argued of Krutch's nature books; it is, in fact, the one which is unmistakably a book, rather than a collection of loosely connected essays. Its goal, Krutch said, was to suggest that "to call man 'an animal' is to endow him with a heritage so rich that his potentialities seem hardly less than when he was called the son of God."[41] A primer of evolution which draws upon a century of post-Darwinian scientific thought, as well as on Krutch's own communion with nature, the book describes the nature of life and the emergence of its manifold forms, starting with growth, sex, and death in the Volox, that colonial enigma at the junction of the plant and animal worlds.

That man has evolved from such "lower" forms is obvious. So, too, is the discovery that natural selection, operating mechanically, has contributed significantly to the process. But Krutch believed that the orthodox Darwinian understanding of natural selection was only a partial explanation of evolution, a phenomenon which, he insisted, was more than a series of blind accidents. In the midst of that apparently inexorable process, evolving organisms intervened to exercise "will" or "preference" in adopting attributes possessing no apparent survival value.

As in *The Modern Temper*, Krutch recognized that insects and other "lower" forms of life which depend upon fixed, conditioned, and largely invariable patterns of behavior have prospects for "survival" far greater than man's. But he had passed beyond his earlier notion that nature is impelled only by "her inscrutable appetite for mere life in itself" and is "extraordinarily fertile and ingenious in devising *means*, but . . . has no *ends* which the human mind has been able to discover or comprehend."[42] Now he insisted that "what nature has been working toward is not merely survival; that, ultimately, it is not survival itself but Consciousness and Intelligence *themselves* — partly at least for their own sake."[43]

Insects — like the ant whose success in life he had admired in *The Modern Temper* — have both a social organization and methods for ensuring the welfare of their kind far more advanced than any other creature except man. "Hence," Krutch said, "by the criteria usually favored by objective scientists, the insects should be called the 'highest' animals — highest from the standpoint of the biologist because most likely to survive; highest from the standpoint of the anthropologist because culturally the most advanced."[44] But such criteria were inadequate. The "higher" animals were "higher because they are capable of something we consider more important than either the elaborateness or the 'survival value' of the instinctive techniques in which creatures 'lower' than they have far surpassed them. . . . What 'higher' really means is 'exhibiting a more extended range of phenomena which cannot be accounted for in terms of mere 'conditioning.'"[45]

In nature Krutch had been reassured to find that creatures other than man enjoyed that more varied, more vivid, nonmechanical psychic life which behaviorism denied. In *The Great Chain of Life* he celebrated the salamander's awareness of others which allows him to be domesticated as a pet; the ground squirrel's capacity, even in the captivity of a cage, to discover devices by which to amuse himself; the Rocky Mountain bighorn's virtues of "courage, daring, and the fight-to-the-death" which are displayed at mating season; and the bird who, to man's eyes at least, takes far more joy in living than does the ant. "If we are ever to regain a respect for ourselves," Krutch wrote, "it may be that we shall regain it by the discovery that the animals

themselves exhibit, in rudimentary form, some of the very characteristics and capacities whose existence in ourselves we had come to
doubt."[46]

Nature's goal, Krutch argued, was something beyond simple
survival and "mere life in itself." Such capacities as emotion, consciousness, and intelligence have a certain "survival value"; but, unlike the mechanical instinct of the insect, those capacities cannot be
explained by the Darwinian principle that no organism develops a
characteristic beyond the point where it is useful for survival. In a nu-
clear age when a "higher" creature like man might well destroy his
kind through the exercise of that intelligence, the Darwinian understanding of evolution seems inadequate. Does not that fact suggest,
Krutch asked rhetorically, that nature "puts a value on things which
do not have any simple survival value? Is it not possible that mam-
mals look after their young with bumbling consciousness rather than
with the expertness of instinct because nature has, in some way, been
interested not merely in the survival of the fittest, but in 'the fittest'
for something more than mere survival?"[47]

Any proper understanding of evolution must allow for the in-
tervention in that process by the nonmechanical "will" and "preference" of creatures who, in order to enjoy a "higher" life, developed in
themselves the non-instrumental capacities most fully realized in
man. Possessed of that knowledge, Krutch had passed beyond modernism's conviction that man was a solitary consciousness in a cold
and indifferent universe. In fact, that humanism on which the modernist prided himself was, Krutch argued, the ultimate expression of
the consciousness, free will, and capacity to prefer which many animals other than man had adopted as their own.

"By contact with the living nature we are reminded of the mysterious, nonmechanical aspects of the living organism," he wrote.
Thence one could trace the ultimate origins of man's creative power
in art, morals, and philosophy; to be reminded of those aspects was to
be freed not only from modernism, but also from the equally paralyzing influence of such deterministic philosophies as Marxism and behaviorism. "By such contact," he continued, in a 1960 essay which
fairly summarizes *The Great Chain of Life* and the message of all his
nature writing, "we begin to get, even in contemplating nature's

lowest forms, a sense of the mystery, the independence, the unpre-
dictableness of the living as opposed to the mechanical. And it is upon
the recognition of these characteristics that he shares with all living
creatures that any recognition of man's dignity has to be based."[48]

The reassurance to be found everywhere in nature was for
Krutch especially abundant in the desert. In *The Modern Temper* he
had remarked that, in its spiritual and emotional sterility, "the human
. . . world grows more and more a desert."[49] However, having left
the metaphoric desert of modernism for the real desert of the Southwest, and having studied its moral as well as natural landscape, he
found it less a wasteland than he had earlier imagined. In his four
desert books, his numerous other uncollected essays, and three hour-
long television programs about the Southwest in which he was fea-
tured, he became widely recognized as America's foremost writer
about and interpreter of that region.

For him and for his readers, the initial appeal of the desert was
the unexpected abundance of life it displayed. He found that the forbidding and apparently desolate wasteland was "teeming with live
things very glad indeed to be right there," that "something lives almost everywhere," and that "the variety which can be achieved within
the limitations imposed by the one invariable condition—scarcity of
water—is astonishing."[50] Like the Desert Museum, his essays displayed the plants and animals of that land and their various strategies
for survival.

Wherever he looked, Krutch found something to see: "the brilliant little flower springing improbably out of the bare, packed sand,
the lizard scuttling with incredible speed from cactus clump to spiny
bush, the sudden flash of a bright-colored bird." Some of the spectacle
was humorous, like the "cocky" road-runner, "the most comic of desert fowl"; the boogum tree, "far more improbable looking as a tree
than the giraffe is as an animal"; or the mating practices of the lizard,
which suggested that "the techniques of courtship have not changed
much in recent years."[51] He was most impressed, however, and his
scientific curiosity was most keenly engaged by the plants and animals which had achieved health and happiness by adapting themselves triumphantly to their hostile environment. The saguaro cactus
towers dramatically above the desert floor and has spread out a net of

shallow roots to capture the maximum amount of water during the infrequent rains. The yucca has roots that go as deep as forty feet. The desert mouse never drinks, but instead manufactures water for himself. The Sonoran spadefoot toad compresses the aquatic life of the tadpole into the few days in which rain puddles last in the desert. As in New England, living things struggled to eke out an existence. But in the desert, Krutch observed, "the contest is not so much of plant against plant as of plant against inanimate nature. The limiting factor is not the neighbor but water; and I wonder," he continued, "if that is, perhaps, one of the things which makes this country seem to enjoy a kind of peace one does not find elsewhere."[52]

The desert also led Krutch to a kind of meditation that the lushness of the natural world in New England had not inspired. "Nothing, not even the sea," he said, "has seemed to affect men more profoundly than the desert, or seemed to incline them so powerfully toward great thoughts, perhaps because the desert itself seems to brood and to encourage brooding."[53] As he observed at another time, "It still brings man up against his limitations and, like the deserts of the East, bids him to turn inward and to contemplate rather than to do. Of all the possible answers to the question 'What is a desert good for?', perhaps the best is just 'Good for contemplation—for that attitude of mind which invited the Arabs to think of the stars and the Hebrews to think of God.'"[54] "Nature's way here," he said, "her process and her moods, corresponds to some mood which I find in myself."[55]

"The desert is conservative, not radical. . . . The heroism which it encourages is the heroism of endurance, not that of conquest."[56] "In the desert," he said, "the very fauna and flora proclaim that one can have a great deal of certain things while having very little of others; that one kind of scarcity is compatible with, perhaps a necessary condition of, another kind of plenty." Desert plants and animals had made their peace with the heat and dryness of their universe. "Let us not say that this animal or even this plant has 'become adapted' to desert conditions," he urged. "Let us say rather that they have all shown courage and ingenuity in making the best of the world as they found it." And, he continued, "Of the desert flora and fauna, let us also add that the best they have made is a very good best." They had mastered "the great art of how-to-do-without."[57]

That was, of course, an art Krutch himself had been mastering in the years since he confessed his own despair in *The Modern Temper* and then found that despair compounded by the apparent collapse of his promising literary career. Lacking both professional success and the capacity to believe in the traditional values modernism and science seemed effectively to have denied, he discovered, in his early communion with nature in Redding, the truth to which the life of the desert also attested: "where some things are scarce others, no less desirable, may abound."[58] In its way, the desert confirmed what Krutch had been learning in his journey beyond his initial modernism: that the losses he had lamented then need not be ultimate; that the gap left by the decay of the values of western humanism, as traditionally formulated, might be filled by the discovery of other values even more fundamental; and that observation of the world not made by man was the starting point for the recovery of such faith and reassurance as man required.

9.

✤ THE PUBLIC THINKER

Summarizing in his autobiography the seven nature books he had published since 1949, Krutch said, "All of them have been, in varying degrees, travel books and descriptive accounts of unusual natural phenomena somewhat belletristic in tone."[1] The modesty and understatement are characteristic of the later Krutch; nevertheless, the descriptive element does predominate over the reflective in nearly all his nature writing, and especially in that about the desert. His two final books about the Southwest, the last of his books devoted wholly to the natural world, could in fact be fairly described as "travel books."

Grand Canyon: Today and All Its Yesterdays (1958), is an amiable vade mecum to the park and provides a potpourri of information for the curious visitor: explanations of the ecology of the area; descriptions of the flora and fauna; discussion of the geological formation of the Canyon and of fossil evidence of early forms of life there; an account of its exploration and of more recent human habitation; suggestions as to how best to relate oneself to the immensity of the spectacle; even reports on tourist amenities and tips concerning spots of particular beauty or interest which "should not be missed."[2]

The Forgotten Peninsula: A Naturalist in Baja California (1961), belongs to much the same genre. "My narrative," Krutch wrote in the prologue, "will include bits of picturesque but out-of-the-way history and rather more of natural history. But primarily it is an account of certain journeys by plane, boat, landing barge, truck, automobile, and burro-back made by a traveler who first saw the country . . . not many years ago and was so struck by its wildness and its beauty that he returned again and again."[3]

Concerned largely with accounts of the history and the natural curiosities of the respective areas, these two last nature books reveal little of Krutch's own thoughts and feelings. Like his other desert books, they were written to introduce the general reader to unfamiliar landscapes. They do, however, reflect the transition in Krutch's interests during the late 1950s from a concern with nature and its human meaning to a broader concern with contemporary society and its values. The desert, with its example of "the great art of how-to-do-without," had led Krutch to question a materialist society which seemed to know little of that art. The Grand Canyon and Baja raised the issue more concretely.

As Krutch wrote his Grand Canyon book, controversy raged over the area's future. Arguing that "human needs come first," many farmers who wanted more water for irrigation were urging construction of dams and clearing of forests in the area. Krutch, however, asked, "Just what needs of just what men should these parks and other natural areas serve?"[4] In describing the historical and natural richness of the Grand Canyon, his book was in part a brief for its preservation. "Conservation," he wrote, "is not likely to mean much to those whose imagination has never been touched by an awareness of the natural world"; in all of his nature writing he had sought to stimulate just such an awareness.[5]

But if *Grand Canyon* was one of Krutch's few direct contributions to the conservation movement, he hardly considered himself a typical conservationist. He sympathized with the ultimate goals of the movement (which honored him, in turn, with many awards), but he felt that the conservationist's concern with nature was largely practical, while his was primarily spiritual. As he wrote in his most extensive essay on the topic, "Conservation Is Not Enough." "What is commonly called 'conservation,'" he said, "will not work in the long run because it is not really conservation at all but rather, disguised by its elaborate scheming, only a more knowledgeable variation of the old idea of a world for man's use only." Properly, Krutch felt, the conservation movement should encourage an understanding of the interrelationship of obvious practical considerations with others

205

"which are commonly called 'moral', 'aesthetic', and even 'sentimental.'"[6] Instead, he found that the movement concentrated on practical arguments for preserving the natural environment, and that most activists were so preoccupied with tactics for addressing the problem they perceived that they had lost the pleasure he found in nature herself. Krutch was eager that the Grand Canyon be protected from the ravages of men whose idea of "human needs" differed from his, but his plea for conservation in the final chapter of the book was characteristic of his approach: "The wilderness and the idea of wilderness is one of the permanent homes of the human spirit."[7]

The forces of "progress" which threatened the Grand Canyon also threatened Baja California, most of which, he said, "is still almost as empty as it was when the white man first saw it."[8] He was not a romantic primitivist, and he recognized that technological progress had allowed him to visit the remote peninsula and to enjoy there some of the creature comforts a man past sixty required. On the other hand, part of the charm Baja held for him—in addition to its natural beauty and curious flora and fauna—existed precisely because the peninsula had largely escaped that "progress" which had despoiled so much of the world.

Krutch was not insensitive to the plight of many natives of Baja who lived on the ragged edge of existence, nor was he blind to the ways in which the padres of the eighteenth century or the tourists and industrialists of the twentieth had improved their lot, economically and otherwise. But he asked whether there was not "some optimum degree of development which it could achieve? Or must it, like the rest of the world, emerge from something like destitution only to find itself all too soon immersed in all the problems, pressures, and perplexities of modern civilization?" The contrast between contemporary American life and that in Baja prompted Krutch to ask whether we must "rest content with the simple assumption that while Baja has much to learn from us, she, on the other hand, poses no questions which it might be worth our while to consider?"[9] In *The Forgotten Peninsula* he insisted, as in much of the social criticism he was also writing by then, that in every society a mean must be sought "between over-development and underdevelopment, between desperate scarcity and almost suffocating abundance."[10]

꽃 Like all good travel books, Krutch's had been based on both conscientious historical research and intimate familiarity with the places he described. Preparatory to writing *Grand Canyon* he had spent a number of months living in a cottage on the South Rim, taken a mule trip with Marcelle to the bottom, and chartered a small airplane to survey the course of the Colorado River and the Canyon through which it cut.

Baja California, however, was considerably less accessible than the Grand Canyon. His visits there—ten by the time he wrote his book, and as many more before he died—were made possible by the generosity of Kenneth Bechtel, a wealthy San Francisco industrialist he met in 1958. During the following years, when Krutch's contact with Mark Van Doren was largely epistolary, Bechtel became Krutch's closest friend.

On the face of it, a captain of industry like Bechtel seems an unlikely candidate for that intimate friendship which Krutch bestowed so parsimoniously. Eleven years Krutch's junior, Bechtel was the son of a Kansas schoolteacher and farmer who had gone to California in the 1890s to make a new life (and a considerable fortune) in construction. By the time Kenneth was a youth, his father's business was booming like California itself; and by World War II, after his father's death, he and his two brothers were running the vast Bechtel empire —including by then not only the construction of highways, dams, and pipelines, but also shipbuilding, airplane manufacture, and an insurance company, Industrial Indemnity.

After the war, Bechtel headed Industrial Indemnity while his brothers attended to the other family enterprises. Although his wealth by then was considerable, he found business increasingly unfulfilling. He devoted much of his time to reading, to round out the education he had interrupted when he had left Berkeley without a degree; to the study of religion, Christian Science in particular; and to civic activities such as the Boy Scouts, of which he became national president. As head of Industrial Indemnity, Bechtel also demonstrated his interests in matters beyond profits and losses. The firm's offices around the country contained well-stocked, carefully selected general libraries to encourage recreational reading by employees, and the company sponsored professionally directed Great Books lectures and discussions for employees, their families and friends. At sales conferences as well, where company executives gathered, Bechtel scheduled lectures by eminent writers or thinkers whose remarks, he hoped, would temper commerce with the humanities.

Several months before the 1958 sales conference, Bechtel read Krutch's *Voice of the Desert*, and he invited Krutch to address the executives who were to be gathering in Phoenix. By February he had read several of Krutch's other books, and he was eager to meet the man whose work he immensely admired — so eager that he flew to Tucson in the company plane to accompany Krutch during the brief flight from Tucson to Phoenix.

To have seen the meeting of the dishevelled writer and the fastidious industrialist would hardly have been to imagine the beginning of a rich and lasting friendship. The one was shy by nature and, from his frequent practice of the enterprise, cynical about lecturing. The other had long lionized great men of science and letters and was possessed of a formidable reserve in its way even more forbidding than Krutch's shyness. By the end of the day, however, they discovered they had much in common.

His hair blown by the gusty winter winds, Krutch spoke outside under the brilliant Arizona sun, rambling informally from one topic to another: the flora and fauna of the Southwest; the austerity of the region's environment and the joy of its natural life; and the contrast between the simplicity suggested by the desert and the complexity of the "Good Life" Americans believed could be achieved only through technological mastery of nature. As Krutch shortly discovered, his ideas about nature and society corresponded closely to Bechtel's own. Bechtel was eager to pursue the discussion they had begun that day, and he asked if he might fly down to Tucson that weekend to talk further with Krutch and meet Marcelle. A few days later the two men met again and spent a mutually agreeable day talking and, of course, visiting the Desert Museum. Having some time at his disposal the following week (as well as a Lockheed Lodestar with two pilots), Bechtel invited the Krutches to fly off with him to any destination they might choose. They were not long in accepting, and soon they were mapping out a trip which Krutch had long aspired to make.

Having just completed his book on the Grand Canyon, he was

eager to trace the entire course of the Colorado River from its source in the Rockies to its mouth in the Gulf of California. He was also eager to see Baja California, which a Columbia student had described to him some years before and whose unspoiled beauty he had more recently heard praised by his friend Lewis Walker, the associate director of the Desert Museum. In Bechtel's plane he was able to see both within a single day. After following the Colorado, they flew down the Gulf of California and along the eastern coast of Baja, landing that evening in La Paz, the capital of that primitive and largely undeveloped area. They spent several nights in one of La Paz's tolerably comfortable tourist hotels and explored by car some of this southernmost part of the Sonoran Desert, which Krutch knew so intimately around Tucson. By the end of the trip Bechtel and the Krutches had come to know and admire not only each other, but also Baja, to which they would frequently return.

A few weeks later Bechtel invited the Krutches to join him for a week there. Supplied with jeeps and power boats, they ventured into more remote parts of the peninsula. Other expeditions followed— twenty-three during the next eleven years. Bechtel's interest in the area grew, and in cooperation with the California Academy of Sciences he underwrote a biological survey of the region. Krutch became the project's unofficial historian; he, and occasionally Bechtel as well, joined the scientists during their explorations. The sixty-eight-year-old Krutch wrote to Mark Van Doren, "I am coming to consider myself quite an explorer to whom wild country, sleeping bags, etc., are a matter of habit."[11] Among so many professional scientists, Krutch was happily still the amateur, asking questions of the specialists and entertaining them around the campfire with the witty anecdotes he delighted to tell. In Baja, Krutch was for Bechtel a model of the amateur naturalist he himself was becoming.

Those trips in 1958 to Baja were the first of many the Krutches would make with Bechtel and, later, his wife Nancy. The following summer they cruised on his ninety-six-foot yacht for five hundred miles along the Alaska panhandle north to the head of Muir Glacier. In 1962 they accompanied the Bechtels on a month-long round-the-world trip to London, Paris, Athens, Beirut, Damascus, Bangkok, Hong Kong, and Tokyo. And in 1965 and 1966 they were again the

Bechtels' guests on two trips to Greece, the Greek Islands, and western Turkey. Enjoying first-class luxury all the way, the Krutches, who had not been to Europe since 1936, were once again world travelers.

The Bechtels valued not only Krutch's lively company but also the humanist's perspective he brought to whatever they saw and did. The trips were valuable for Krutch as well. As his interest turned from nature writing to social criticism, he found in his travels a context for his critique of contemporary America. Returning from his round-the-world trip, he wrote Mark Van Doren concerning two of his "principal conclusions": "the variety possible to the human condition both physically and in mores," and the absence of any "obvious connection between contentment and 'the standard of living.'"[12] In 1959, only a year after the two men had met, Krutch dedicated *Human Nature and the Human Condition* "To Kenneth Bechtel, who introduced me to some new country both geographical and spiritual."

During the following years, the nature and extent of Krutch's debt would become even clearer. The excursions to Baja that he underwrote, the travels on which he invited the Krutches to accompany him, the lectures he arranged, and the secretarial assistance he provided were but several of Bechtel's many generosities to Krutch. If, as he said in the 1940s, Johnson had helped free the man of letters from the suffocating embrace of the patron, Krutch in the 1960s discovered that the patronage of a man like Bechtel was not to be scorned. But beneath the literary patronage lay a deep friendship and mutual respect. As between Krutch and Van Doren, so between Krutch and Bechtel two men, in many ways quite different from each other, were in fact complementary.

Bechtel undoubtedly appreciated the admiration of a distinguished writer like Krutch, a respect which no amount of money could buy. Moreover, feeling that the world of commerce was not in itself fulfilling, Bechtel valued the entree Krutch offered to a literary and intellectual world for which he thirsted. For Bechtel, Krutch was not only a friend whose witty company and anecdotes he enjoyed, but also an intellectual mentor who helped him to define for himself values beyond the credits and debits of which he had long ago wearied.

Bechtel, on the other hand, held a certain fascination for Krutch as well. Having long aspired to wealth and having recently begun to achieve it as a successful literary entrepreneur in Tucson, Krutch enjoyed a glimpse of how the truly wealthy live and think. But had he been merely a typical successful businessman, Bechtel would have been for Krutch at best a curiosity. In fact, Krutch admired Bechtel's intelligence, the breadth of his interests, and the earnestness with which he pursued his self-education and brought his humanistic concerns to the libraries and discussion groups at Industrial Indemnity.

Talking with Bechtel, Krutch valued the perspective and insights his friend brought from his experience in the world of commerce. At the end of his career, that world seemed to Krutch at least as real as the literary and academic world he had left behind in coming to Tucson. Having discounted the pretensions of New York's professional intellectuals, Krutch found refreshing the enthusiastic amateurism with which Bechtel pursued his interest in nature, literature, and ideas. For Krutch, Bechtel was not only a generous and valued friend, but also a type of the person for whom he was now writing: a curious, literate, intelligent layman who was sympathetic to Krutch's own humanist perspective and who was eager critically to examine contemporary society by the light of that humanism and the dictates of common sense.

The Grand Canyon and *The Forgotten Peninsula* are admirable books of their kind, informed, informative, and immensely readable. They also suggest, however, that by the late 1950s Krutch had largely exhausted the lode of literary (if not personal) inspiration he had found in nature a decade earlier. Although he continued to publish the occasional nature essay during the following years, after the midfifties his writing, like his lecturing, was largely devoted to social commentary and the consideration of "things in general."

The first of his major Tucson books, *The Measure of Man*, was an excursion in this direction; its recognition encouraged Krutch to devote more of his efforts to such writing. In spring 1955, he deliberately began this final phase of his career when he became "Editor at Large" of the *Saturday Review* and a columnist for the *American Scholar*. Until his death in 1970 his essays appeared regularly in both magazines, and his quarterly column in the *Scholar* was soon the most popular of that journal's regular features. As a social commentator in those and many other magazines, his popular reputation grew still greater.

The familiar essay, Krutch acknowledged in 1960, is "probably the least respected of all literary genres." But it remained among the most widely read, and it was the form which, having proved so congenial for his nature writing, he adopted for most of his social commentary as well. However low its prestige in the hierarchy of literary kinds, it was "the very best of all possible forms for the personal statement of observations and opinions," just such personal statements as Krutch now sought to make. Though their basis was often sociological and topical, his essays invariably became philosophical and reflective. They were addressed, he said, to "eternal problems in their contemporary forms."[13]

"Even a casual reading of newspapers and magazines will keep you constantly supplied with new occasions for pet indignations," he once remarked.[14] The inspiration for his essays was as likely to be an article in *TV Guide* as a treatise in some scholarly journal, a friend's casual remark as the report of a comment by some noted public figure. As in his nature writing, he was here a vigilant observer of the commonplace. His essays explored some of the implications of things that were seen, heard, and believed, but too rarely, he thought, critically scrutinized.

In his social commentaries, as in his nature writing, Krutch was patently the amateur. His essays were strictly attempts to define for himself and his readers his reactions to the passing scene. The very title of his *American Scholar* column, "If You Don't Mind My Saying So," suggests the engaging modesty with which he generally wrote. His essays never pretended to the authority of fact. He offered not the last word on a topic, but his own admittedly personal perspective, beginning his paragraphs with such remarks as "So far as I can see," "Sometimes I wonder," "What really interests me in this is," or "My theory is." He was, then, long on opinions but short on conclusions. The highly wrought style and labored speculation of his *Modern Temper* essays were replaced here by a style far more casual and thoughts apparently far less stunning. For Krutch, as for his predecessor Johnson, the essay was a loose sally of the mind. Rambling freely from one topic to another, digressing frequently from his ostensible topic to ponder some tangentically related matter, and drawing often upon some favorite literary anecdote or allusion, Krutch the writer was Krutch the talker. Many of his essays seem to be simply literary extensions of the leisurely, candid conversation he enjoyed among his Tucson friends.

The role he adopted was that of gadfly, doubter and questioner, rather than advocate. He was less interested in persuading his readers to accept some novel ideology than in stimulating them to measure, as he had, the current fashions in thought, taste, and behavior against an implicit standard of common sense. The premise of Krutch's social commentary was much like that which he described as the foundation of the lively conversation of Johnson and his circle: "acceptance of a doctrine which we have rejected— namely, the doctrine . . . that every normal mind is prepared to recognize truth when it is presented."[15]

Because Krutch himself had clearly formulated an opinion about most matters, his essays reflect not so much the vigor of original thinking as the application of his commonsense perspective to the often perverse world in which he lived, not entirely comfortably. In one of his first *American Scholar* columns he wrote: "Don't, say I, fight too hard against the growing conservatism which seems to come naturally. It's perfectly all right for the aged to believe in the good old days— social, moral, and artistic."[16] While he often presented himself as an amiable curmudgeon, his conservatism was not merely that of old age. It was a fundamental part of his character and had expressed itself decades before when, faced with modernism and then Marxism, he also looked longingly to those "good old days."

Pursuing the kind of inquiry begun in *The Measure of Man*, Krutch during the last fifteen years of his career produced well over a hundred essays and one book of social criticism. Like his previous such effort, *Human Nature and the Human Condition* was widely praised when it appeared in 1959; shortly it was in its fifth printing. Like his essays, that book rehearsed many of the topics which preoccupied Krutch's writing in Tucson: the spiritually paralyzing and artistically pernicious influence of modernism; the impossibility of ever realizing utopian ideals; the responsibility of the intellectual and the place of the humanities in an age of science; the relationship between fact and value judgment; the futility of sociology's efforts to quantify happiness; the fallacy of mechanistic, deterministic philosophies of man; and the environmental dangers of pollution, overpopulation, and diminishing resources.

His essays also considered a wide variety of other topics, including capital punishment, pacificism, the development of the electron microscope, the Russians' interest in Mark Twain, euphemisms and clichés, as well as the obsession of Americans with "fun," and the curious ways in which they find it. A number of his essays were primarily autobiographical, ranging from his reflections on rereading Bishop Paley's *Natural Theology* to a series of verbal home-movies taken during his travels with the Bechtels. Some were simply *jeux d'esprit*, like those dialogues in which he imagined meetings between Johnson and Thoreau, Shaw and Thoreau, and Thoreau and Krutch.

One topic conspicuously absent was politics. Such issues as McCarthyism, the civil rights movement, and the Vietnam war received little attention. In one of his earliest essays Krutch asked, "Wouldn't a really healthy citizen in a really healthy country be as unaware of the government as a healthy man is unaware of his physiology?" Against what he felt was the excessive political awareness of most people, he suggested that "We ought not have as our ideal the state of universal hypochondria."[17] His essays attested to his recognition that his was not "a really healthy country," but for Krutch the national malaise was more fundamental than that addressed by most politicians.

In *Human Nature and the Human Condition* and in a number of the essays which followed from it, he addressed himself squarely to that malaise. For Krutch, the problems of American society were primarily spiritual and philosophical, rather than political; to resolve them would require more than legislative tinkering. In much of his later writing the genial social commentator became an impassioned social critic. As in his earlier essays, he candidly and unsystematically set forth his own prejudices, offering neither closely argued treatises nor any coherent program for social reform. He remained an independent, questioning mind whose doubts about the present were far clearer than his faith in some utopian future. However, the urgency with which he voiced those doubts during the last decade of his career reflects the renewal, now that he was once again writing extensively about contemporary society, of that despair he had felt while analyzing the modern temper. Returning to study the modern world from which he had so fruitfully fled to nature, he found that world as uncongenial as he had before.

The elder Krutch rejoiced in the recent "progress" of American society no more than had the younger man three decades before. *The Modern Temper* had expressed his uneasiness with what passed for progress in thought; and even earlier, in one of his first *Nation* editorials, Krutch in 1924 had asked more generally, "What does 'progress' mean? . . . When progress became the religion of the modern world . . . the present age of confusion began," he said. "We can go anywhere we like and faster than we need to go; few realize that it is time to ask where it is most worth while to go."[18] Half a lifetime later he returned to pose the same question and issue the same reminder. His social criticism offered a quiet, reasoned, and persuasive indictment of the crass materialism, moral relativism, and artistic nihilism he found in contemporary society.

By some criteria, he recognized, America had progressed impressively. The "standard of living" was high, life expectancy was long, and the nation was "astonishingly kindly and generous" in sharing its wealth with others. But those were not, for him, the true criteria by which a society should be judged. Many Americans felt, like himself, "that there is something lacking in our society" — "that, for all its prosperity and for all its kindliness, generosity, and good will, it is somehow shallow and vulgar; that the vulgarity is superficially evidenced in the tawdriness, the lack of dignity and permanence in the material surroundings of our lives, and more importantly in our aims and standards."[19] As a social critic, Krutch examined some symptoms of those shallow and vulgar aims and standards.

In the three decades since writing *The Modern Temper*, Krutch had been confirmed in the humanism which even there had contested his studied modernism. He was as disillusioned with technology now as he had been with science then, but he now spoke with a new conviction. As a humanist, he was distressed to recognize that for most Americans "progress" was simply equated with the advance in technology, which was seen uncritically as a good in itself. Man, he said, was "hypnotized" by the machine: "we do not want to control it because in our hearts we believe it more interesting, more wonderful, more admirable, and more rich in potentialities than we ourselves are." Infatuated with its apparent enrichment of life, man was blind to technology's equally great power to debase and destroy that life. Drunkenly piling one technological advance upon another, man had become "*Homo faber*, not *Homo sapiens*; man the maker, not man the thinker. He is," Krutch said, in a tone characteristic of much of his later social criticism, "the great master of know-how but incapable of Reason or Wisdom. . . . Truly he is, for all his wealth and power, poor in spirit."[20]

Both handmaiden and creature of technology, advertising offered a constant reminder of America's crass materialism. Producing more things than it needs or can naturally consume, the nation was forced to create an artificial demand for its surfeit of material goods. The advertisers, Krutch frequently complained, had taken a measure of man different from his own and had found that man could be subtly coerced into behaving like the machine he so admired. A new kind of child slavery was replacing the old: "Millions of children instead of standing in front of looms are seated in a seemingly milder enslavement before 'giant twenty-one inch screens,' hypnotized by distant and usually anonymous masters."[21]

The epitome of America's perverse obsession with technology was, for Krutch, space travel. In 1958 he wrote that it "represents the most grandiose escape mechanism yet elaborated by the ingenious but self-defeating human mind. . . . I am still patriotic enough to hope that if anyone gets to the moon and beyond, it will be one of our boys," he said. "But I am also a member of that minority which would prefer to have nobody at all get there."[22] For most people, he wrote nine years later, landing on the moon was, "the one accomplishment most worth achieving . . . today's equivalent for the Crusades or the search for the Holy Grail."[23] For him it was another example of technology run amok.

Less than a year before Krutch died, men first stepped onto the moon; but for him it was hardly a giant leap for mankind. He followed the landing on television, and in a letter to his brother he confessed that he found it "astonishing." A person with Krutch's amateur interest in science could hardly have failed to be impressed, but as a humanist he regretted the act's "unfortunate tendency to suggest that we can do anything, whereas we can do only things which depend upon technology, not the important things which depend not on technology alone but upon our willingness to apply it in the realm of human betterment."[24] The moon landing seemed to him yet another example (and hardly the least costly) of America's misplaced priorities; of the fact, as he wrote earlier of the project, that "ours is an age devoted to all sorts of unexamined enterprises."[25]

He saw other examples closer to home. In Tucson, nature's beauty was being replaced by man's squalor; the pure desert air and sparkling night skies were being sacrificed to "progress." In 1956 Krutch had spoken to a meeting of the local Rotary Club, arguing against the efforts of Tucson's city fathers to attract more industry, commerce, and people there. The local newspaper (speaking, Krutch recognized, for many) found it "a rather unusual address" and wondered "whether to take him seriously or whether he was speaking more or less in a humorous vein."[26]

By 1970 the area's population had grown more than five-fold, to 250,000; and much that Krutch had valued when he first came there in 1950 had been lost. As hamburger stands, filling stations, shopping centers, and housing "developments" spread out toward his formerly isolated desert home, he described Tucson as a "sort of anti-city," more and more like the other "sloburbs" which were "the most characteristic aspect of modern America." In Tucson he saw the spiritless functionalism he disliked in all modern architecture. Writing like a disillusioned lover, he lamented that "Everything looks improvised, random, unrelated to everything else, as though it had no memory of yesterday and no expectation of tomorrow." He wondered whether "ever before in history a prosperous people had consented to live in communities so devoid of every grace and dignity, so slum-like in everything except the money they represent."[27]

For Krutch, the shabbiness of America's cities was merely a concrete sign of the vulgarity of her people's taste. The American preoccupation with "welfare" also reflected the shallowness of the nation's ideals. Krutch truly admired the generosity with which the United States shared its riches with its own citizens and disadvantaged people elsewhere in the world. But for him it was significant that the "welfare" America provided was almost wholly material, and that the citizen's traditional right to the pursuit of happiness had become the right to attain welfare. "To define welfare as whatever most people seem to want," he wrote, "tends to mean more things and fewer ideas and, in general, tends toward the vulgarest possible conception of what constitutes the good life."[28] The enshrinement in legislation of that materialistic notion of the good life implicitly denied any higher ideals. "The nearer the welfare state comes to achieving its ideal, the less likely it becomes that happiness can be achieved by anyone whose conception of it does not coincide with that of the majority."[29]

The free public education in which Americans so passionately and uncritically believed was for Krutch another example of aspiration to little better than the prevailing common denominator, to "preparation for contented living on whatever level the world had sunk to."[30] Examining (as he did in many of his essays) recent trends in educational thought and practice, he found little evidence that the schools sought "to produce that maladjustment which consists in the cultivation of tastes, standards, and habits different from and superior to those prevailing."[31] The linguistic permissiveness of teachers who insisted that children had a "right" to "their own language" was for Krutch another symptom of "the far more inclusive phenomenon of our age: namely, the doubt that any one thing is in itself better than any other."[32]

"Churches," like schools, he remarked in another essay, "never before demanded so little—in the way of professed belief, unworldly ideals, or change of life." The truth, he said of the much-discussed religious revival of the 1950s, "is not that 'more people are joining the church' as that the church is joining more people."[33] The academic and spiritual leaders to whom he hoped a drifting society might look for guidance and inspiration offered little of either. Nor, finally, did the artist, who—as Krutch had suggested in his earliest reviews and more recently in his Cornell lectures on modern drama—was both symptomatic of and contributory to the malaise of the age. "Never, with the possible exception of the world of the Roman Empire, has so large a part of the best artistic creation been bitter, despairing, contemptuous, and destructive," he wrote in 1964. "With rare exceptions, the works most, and most justly, admired by intellectuals are counsels of despair. . . . Our best artists are engaged in disrupting patterns, smashing forms, and deliberately cultivating dissonances in painting and music, as well as in poetry, fiction and drama."[34] In various essays he maligned the "taste for violence," the "all-inclusive hatred," the "perverse eroticism" and the "terrible monotony" of contemporary literature. "At the risk of being dismissed as pathetically unperceptive," he confessed that the intellectual world of Sartre, Camus, Tennessee Williams, Beckett, and Genêt "is simply not the world I know and that their problems are not mine."[35]

As he surveyed the contemporary human situation and gathered his thoughts for his essays, Krutch's pessimism grew. "The world of my day has moved pretty steadily in directions which I find distressing," he wrote in 1967; it was, he said, "increasingly alien." "Those aspects of the physical world that make me happiest are certainly disappearing as a result of industrialization, exploding population, and urban sprawl. . . . The majority of my fellow citizens are crassly and cynically materialistic, while most of the intellectual minority which one might expect to oppose them are nihilists interested chiefly in destruction and violence, in non-art, non-music, and non-painting." In the late 1920s the apparent withering of man's spirit in the face of science had occasioned Krutch's despair. Now, in the age of the atom bomb, Krutch feared for man's very existence. "A case could certainly be made out for the contention that modern man as a race has the death wish," he wrote in 1967.[36] Two years later, in an article written for Field Enterprises and syndicated to many American newspapers, he described the decade then ending as "the most troubled, the most insecure, the least optimistic, and the most threatened decade of the last 300 years." To Krutch, at least, the statement was not hyperbolic.

The disillusionment with the human condition reflected in much of Krutch's later public writing was apparent in letters to friends as well. "Sometimes I can't help being depressed these days," he wrote Mark Van Doren in 1968. "I can't seem to agree with either the left or the right. They both," he explained, "seem to me to lack all common sense."[37] It was against that measure of common sense, rather than according to some body of carefully formulated convictions, that he

219

judged the drift of contemporary society. "I am convinced," he wrote
Van Doren nine months later, "that we cannot be saved by either of
the remedies commonly proposed—technology or political change.
. . . It would not be enough to end discrimination, the Vietnam War,
etc., etc., desirable as such ends would be. We would still be lost."
The only hope was for man "to be born again—by which I mean accept a new set of values."[38]

Neither in his social criticism nor in his letters did he explain of
what that "new set of values" might consist. In fact, it is not clear
that Krutch himself knew, and that very uncertainty suggests both
the strength and the weakness of his social criticism: the strength, for
readers who are skeptical of any ideology which pretends to have arrived at Final Truth about the nature of things, and who prefer an
open, questioning mind like Krutch's to one closed and dogmatic;
and the weakness, for those who search in Krutch's writing for a philosophical precision and a specificity of assertion largely absent there.

As a social critic, Krutch was more concerned with diagnosing
some of the ills of his society than with proposing any easy cure. He
had no more a comprehensive philosophy of man and society than he
did of nature. Drawing upon his commonsense humanism, he simply
and unpretentiously surveyed a world which seemed to live by values
different from his. In the plain-speaking manner which characterized
his later writing, he registered his uneasiness; but he asserted only as
much as he honestly could. He had no Final Answers; moreover, he
believed that, with such modest assertions as that of Minimal Man,
he could reach more readers and stimulate more thought than by dis-
ingenuously proposing sweeping half-truths.

By the end, Krutch's quest for values, which had taken many
different forms in his life, was still not complete. Although Johnsonian common sense and Thoreauvian pantheism had taken him far beyond his earlier, thoroughgoing modernist skepticism, he remained a
man of "robust but serious mind." Just as he had doubted in childhood that the lion and the lamb would ever lie peacefully together, he
doubted in his late writing that there were simple answers to complex problems. In his social criticism he could, at best, look to the humanities as man's last best hope: "'The humanities' are not the orna-
ments of civilization; they are its salvation—if indeed it is to be saved.

. . . Even if there is no Truth, no Right, no Wrong, and no Justice, then, at least, arts and letters are in any society the principal source of those illusions concerning Truth, Right, Wrong, and Justice which guide its conduct."[39] For Krutch, the moral concepts he had earlier dismissed as illusory now had something of the power of truth.

But in his social criticism he never made clear just what those terms meant to him. As in *The Measure of Man*, he was more concerned to insist upon the importance of man's having and honoring values than to describe just what their content might be. The comfort, wisdom, and inspiration he had gained from nature had no simple application to the world of contemporary society and ideas. As he returned, at the close of his career, to address himself once again to "the experiment which we are at present making in the art of living," he found himself hardly more able then than he had been in the 1920s to assert some beliefs as forcefully as he rejected others. Because he remained infected with something of the doubt of his earlier modernism, in his last years he felt again something of the despair he had described four decades earlier. Krutch's social criticism remains valuable, then, not for the answers it proposes, but for the questions it raises; not for the profundity of its assertions, but for the example it offers of an honest and earnest humanist allowing his mind to play freely over contemporary society.

If the essays Krutch wrote at the close of his career lack the permanent value of those at the beginning—if they are neither as polished in form nor as strikingly original in content—they nonetheless enjoyed a popularity quite as great as any achieved by his remarkable essays on modernism. No longer straining to appear "distinctly highbrow," he was now writing naturally in his own voice as he presented a brief for values beyond the quantifiable; for the importance of moral discourse even (indeed, especially) in an age of technology; and for the social, intellectual, and spiritual stability that "progress," in its many forms, undermined. He was less eager to address posterity and make some permanent contribution to letters than to address his day and set other minds in train upon the kind of humanist critique in which he himself was engaged.

221

Krutch discovered that many readers in the late 1950s and 1960s were hungry for just such a humanistic perspective on contemporary society as he offered. His social criticism reached an immense and admiring audience—one larger than he had ever before achieved. As a popular and respected literary journalist, he enjoyed not only the gratification of reputation but also the financial rewards such reputation brought. Never before had his writing been in such demand as at the end of his career. In addition to his regular contributions to the *Saturday Review* and the *American Scholar*, his writing on various topics appeared in other journals of national circulation such as *Commentary, Life*, the New York *Times Book Review* and *Magazine*, the *Saturday Evening Post*, and *Theatre Arts;* in women's magazines like *Family Circle, House Beautiful, House and Garden*, and *McCalls;* in Sunday supplements like *Family Weekly* and *This Week;* in corporate publications like the *Bell Telephone Magazine*, the *Chrysler Magazine, Ford Times*, and IBM's *THINK;* in regional journals like *American West, Arizona Highways*, and *Westways;* and of course in nature magazines like *Audubon, National Forests, National Wildlife*, and *Natural History*. It was a rare reader who, during the fifties and sixties, did not somewhere encounter Krutch's prose.

Inevitably, the impressive quantity of his later writing led to a distinct unevenness in its quality. Many of his essays were repetitive in both conception and expression; more than a few of them were, one imagines, the product of little more than a morning's thought and writing. But toward the end Krutch was generously rewarded for even his most modest efforts; occasionally he was offered as much as a dollar a word for a contribution to a nationally syndicated Sunday newspaper supplement. He enjoyed not only the public recognition, but also the wealth he had long sought. To have left behind an estate of well over $300,000 was at least one mark of the success of a professional writer's career.

As one reads some of his writing from Tucson, however, it is difficult to escape the suspicion that Krutch was occasionally exploiting —perhaps even cynically—the reputation he had come to enjoy. Shortly after he arrived there, he published in *House Beautiful* several self-help articles: "How to Make an Art of Daily Living," "How to Develop Discrimination," and "Every Day Is Full of Wonder and

Delight"—hardly the work one might expect of a man just retired from one of America's most distinguished literary professorships. "I have done a lot of odd jobs and in one way or another pulled in more income than I expected," he wrote Mark Van Doren in 1955. "But," he added somewhat apologetically, "a lot of these jobs have not been things I wanted to do or that were really worth doing."[40] He proudly wrote a friend that he had once refused an offer of $500 from the *Reader's Digest* for two sentences endorsing their condensed books. Still, in Tucson such scruples were often set aside. He allowed the *Digest* to reprint some paragraphs on walking from the *American Scholar*, consenting to their editorial mutilation of his essay because, he said, a writer is so well paid for permitting such indignities. Lacking the assured income of his position on the *Nation* or his professorship, he was wholly dependent upon the literary marketplace, and his sense of that market was usually sound. On one occasion, however, when he sent off an unsolicited article on modern literature to *Playboy*, he was asked to revise it to eliminate some of the more vivid discussion of the sexual attitudes of the authors he considered. Of course, he promptly complied.

Though Krutch knew that many of the jobs he undertook in his retirement were not "really worth doing," he continued to pursue them both for their contribution to his and Marcelle's financial security and for the occasion they provided for that several hours of writing each morning, which had by now become a nearly automatic activity. The appearance of an essay or a review, however modest, reminded him that he was still the man of letters he had set out to become in the 1920s, and in some ways he was more successful than he had ever dared dream he might be. The mailbox several hundred yards from his home was the umbilical cord connecting him to the New York literary world he had left behind on his retirement; as he trod the path to it through desert brush, he was reassured to know that editors would be awaiting his latest work with an eagerness they had not always displayed.

To capitalize on the reputation he now enjoyed, Krutch brought out *If You Don't Mind My Saying So* (1964), a collection of his recent *American Scholar* and *Saturday Review* essays as well as other articles published elsewhere since 1936 on contemporary society, literature, the theater, and nature. The success of that volume led to the publication three years later of a sequel, *And Even If You Do*. Inevitably, many of these unrevised essays are dated and repetitive, although they offer a useful selection of what Krutch judged to be some of his best efforts in the form.

Numerous other books during the 1960s also bore his name. For the burgeoning college market he edited two paperback anthologies, one of eighteenth-century drama, the other of Thoreau's prose. He also served as consulting editor for Prentice-Hall's ambitious "Series in Nature and Natural History," of which seven volumes appeared with Krutch's introductions before he died.

Other projects were distinctly less ambitious. For the elegant Sierra Club series of nature books he selected passages from his nature writing and social criticism to accompany color photographs of Baja scenes. For the 1961, 1962, and 1965 Christmas seasons he lent his name, some introductory material, and his skill with scissors and paste to three handsome and costly gift books: *The World of Animals* ("a treasury of lore, legend and literature by great writers and naturalists from the 5th century B.C. to the present"); *A Treasury of Birdlore* (an anthology of writings on birds and bird-watching); and an *Herbal*. In 1967 he selected lines from forty-three English and American poems referring to bird songs which, together with the songs themselves as recorded by the Cornell Laboratory of Ornithology, were issued on a phonograph record, "Bird Songs in Literature." Like several of his other projects in the sixties, this one was, he admitted to Van Doren, "a gimmicky affair."[41]

Having appeared frequently on radio and television interview and discussion programs, most often to promote his latest book, Krutch was by the 1960s no stranger to the media. He became, however, something of a star in three hour-long NBC telecasts devoted to his observations on the natural world of the Southwest. Gerald Green—one of Krutch's admiring students at Columbia in the early 1940s, and by 1961 a producer at NBC—wrote to propose the first such program. Krutch's reading of a script composed largely of passages from his writing about the desert would be accompanied by film of Krutch admiring the beauties of the region. Krutch agreed, and the filming took place in spring 1962. The glowing reviews of that first program led to a second, this time about the Grand Canyon; again Green prepared the script from Krutch's published writing, and Krutch contributed his presence to the scenery. When the Grand Canyon program was shown in 1964, it received more critical praise and the Edison Award for Excellence in Television. A third program in collaboration with Green followed, filmed in Baja and broadcast in 1967. The handsome fees Krutch received for his modest efforts and the national exposure the programs brought him apparently outweighed any scruples he might have felt about being an accomplice of the television industry he was criticizing in his essays.

Given his many other kinds of activity then, it is hardly surprising that during the 1960s Krutch found little time for the extended concentration necessary to write books. In addition to his travel book on Baja, he published only two wholly original volumes during that final decade of his life: his autobiography, *More Lives Than One* (1962), and *The Most Wonderful Animals That Never Were* (1969), a charming study of unicorns, mermaids, dragons, and other creatures of the lore of "unnatural history."

Of the three, his autobiography is naturally of greatest interest. The title refers of course to Krutch's several careers as drama critic, book reviewer, essayist, *Nation* editor, professor, biographer, nature writer, and social commentator. Rehearsing some of the more memorable episodes in his professional journey from Knoxville to Greenwich Village and then on to Redding and Tucson, *More Lives Than One* provides — as he said at the beginning, quoting Thoreau — "'a simple and sincere account of his own life.'"[42]

Krutch, however, was more a writer than a literary personality, and he will be remembered more for the achievement of his books than for any famous or infamous acts. The outward life of a man who went to England three times armed with letters of introduction to Shaw and never presented any of them was not, as Krutch recognized, in itself likely to make for compelling reading. ("I did not know what on earth I would say to him," he remarked of his failure to meet Shaw, and he was "quite sure there was nothing he would want to say to me."[43]) Thus, the purely biographical part of the book is of less interest than that which describes the intellectual context of his life of writing: his inner journey from the provinciality of his youth to the smart sophistication he labored to affect as he began his career, and then from the pessimism of his early modernism to the spiritual peace he later came to enjoy. Written before he again yielded to pessimism in his final years, his autobiography radiates that serene contentment he enjoyed during his first decade in Tucson. Reading the book, one can well imagine Krutch sitting on his terrace under a paloverde, reminiscing with friends, telling (hardly for the first time) some anecdotes in which he especially delighted, and interrupting himself occasionally to go to his study to retrieve a passage he had published some years ago and now wanted to read verbatim. Having found among his Tucson friends an appreciative audience for his reminiscences, he hoped readers might enjoy them as well.

Krutch's autobiography shares throughout the cordial familiarity, modest self-presentation, engaging wit, and tendency to commonsense speculation on ideas and events which distinguished his work as an essayist. One brief passage will stand as an example of many longer ones. While discussing his college days, he noted that he had been elected to Phi Kappa Phi, the academic honorary. He then digressed to remark that he had many years later seen on a brass plaque at another university the motto of the fraternity: "The Love of Learning Rules the World." "Of all the lies which have been cast in eternal bronze," he observed characteristically, "this is probably the most barefaced."[44] In such asides lies much of the charm of the book.

Like most of his later writing, his autobiography sought to charm rather than to impress. The very act of preparing such a book suggests that the author imagines his life and ideas might be of interest to others. But here, as in his nature writing and his social criticism, Krutch's literary pretensions were few. By the early 1960s, perfection of the private life had become far more important to him than perfection of the public work. While More Lives Than One is hardly a classic of the genre, it is impressive as a human if not as a literary document, as an account of a man's discovery of how one could transcend a temperamental pessimism to enjoy an enormous zest for living, and of how as an individualist Krutch achieved the personal happiness which at the end he valued far more than the literary fame he had earlier so strenuously sought.

As he wrote his autobiography in Tucson in the early sixties and basked in the popular reputation he enjoyed along with that happiness, he had few regrets over his life. He was, he said, "rather more satisfied than most with both my past and my present. . . . I have been unusually fortunate in being able to live a good deal of my life as I chose to live it. . . . I have had an interesting life," he continued, "in the special sense that I myself have usually been interested in it. This, I think, is what I have most wanted . . . though," he added with characteristic understatement, "I do not scorn the modest popularity my books have achieved."[45]

During the next eight years that popularity continued to grow. Almost all of Krutch's books were still in print or were reprinted — many of them, including even his Columbia dissertation, in paperback. Royalty checks grew steadily larger. Even the literary and academic establishment, whose approval Krutch welcomed but no longer deliberately courted, bestowed upon him the honors that some years earlier would have meant to him far more.

Hardly a year passed in the 1960s when Krutch was not invited to accept an honorary degree. Numerous other awards came as well, including in 1967 the American Academy of Arts and Sciences' Emerson-Thoreau Medal for "distinguished achievement in the broad field of literature." Previous recipients since the award was first made in 1958 had included T.S. Eliot, Robert Frost, Lewis Mumford, Katherine Anne Porter, and Edmund Wilson. Krutch felt deeply moved to be included in their ranks.

But the pleasure he took in the professional recognition he received in the late 1960s was clouded by other, darker feelings: by his renewed sense of alienation from contemporary society, and above all by his certain knowledge that the many ailments of old age with which he was now afflicted were harbingers of his approaching death. Even during his first years in Tucson, when he enjoyed more consistently good health than ever before, he remained a fretful valetudinarian. By the sixties, however, his complaints were unmistakably real. Five times in as many years he was hospitalized for various surgical procedures: removal of a benign tumor from his jaw, a prostate operation, a hernia repair, and the removal of cataracts from both eyes. In each case, Krutch recovered rapidly and continued to write and travel with a vigor more befitting a man half his age.

But in the fall of 1968 he learned that he had a highly malignant cancer of the colon, from which he was never to recover. Radical surgery and intense chemotherapy seemed for a time to have arrested the spread of the cancer; hoping against hope that he might be able to resume his normal activity, he made yet another trip to Baja and realized a longstanding ambition to see the Bristlecone Pines near Bishop, California—the longest-lived organisms on earth. But if Krutch hoped for the best, he characteristically feared the worst, and he began preparing two valedictory collections of his favorite work: *The Best Nature Writing of Joseph Wood Krutch*, and a companion volume of other, miscellaneous prose, *A Krutch Omnibus*. He lived to see the publication of only the former.

By September 1969, it was clear that the cancer had not been arrested, and he was hospitalized again for further surgery that left him a semi-invalid. He was grateful, though, to be able to return home to pass his last, often painful months surrounded by that desert which still spoke to him of joy as well as of endurance. He was comforted as well to be attended in his last illness, as he had been in so many previous ones, by Marcelle, whose loving devotion was inexhaustible. Reading to him, taking dictation for the essays and letters he continued to write, and tending to his every need, she sustained both spirit and body during his long but steady decline.

Krutch faced death with resignation, if not with willingness, making a studied effort to seize what little pleasure he could from the days that remained. Shortly after he first learned he had cancer he wrote, "I think I should prefer to go out laughing, not at death itself but at something irrelevantly funny enough to make me forget it."[46] So even as he was writing dour essays about the prospects of civilization, he wrote for his own amusement limericks "referring to some . . . aspects of contemporary manners":

A Certain Difficulty with Difficulties
   An Ambitious young poet and seer
   Said dear, oh dear, oh dear,

If you want to endure
You must be obscure,
And I'm so disgustingly clear.

On the Tendency of Pot Smokers to Prefer Meditation to Action
Said a well-known hippie and dove,
I've lost all my interest in love.
I'd rather have grass
Than any girl's ass
With all that pushing and shove.

Nature also sustained him, as it had for nearly four decades. In his journal he continued to record matter-of-factly his observation of the commonplace phenomena of a natural world he knew would endure long after he had gone. But even as he chronicled the rising temperatures, the reappearance of animals and flowers, and the other evidences of spring, 1970, he knew he would not see another like it. By May 21, he and Marcelle recognized that his death was imminent. They agreed that he should go out as he had lived: lucidly. He stopped taking all drugs, save the morphine he required to dull the excruciating pain. The following morning, with Marcelle at his side, he died. "I suppose I am dying," he said quietly. "It is not as bad as I thought." The statement sums up the later man: candid, curious, and unpretentious.

The national standing and popular reputation Krutch by the end enjoyed was suggested by the appearance, shortly after his death, of an editorial tribute in the New York *Times*. It concluded: "The current wave of concern for the environment, the contempt for materialism voiced by so many youthful Americans, and now perhaps their growing rejection of nihilism as well — these should turn a generation unfamiliar with Joseph Wood Krutch to a reading of his books with delight to themselves and profit to the world."[47] Although the *Times* was, of course, referring to the nature writing and the social criticism with which Krutch had won his most recent and widest fame, his total achievement was greater even than the *Times* suggested. Had Krutch written only *The Modern Temper*, he would deserve a respected place in the history of twentieth-century American letters. But in fact there remains much else of interest and value: his compelling psychoanalytic study of Poe; his civilized essays on the novel and on aesthetics; his prescient analysis of the Marxist enthusiasm of the 1930s; his extensive writing on drama; his masterly biographies of Johnson and Thoreau; and of course the nature writing and social criticism with which he brought his long and fruitful career to a close.

Looking back on that career, one must acknowledge certain shortcomings. Perhaps, by the most austere standards of literary history, Krutch falls short of deserving a place in the very first rank of American writers. After abjuring the effort to become "distinctly high-brow" — an effort which brought him his earliest fame but hardly his greatest happiness — his literary ambition, like his thought, became more modest and also more genuine. His search as a man for values prevailed over his search as an artist for literary perfection. As a man of letters, he wrote to his day, rather than to posterity; he hoped to be read by his contemporaries, rather than studied by his successors. And he sought to bring delight to his readers and, indirectly, profit to the world, rather than (as in his writing in the 1920s) literary glory to himself.

If he was absolute master of no single literary genre, he worked skillfully in many. The versatility of his writing, the many-sidedness of his interests, and the range of topics treated in his works — a breadth which makes his career as a whole such an interesting one — prevented Krutch from achieving that depth which might have brought him even greater, if different, recognition as a clearly preeminent figure on any one ground. Intellectual fashion may underrate the value of the nonspecialist perspective Krutch brought to so much of his writing. But for many readers the modest, earnest enthusiasm and conviction of the amateur that characterized both his life and his writing was precisely the quality which constituted the distinctive attraction of his later essays and books.

It may, in fact, be fair to say that Krutch's gifts were more verbal than intellectual. He broke little new ground in the history of thought, and in many of his works his greatest achievement was to gather and synthesize some of the best that others had thought and said, revivifying and making popularly available that traditional wisdom. His effort as a popularizer was so successful largely because of Krutch's extraordinary verbal gift—his capacity, that is, for forceful and peculiarly unhackneyed utterance. As he addressed his general reader, he employed a prose as warm and unpretentious as his ideas, a style which, like his mind, was clear, sober, flexible, and tempered by unobtrusive wit and self-effacing irony. If (as someone once said) literature is journalism worth reading twice, even Krutch's essentially journalistic reviewing often achieves the state of literature. Had he no other distinction, Krutch will be remembered as the author of some of the most distinguished prose in modern letters.

To read and study from beginning to end the entire corpus of Krutch's fifty enormously productive years as a man of letters is to put his writings to a severe test. Inevitably, the nearly three dozen books he wrote or edited and his several thousand reviews, editorials, and essays are not all of equal excellence. Indeed, his most substantial accomplishments, his unquestionably significant work, might seem even greater were it not surrounded by other writing which seems trivial and ephemeral by comparison. But whatever the shortcomings of Krutch's career, one is inclined to regret rather than to scorn them in one's admiration for the achievement his life of writing represents.

In retrospect, it is perhaps less any single work than the shape of Krutch's life and works as a whole which remains most memorable. Coming up from Tennessee with an acute and capacious but relatively unstocked mind, he spent the better part of the following half-century defining an intellectual position that was authentically his own. Most of his works—including many of those with apparently slight autobiographical significance—reflect that lifelong effort at self-discovery. Early on, even as he tried to embrace modernism, he was confounded by his age and sought to achieve an understanding, different from that of many of his contemporaries, of what it means to be human. His life was one of continuous discovery—or, more precisely, rediscovery—of what is truly essential. Believing in that individualism of which he had written as an undergraduate, he found happiness in a world in which he never felt wholly at home. And through Johnson, Thoreau, and his study of nature he found a new faith in some of those basic human values effectively denied by modernism, Marxism, behaviorism, and other contemporary -isms. For many other people who shared his sensibility and, through his books and essays, followed him in his quest, Krutch's intellectual and spiritual odyssey was exemplary.

His revelation of that quest was neither maudlin nor truculently self-advertising. Like the man, it was modest and understated, earnest and sincere. He was such a popular writer (and, for many readers, so important a thinker) because, in ambitiously tackling difficult intellectual and social problems, he was able to address some of the crucial issues of his day in terms comprehensible for the general reader. Refusing to align himself with any literary or intellectual school or coterie, and never resting complacently in any simple doctrine or dogma, he remained steadfastly his own man. As an independent thinker he resisted the pressures of his times. As a humanist he bore witness to convictions about man and nature, convictions he found more fundamental than those of an age which tried to live by principles different from his own. And as a writer he offered an account of the possibility of that resistance and the importance of those convictions—an account to which many readers will continue to turn, with delight to themselves and with profit to the world.

NOTES

NOTES TO CHAPTER I.

1. *Partisan Review* 5 (1938), 22, 24.
2. "Drama," *Nation,* 15 April 1950, p. 335.
3. Knoxville *Evening Sentinel,* 25 Nov., 1 Dec. 1893.
4. *More Lives Than One,* 13.
5. Ibid., 5.
6. Ibid., 10, 16, 14.
7. Ibid., 9.
8. Ibid.
9. Ibid., 36.
10. Ibid., 23.
11. Ibid., 16.
12. "Blood and Thunder," *Nation,* 20 Oct. 1929, p. 574.
13. *More Lives Than One,* 28.
14. *And Even If You Do,* 305.
15. *More Lives Than One,* 19.
16. Ibid., 35.
17. Ibid., 14.
18. Ibid., 15.
19. Ibid., 14.
20. New York *Times Book Review,* 30 July 1950, p. 2.
21. *University of Tennessee Magazine* 23 (1920), 372–73.
22. Ibid., 397.
23. *More Lives Than One,* 44.
24. *Orange and White,* 20 Nov. 1913, p. 2.

25. Ibid., 18 Dec. 1913, p. 4.
26. "Prepare Your Facile Pen," ibid., 20 May 1914, p. 3.
27. "On Editorials," *University of Tennessee Magazine* 18 (1914), 30–31.
28. "Editorial," ibid., 62.
29. "Editorial," ibid., 95.
30. *More Lives Than One*, 50.
31. "Papa Shaw," *Nation*, 14 Dec. 1927, p. 690.
32. *More Lives Than One*, 50–51.
33. "Androcles and the Lion," *University of Tennessee Magazine* 18 (1915), 79, 78, 79.
34. "Being One's Brother's Keeper," ibid., 148–49, 150, 152.
35. "Editorial," ibid., 162–63.
36. "Editorial," ibid., 194.
37. *More Lives Than One*, 56.
38. "Editorial," *University of Tennessee Magazine* 18 (1915), 230, 229, 230.
39. *More Lives Than One*, 63.
40. Ibid., 46.
41. Ibid., 49.
42. "Salvation by Grace," *Bookman* 57 (1923), 175.
43. Ibid.
44. *More Lives Than One*, 48.
45. Ibid., 58.

Notes to Chapter 2.

1. *More Lives Than One*, 81.
2. "George Henry Boker," *Sewanee Review* 25 (1917), 457.
3. *More Lives Than One*, 82.
4. Ibid., 63.
5. *Johnson*, 342–43.
6. Mark Van Doren, *Autobiography* (New York: Harcourt, Brace, 1958), 72–73.
7. *More Lives Than One*, 65–66.
8. Van Doren, *Autobiography*, 73.
9. Ibid., 99.
10. Quoted in *More Lives Than One*, 101.
11. Ibid., 105.
12. *Comedy and Conscience after the Restoration* (New York: Columbia Univ. Press, 1924), 39, 25.
13. Ibid., 120, 249, 253, 258.

14. "Threnody upon a Decadent Art," in *Smart Set Anthology,* ed. Burton Rascoe and Groff Conklin (New York: Reynal and Hitchcock, 1934), 225–29. (First published Jan. 1921.)
15. Quoted in *More Lives Than One,* 113.
16. "A Note on Irony," *Nation,* 1 Nov. 1922, pp. 473–74.
17. New York *Evening Post Book Review,* 20 July 1920, p. 1.
18. "Salvation by Grace," *Bookman* 57 (1923), 176.
19. Ibid., 175.
20. *More Lives Than One,* 92.
21. *Autobiography,* 137.
22. "Plain and Colored," *Nation,* 13 Feb. 1924, p. 176.
23. "The Humble Critic," ibid., 8 April 1925, p. 374.
24. "The Nathanism of Mr. Nathan," New York *Herald Tribune Books,* 1 Sept. 1929, p. 3.
25. "The Critic in the Marketplace," *Nation,* 26 April 1922, p. 500.
26. "Pseudo-Classic," ibid., 15 Aug. 1923, p. 168.
27. "Two Sophisticates," ibid., 11 June 1924, p. 685.
28. "Devil's Disciple," ibid., 25 April 1923, p. 497.
29. "Slaying the Slain," ibid., 20 Dec. 1922, p. 694.
30. "Wasteland," ibid., 7 Nov. 1923, pp. 626–27.
31. "A Voice from Limbo," *Literary Review,* 11 Sept. 1920, p. 2.
32. *Nation,* 25 June 1924, p. 735.

NOTES TO CHAPTER 3.

1. "A Via Media for Americans," *Nation,* 4 Oct. 1922, p. 339.
2. "Cultural History of an Era of Optimism," New York *Herald Tribune Books,* 24 Aug. 1947, p. 1.
3. "The Writer's Dilemma," *Nation,* 26 June 1926, p. 572.
4. "Books and Universities," ibid., 1 Feb. 1928, p. 114.
5. "The Business of Book-Making," ibid., 20 April 1927, p. 414.
6. "The Writer's Dilemma," ibid., 26 June 1926, p. 572.
7. *Samuel Johnson,* 169.
8. 11 June 1929, Library of Congress.
9. "The Social Value of the Literary Guild," *Wings* 1 (1927), 12.
10. "Books and Things," New York *Herald Tribune,* 13 Dec. 1950.
11. Ibid.
12. "The Peasants," *Saturday Review of Literature,* 28 Aug. 1926, p. 69.
13. "In the Driftway," *Nation,* 4 Nov. 1925, p. 514.
14. *More Lives Than One,* 172.

15. 14 March 1930, Harvard University Library.
16. *More Lives Than One*, 172.
17. "Breaking Ranks," *Nation*, 12 Nov. 1924, pp. 511–12.
18. "Paging the Censor," ibid., 4 Mar. 1925, p. 232.
19. "Mr. Bryan's Religion," ibid., 5 April 1922, p. 387.
20. "The Perfect Censor," ibid., 22 April 1925, p. 457.
21. *More Lives Than One*, 144.
22. "Darwin in Dayton," *Saturday Review*, 24 May 1958, p. 19.
23. "Darrow vs. Bryan," *Nation*, 29 July 1925, pp. 136–37.
24. "Tennessee's Dilemma," ibid., 22 July 1925, p. 110.
25. "Tennessee: Where Cowards Rule," ibid., 15 July 1925, pp. 88, 89.
26. "Topics of the Times," New York *Times*, 10 July 1925.
27. Knoxville *Sentinel*, 10 July 1925.
28. "The American Classic," New York *Herald Tribune Books*, 2 March 1947, p. 1.
29. "The Mystery of Poe," *Nation*, 10 Dec. 1924, p. 616.
30. *Edgar Allan Poe: A Study in Genius* (New York: Knopf, 1926), 15.
31. Ibid., 17, 98, 200.
32. Ibid., 38.
33. "Confusion Worse Confounded," *Nation*, 22 March 1922, p. 348.
34. "The Mystery of Poe," 616.
35. *Poe*, 16.
36. Ibid., 8, 15, 36.
37. Ibid., 68, 24.
38. Ibid., 82, 86.
39. Ibid., 117, 106–7.
40. Ibid., 115.
41. Ibid., 234, 192–93.
42. Ibid., 97, 77, 114, 19.
43. Ibid., 235.
44. "Genius and Neuroticism," *Saturday Review*, 19 Jan. 1963, p. 12.
45. *Nation*, 17 March 1926, p. 289.
46. *New Masses* 1 (June, 1926), 23.
47. *New Republic*, 8 Dec. 1926, p. 77.
48. Hervey Allen, New York *Times Book Review*, 21 Mar. 1926, p. 7.
49. *Saturday Review of Literature*, 5 June 1926, p. 834.
50. New York *Herald Tribune Books*, 21 March 1926, p. 1.
51. "An American Paradox," *Nation*, 11 Nov. 1925, p. 532.

Notes to Chapter 4.

1. "Twenty Years of the American Drama," *Saturday Review of Literature*, 5 Aug. 1944, p. 36.
2. *More Lives Than One*, 136.
3. "Summary: I," *Nation*, 10 June 1925, p. 672.
4. "Review," ibid., 16 June 1926, p. 675.
5. *More Lives Than One*, 134–35.
6. "On Contemporary Books," *Nation*, 9 June 1926, p. 626.
7. "Our Literature and Ourselves," ibid., 28 Oct. 1925, p. 480.
8. "A Voice from Limbo," *Literary Review*, 11 Sept. 1920, p. 2.
9. "Jazz of the Spirit," *Nation*, 28 Jan. 1925, p. 99.
10. "Figures of the Dawn," ibid., 11 March 1925, p. 272.
11. "A Passionate Mystic," ibid., 4 March 1925, p. 244.
12. "Bitter Mirth," ibid., 8 Oct. 1924, p. 382.
13. "Hard Facts," ibid., 17 March 1926, p. 295.
14. "Second Best," ibid., 23 Sept. 1925, p. 336.
15. "Simplicity Farewell," *Saturday Review of Literature*, 24 Jan. 1925, pp. 475–76.
16. "The Long Journey," *Nation*, 7 Oct. 1925, p. 389.
17. "Unspacious Days," ibid., 4 Nov. 1925, pp. 521–22.
18. This and subsequent passages will be found in the specified essay in *The Modern Temper*. Where a passage is cited other than in the course of the summary of an essay, page reference will be given.
19. Quoted in *More Lives Than One*, 209–10.
20. Correspondence in the files of the *Atlantic Monthly*.
21. 2 Oct. 1927, in files of the *Atlantic Monthly*.
22. 3 May 1928, Harvard University Library.
23. 14 May 1928, Columbia University Library.
24. *Modern Temper*, 18.
25. *If You Don't Mind My Saying So*, 49.
26. *Modern Temper*, xvi, xv.
27. Ibid., 77.
28. 9 June 1928, Library of Congress.
29. "The Case of Frank Harris," *Nation*, 5 July 1922, p. 19.
30. 24 March 1929, p. 1.
31. *Outlook*, 10 April 1929, pp. 587–88.
32. *New Republic*, 22 May 1929, p. 36.
33. *Christian Century*, 1 May 1929, p. 587.

34. *Nation,* 10 April 1929, p. 428.

35. *Forum,* June, 1929, p. x.

36. To Oswald Garrison Villard, n.d., Harvard Univ. Library.

Notes to Chapter 5.

1. *Samuel Johnson,* 454.

2. *TLS,* 7 May 1931, p. 370.

3. *Five Masters: A Study in the Mutations of The Novel* (Gloucester, Mass.: Peter Smith, 1968), 158, 131.

4. Ibid., 63, 178.

5. Ibid., 257, 254, 323–24, 315.

6. Ibid., 323, 316, 267.

7. Ibid., 327.

8. *Modern Temper,* 124.

9. *Experience and Art: Some Aspects of the Esthetics of Literature* (New York: Harrison Smith and Robert Haas, 1932), 7–8.

10. Ibid., 41, 33.

11. Ibid., 50, 54, 123.

12. Ibid., 143, 131–32.

13. Ibid., 216, 220, 208.

14. Ibid., 221–22.

15. 12 Dec. 1931, in files of the *Atlantic Monthly.*

16. 29 Jan. 1933, Columbia University Library.

17. *And Even If You Do,* 283, 286.

18. "Summary: I," *Nation,* 31 May 1933, p. 622.

19. *Comedy and Conscience after the Restoration* (New York: Columbia Univ. Press, 1924), 72.

20. "Another Modern," *Nation,* 17 Feb. 1926, p. 187; "Clemence Dane Discourses," ibid., 13 April 1927, p. 405; "The Season in Moscow," ibid., 27 June 1928, p. 717.

21. "The Prosecution Rests," ibid., 8 Feb. 1933, pp. 158–59.

22. "The New Dispensation," ibid., 25 Sept. 1935, p. 352.

23. "The Drama as a Social Force," ibid., 20 April 1932, p. 467.

24. "For Art's Sake," ibid, 2 Jan. 1935, p. 6.

25. "Art for Art's Sake," ibid., 19 Dec. 1936, pp. 735–36.

26. *Forum* 90 (1933), 80.

27. Ibid., 82–84.

28. *More Lives Than One,* 179.

29. "Tactics and the Clerk," *Nation,* 13 May 1936, p. 616.

30. "Havelock Ellis," ibid., 11 Jan. 1933, p. 43.
31. "Towers for Looking," ibid., 6 June 1934, p. 636.
32. *Was Europe a Success?* (New York: Farrar and Rinehart, 1934), 1–3.
33. Ibid., 36.
34. Ibid., 46, 44, 46.
35. Ibid., 11, 10, 1.
36. Ibid., 15.
37. Ibid., 20–22.
38. Ibid., 27, 21.
39. Ibid., 31, 14.
40. Ibid., 54.
41. Ibid., 48, 57–58.
42. "What Is the West?," *Nation,* 22 Feb. 1928, p. 214.
43. "Was Europe a Success?" ibid., 31 Oct. 1934, pp. 373–75.
44. *New Republic,* 9 Jan. 1935, p. 253.
45. "A Confession of Faith," *Nation,* 2 Aug. 1933, p. 134.
46. "Unnatural History," ibid., 9 May 1934, p. 523.
47. "Nature and the Modern Mind," ibid., 22 Aug. 1936, p. 215.
48. *Henry David Thoreau,* 148.
49. *More Lives Than One,* 238, 253, 250.
50. "A 'Nation' Divided," *New Masses Literary Supplement,* 7 Dec. 1937, pp. 8–11.

NOTES TO CHAPTER 6.

1. New York *Times,* 30 Dec. 1938.
2. "Drama," *Nation,* 15 Oct. 1938, p. 388.
3. "Drama Note," ibid., 11 Nov. 1939, p. 535.
4. "Soldier's Wife," ibid., 21 Oct. 1944, p. 482.
5. "Theater Yearbooks," ibid., 20 Jan. 1945, p. 78.
6. "Drama," ibid., 10 April 1948, p. 402.
7. "The First Twenty-Five Years," ibid., 22 Oct. 1949, p. 398.
8. "How I Stand It," ibid., 10 Feb. 1940, p. 222.
9. "A Defence of the Professional Reviewer," in *Theatre Annual* (New York, 1943), 22.
10. Ibid., 25.
11. Ibid., 22.
12. "Minerva, 1953," *Freeman,* 28 Dec. 1953, p. 248.
13. *More Lives Than One,* 300.
14. *O'Neill* (London: Jonathan Cape, 1962), 412.

15. 9 May 1933, Library of Congress.
16. "Our Electra," *Nation,* 18 Nov. 1937, pp. 551–52.
17. *Literary History of the United States* (New York: Macmillan, 1974), 1249.
18. "The Legacy of the Living Theatre," *Theatre Arts* 40 (1956), 73.
19. *More Lives Than One,* 282–83.
20. *Was Europe a Success?,* 31.
21. *More Lives Than One,* 285.
22. "The Great Cham," *Nation,* 14 March 1934, p. 306.
23. *Samuel Johnson,* v.
24. Ibid., 118.
25. Ibid., 39, 198.
26. Ibid., 109, 497.
27. Ibid., 293.
28. Ibid., 492–93.
29. Ibid., 1, 273.
30. *More Lives Than One,* 283.
31. *Samuel Johnson,* 363.
32. Ibid., 246.
33. Ibid., 26.
34. "Dr. Johnson," *New Yorker,* 18 Nov. 1944, p. 81.
35. "Dr. Johnson," *Kenyon Review,* 8 (1946), 637–38.
36. *Henry David Thoreau: A Critical Study* (Boston: Houghton Mifflin, 1916), 108.
37. *More Lives Than One,* 289.
38. *Walden,* ed. J. Lyndon Shanley (Princeton: Princeton Univ. Press, 1971), 131.
39. *Modern Temper,* 6.
40. "Walden Revisited," *Nation,* 3 May 1933, p. 506.
41. "The Usable Past," ibid., 14 Feb. 1934, p. 191.
42. *Henry David Thoreau,* 11, 239.
43. Ibid., 239, 8.
44. Ibid., 10, 257.
45. Ibid., 258.
46. Ibid., 107, 146, 115.
47. *Modern Temper,* 6.
48. *Henry David Thoreau,* 175, 185.
49. Ibid., 145, 172.
50. Ibid., 79, 139.
51. Ibid., 277.
52. Ibid., 279, 283.

Notes to Chapter 7.

1. *Twelve Seasons,* 3–13.
2. *More Lives Than One,* 294–95.
3. Files of *Atlantic Monthly.*
4. *Twelve Seasons,* 29.
5. Ibid., 175.
6. *Great American Nature Writing* (New York: William Sloane, 1950), 2.
7. *Best of Two Worlds,* 18.
8. Ibid., 113, 164, 165, 15.
9. Ibid., 28.
10. *Desert Year,* 5–6.
11. *More Lives Than One,* 308.
12. 28 June 1950; 11 Jan. 1951, Columbia Univ. Library.
13. *Desert Year,* 9, 20, 11.
14. Ibid., 265.
15. "Drama," *Nation,* 3 May 1952, p. 436.
16. 29 Feb. 1952, Bollingen Foundation Archives, Library of Congress.
17. *"Modernism" in Modern Drama: A Definition and an Estimate* (Ithaca: Cornell Univ. Press, 1953), 2.
18. *Samuel Johnson,* 499.
19. *"Modernism" in Modern Drama,* viii.
20. Ibid., 131, 5.
21. Ibid., 100, 5.
22. Ibid., 12, 30.
23. Ibid., 76, 62.
24. Ibid., viii, 89.
25. *Desert Year,* 127.
26. *Measure of Man,* 194.
27. *Modern Temper,* 50.
28. *Measure of Man,* 34, 37.
29. Ibid., 32, 165.
30. Ibid., 145.
31. Ibid., 82.
32. Ibid., 97, 99.
33. *Modern Temper,* 16.
34. *Measure of Man,* 257.
35. Ibid., 224, 195, 258, 244.
36. Ibid., 197.

37. "We Were Not Skeptical Enough," in *This I Believe* (New York: Simon and Schuster, 1954), 78.
38. *Samuel Johnson*, 363.
39. "Man's Role in an Age of Anxiety," New York *Post*, 4 Apr. 1954.
40. New York *Times*, 26 Jan. 1955.

NOTES TO CHAPTER 8.

1. *Best of Two Worlds*, 14–15.
2. "The Mystique of the Desert," *Saturday Review*, 17 April 1954, p. 46.
3. To Emery Neff, 14 Dec. 1955, Library of Congress.
4. To Mark Van Doren, 1 June 1953, Columbia Univ. Library.
5. 18 Dec. 1955, ibid.
6. *More Lives Than One*, 329.
7. *Forgotten Peninsula*, 201.
8. *Best of Two Worlds*, 143–55.
9. *Twelve Seasons*, 131.
10. *If You Don't Mind My Saying So*, 369.
11. *Voice of the Desert*, 149; *Twelve Seasons*, 178.
12. *Best of Two Worlds*, 121.
13. *Voice of the Desert*, 219.
14. *Desert Year*, 38.
15. Ibid., 268.
16. *Voice of the Desert*, 216.
17. *Twelve Seasons*, 178.
18. Ibid., 3.
19. *Desert Year*, 106.
20. *Great Chain of Life*, 161.
21. "The Thought of Turtles," *Nation*, 12 June 1948, p. 664.
22. *Great Chain of Life*, x.
23. *Voice of the Desert*, 218.
24. *Desert Year*, 230.
25. *Best of Two Worlds*, 84.
26. Ibid., 39.
27. *Twelve Seasons*, 44, 45.
28. Ibid., 19.
29. Ibid., 29.
30. *Best of Two Worlds*, 16.
31. *Great Chain of Life*, 227.
32. *Twelve Seasons*, 177.

33. *Best of Two Worlds,* 17.
34. *If You Don't Mind My Saying So,* 372.
35. Ibid., 345.
36. *Best of Two Worlds,* 128.
37. *If You Don't Mind My Saying So,* 371.
38. *Twelve Seasons,* 125.
39. *Best of Two Worlds,* 95.
40. *Great Chain of Life,* ix.
41. Ibid., 153–54.
42. *Modern Temper,* 26–27.
43. *Great Chain of Life,* 122.
44. Ibid., 108.
45. Ibid., 109, 137.
46. Ibid., 143.
47. Ibid., 120–21.
48. "If You Don't Mind My Saying So," *American Scholar* 30 (1960), 409.
49. *Modern Temper,* 97.
50. *Desert Year,* 29, 86, 176.
51. Ibid., 20, 14, 64, 44.
52. Ibid., 23.
53. *Voice of the Desert,* 220.
54. "The Lure of Sun, Sand and Stars," New York *Times Magazine,* 8 Nov. 1959, p. 62.
55. *Desert Year,* 11.
56. *Voice of the Desert,* 221.
57. *Desert Year,* 181–82, 28–29, 56.
58. Ibid., 184.

Notes to Chapter 9.

1. *More Lives Than One,* 330.
2. *Grand Canyon,* 192.
3. *Forgotten Peninsula,* 6.
4. *Grand Canyon,* 257.
5. "Windows on the World of Nature," New York *Times Book Review,* 9 June 1957, p. 26.
6. *Voice of the Desert,* 199, 200.
7. *Grand Canyon,* 275.
8. *Forgotten Peninsula,* 6.
9. Ibid., 276, 263.

10. Ibid., 263.

11. 26 May 1959, Columbia Univ. Library.

12. 27 July 1962, ibid.

13. "The Voice of His Own," New York *Times Book Review*, 25 Sept. 1960, p. 20.

14. "If You Don't Mind My Saying So," *American Scholar* 30 (1960), 241.

15. *Samuel Johnson*, 364.

16. *If You Don't Mind My Saying So*, 8.

17. Ibid., 24.

18. "Advancing Backward," *Nation*, 31 Dec. 1924, p. 723.

19. *Human Nature and the Human Condition*, 5, 115.

20. Ibid., 208, 101.

21. Ibid., 144.

22. "If You Don't Mind My Saying So," *American Scholar* 28 (1958), 93, 92.

23. "Who Was Henry Thoreau?," *Saturday Review*, 19 Aug. 1967, p. 18.

24. Letter to Charles Krutch, 25 July 1969, Library of Congress.

25. *And Even If You Do*, 3.

26. *Arizona Daily Star*, 4 Oct. 1956.

27. *And Even If You Do*, 67, 66.

28. "Life, Liberty, and the Pursuit of Welfare," *Saturday Evening Post*, 15 July 1961, p. 56.

29. *Human Nature and the Human Condition*, 119.

30. Ibid., 79.

31. "If You Don't Mind My Saying So," *American Scholar* 36 (1967), 533.

32. "Who Says It's Proper English," *Saturday Review*, 14 Oct. 1967, p. 132.

33. *Human Nature and the Human Condition*, 87.

34. "The Creative Dilemma," *Saturday Review*, 8 Feb. 1964, p. 17.

35. *If You Don't Mind My Saying So*, 203.

36. *And Even If You Do*, 335–36.

37. 26 Sept. 1968, Columbia Univ. Library.

38. 4 June 1969, ibid.

39. *Human Nature and the Human Condition*, 206.

40. 29 March 1955, Columbia Univ. Library.

41. 3 March 1967, ibid.

42. *More Lives Than One*, 4.

43. Ibid., 260.

44. Ibid., 56.
45. Ibid., 364, 370.
46. "If You Don't Mind My Saying So," *American Scholar* 38 (1969), 188.
47. "Joseph Wood Krutch," New York *Times,* 26 May 1970.

✥ BIBLIOGRAPHICAL ESSAY

A NOTE ON SOURCES

Many of Krutch's papers were destroyed in a 1952 fire at his Connecticut home. Those that survived, and papers from 1952 to 1970, have been deposited in the Manuscript Division of the Library of Congress. The materials there include typescript and published copies of many of the essays he wrote in Tucson, the scribbled notes and clippings from newspapers and magazines which were the raw material for many of his essays and books, reviews of his books, and his voluminous correspondence with his publishers. The Library of Congress collection also includes several boxes of his Columbia lecture notes and much of the "fan mail" he received from admiring readers. While traveling with the Bechtels in the American Southwest, in Baja California, and abroad, Krutch dictated into a recorder diaries of what he saw and did. Transcriptions of more than two dozen such diaries, from 1958 through 1969, are also included in the Library of Congress collection.

Since he reserved most of his literary energy for his public writing, Krutch was not a great writer of letters. Most of his surviving correspondence concerns professional rather than personal matters—lectures he was to deliver, or essays and books he had agreed to write. The most revealing of his letters are those to Mark Van Doren; many of them are available in the Van Doren Papers in the Columbia University Library. The Columbiana Collection there also contains numerous papers concerning Krutch's tenure on the Columbia faculty.

Some correspondence dating from Krutch's first ten years on the staff of the *Nation* can be found in the Oswald Garrison Villard Papers in the

246

Houghton Library, Harvard University. The files of the *American Scholar*, which also contain some letters to, from, and about Krutch, are deposited in the Library of Congress.

No comprehensive bibliography of Krutch's writing has yet been published. Given his prolificacy and the fact that any such work would contain several thousand entries (including reviews, essays and books), it is doubtful that any such work will soon appear. A thirty-three-page typed bibliography by Professor Richard C. Kohler is among the Krutch papers in the Library of Congress. Dealing only with his writing through 1962, it lists books by Krutch, books edited or compiled by him, essays by Krutch included in books edited or compiled by others, and an incomplete list of reviews of Krutch's books.

In preparing the present work, I undertook to locate as many of Krutch's writings as possible. The result of that quest — contained in two long file drawers of 3x5 cards — is deposited in the Special Collections Department of the Northwestern University Library. The several thousand cards include not only signed essays in commonly indexed periodicals like the *Nation*, *Saturday Review*, *American Scholar*, and *New York Times*, but also more fugitive pieces which were published in various specialized periodicals of limited circulation. The file cards available at Northwestern also identify several hundred unsigned contributions by Krutch in the *Nation* — especially notes on "Books in Brief" and editorials. These unsigned contributions were identified as Krutch's through a study of *Nation* "Contributors' Pay Books" deposited in the New York Public Library.

A NOTE ON WRITINGS ABOUT JOSEPH WOOD KRUTCH

For a man who wrote so much, Krutch has been relatively little written about. Four dissertations discuss various aspects of his career. In his "Analytical Study of the Dramatic Criticism of Joseph Wood Krutch as Published in the *Nation*, 1924-1952" (University of Southern California, 1959), Gordon C. Green sets forth Krutch's opinions on various plays, playwrights, and theatrical topics. Joseph G. Green's rather more ambitious "Joseph Wood Krutch: Critic of the Drama" (Indiana University, 1965) has a wider scope and places Krutch's dramatic criticism (in the *Nation* and elsewhere) in the broader context of his philosophy of literature and art. John Richard Harley's "Joseph Wood Krutch: Nature and Man" (Texas Christian University, 1971) offers a thorough and thoughtful study of Krutch's philosophy of nature, while Kenneth Johnson's "The Lost Eden: The New World in American Nature Writing" (University of New Mexico, 1973) includes a chapter on Krutch along with chapters on William Bartram, Henry David Thoreau, John Muir, and Rachel Carson.

Several articles also discuss Krutch's life and work. Durant da Ponte's "Quest for Values: The Pilgrimage of Joseph Wood Krutch" (*Tennessee Studies in Literature*, Special Number [1961], 185–97) is a brief but suggestive essay describing the broad outlines of Krutch's intellectual development. René Dubos's "The Despairing Optimist" (*American Scholar* 40 [1971], 16–20) is an eloquent tribute to Krutch as "one of the first representatives of a new class of scientific humanists." Charles I. Glicksberg's "Joseph Wood Krutch: Critic of Despair" (*Sewanee Review* 44 [1936], 77–93) is one of the earliest extended discussions of Krutch and deals with his books through *Was Europe a Success?*

Gerald Green's "A Pessimist with a Zest for Life" (*Columbia College Today*, Winter 1972, pp. 16–19) is an admiring reminiscence by a former student who later collaborated with Krutch in the production of three television programs on the Southwest. William Holtz's "Homage to Joseph Wood Krutch: Tragedy and the Ecological Imperative" (*American Scholar* 43 [1974], 267–79) is a learned and thoughtful discussion of Krutch's attraction to Johnson and Thoreau and of his later nature writing. Anthony L. Lehman's "Joseph Wood Krutch: A Personal Reminiscence" (*The Book Club of California Quarterly News-Letter* 37 [1972], 51–63) is an account of a 1968 visit to Krutch's Tucson home and of their discussion of Krutch's interest in nature.

My own "Joseph Wood Krutch: A Writer's Passage beyond the Modern Temper" (in *Romantic and Modern: Revaluations of Literary Tradition*, ed. George Bornstein [Univ. of Pittsburgh Press, 1977], pp. 223–40) reviews the development of Krutch's thought. Paul N. Pavich's "Joseph Wood Krutch: Persistent Champion of Man and Nature" (*Western American Literature* 13 [1978], 151–58) considers the humanistic and ecological concerns of Krutch's later writing. Lawrence Clark Powell's "Southwest Classics Reread: Joseph Wood Krutch's *The Desert Year*" (*Westways*, June 1971, pp. 14–17, 66–67) is a brief review of Krutch's life and works, with particular attention to his years in Tucson and his desert writing. Krutch is also the subject of a thinly disguised *roman à clef*, Gerald Green's *An American Prophet* (Doubleday, 1977), which draws upon people and incidents from Krutch's Tucson years.

Fred Y. Osborne's "Index of Twelve Books by Joseph Wood Krutch" (Tucson: Arizona-Sonora Desert Museum, 1977) covers Krutch's nature books and autobiography and lists the appearance of selected words and phrases ranging from "Cartesianism" to "Caruso, E., widow of" to "Cat."

Books Written or Edited by Joseph Wood Krutch
(in order of publication)

Comedy and Conscience after the Restoration. New York: Columbia Univ. Press, 1924.

Edgar Allan Poe: A Study in Genius. New York: Knopf, 1926.

(ed.) *The Comedies of William Congreve.* New York: Macmillan, 1927.

The Modern Temper: A Study and a Confession. 1929; rpt. Harvest ed. with a new preface, New York: Harcourt, Brace, 1956.

Five Masters: A Study in the Mutations of the Novel. 1930; rpt. with a new preface, Gloucester, Mass.: Peter Smith, 1968.

Experience and Art: Some Aspects of the Esthetics of Literature. New York: Harrison Smith and Robert Haas, 1932.

Was Europe A Success? New York: Farrar and Rinehart, 1934.

The American Drama Since 1918: An Informal History. 1939; rev. and expanded ed., New York: Braziller, 1957.

Samuel Johnson. New York: William Sloane, 1948.

Henry David Thoreau. New York: William Sloane, 1948.

The Twelve Seasons: A Perpetual Calendar for the Country. New York: William Sloane, 1949.

(ed.) *Great American Nature Writing.* New York: William Sloane, 1950.

The Desert Year. New York: William Sloane, 1952.

(ed.) *Selected Letters of Thomas Gray.* New York: Farrar, Straus, 1952.

"Modernism" in Modern Drama: A Definition and an Estimate. Ithaca: Cornell Univ. Press, 1953.

The Best of Two Worlds. New York: William Sloane, 1953.

The Measure of Man: On Freedom, Human Values, Survival, and the Modern Temper. New York: Bobbs-Merrill, 1954.

The Voice of the Desert: A Naturalist's Interpretation. New York: William Sloane, 1955.

The Great Chain of Life. Boston: Houghton Mifflin, 1956.

Grand Canyon: Today and All Its Yesterdays. New York: William Sloane, 1958.

(ed.) *The Gardener's World.* New York: Putnam's, 1959.

Human Nature and the Human Condition. New York: Random House, 1959.

The Forgotten Peninsula: A Naturalist in Baja California. New York: William Sloane, 1961.

(ed.) *The World of Animals: A Treasury of Lore, Legend, and Literature by Great Writers and Naturalists from 5th Century B.C. to the Present.* New York: Simon and Schuster, 1961.

Modern Literature and the Image of Man. San Francisco: Industrial Indemnity, 1962.

More Lives Than One. New York: William Sloane, 1962.

(ed.) *Thoreau: Walden and Other Writings.* New York: Bantam, 1962.

(ed.) with Paul S. Eriksson. *A Treasury of Birdlore.* New York: Paul S. Eriksson, 1962.

If You Don't Mind My Saying So: Essays on Man and Nature. New York: William Sloane, 1964.

Herbal. New York: Putnam, 1965.

(ed.) *Eighteenth-Century English Drama.* New York: Bantam, 1967.

And Even If You Do: Essays on Man, Manners, and Machines. New York: William Morrow, 1967.

The Best Nature Writing of Joseph Wood Krutch. New York: William Morrow, 1969.

The Most Wonderful Animals that Never Were. Boston: Houghton Mifflin, 1969.

A Krutch Omnibus: Forty Years of Social and Literary Criticism. New York: William Morrow, 1970.

# INDEX